Psychology and Culture

With increasing globalization, countries face social, linguistic, religious, and other cultural changes that can lead to misunderstandings in communication, the workplace, health care, and education. These cultural changes can have broader implications across the world, leading to changing dynamics in identity, gender, relationships, family, and community. This book addresses the subsequent need for a basic understanding of the cultural dimensions of psychology and their application to everyday settings.

Dr Vaughn provides an up-to-date overview of psychology and culture, emphasizing the cultural influences on our thinking and behaviour during intercultural interactions. The book discusses the basis of culture and presents related theories and concepts, including a description of how cognition and behaviour are influenced by sociocultural contexts in the areas of identity, human development, intercultural interactions, and basic psychological processes. The text explores a broader definition of culture which includes social dimensions (e.g., gender, religion, socioeconomic status) and provides practical models to improve intercultural relations, communication, and cultural competency in education, organizations, relationships, and health.

Each chapter contains an introduction, a concise overview of the topic and its theoretical construct, a practical application of the topic using current global examples, and a brief summary. The book is ideal reading for undergraduate and graduate students and academics interested in culturally related topics and issues.

Lisa M. Vaughn is Associate Professor in Paediatrics at the University of Cincinnati College of Medicine/Cincinnati Children's Hospital Medical Center. She is trained as a social psychologist, counsellor and medical educator and her primary interests are sociocultural issues affecting the health and well-being of families, especially immigrant and minority populations.

Psychology Focus

Series editor: Perry Hinton, Oxford Brookes University

The Psychology Focus series provides students with a new focus on key topic areas in psychology. It supports students taking modules in psychology, whether for a psychology degree or a combined programme, and those renewing their qualification in a related discipline. Each short book:

■ presents clear, in-depth coverage of a discrete area with many applied examples
■ assumes no prior knowledge of psychology
■ has been written by an experienced teacher
■ has chapter summaries, annotated further reading and a glossary of key terms.

Also available in the series:

Friendship in Childhood and Adolescence
Phil Erwin

Gender and Social Psychology
Vivien Burr

Jobs, Technology and People
Nik Chimiel

Learning and Studying
James Hartley

Personality: A Cognitive Approach
Jo Brunas-Wagstaff

Intelligence and Abilities
Colin Cooper

Stress, Cognition and Health
Tony Cassidy

Types of Thinking
S. Ian Robertson

Psychobiology of Human Motivation
Hugh Wagner

Stereotypes, Social Cognition and Culture
Perry R. Hinton

Psychology and 'Human Nature'
Peter Ashworth

Abnormal Psychology
Alan Carr

Attitudes and Persuasion
Phil Erwin

The Person in Social Psychology
Vivien Burr

Social Psychology of Behaviour in Small Groups
Donald C. Pennington

Attention: A Neuro-
psychological Perspective
Antony Ward

Attention, Perception and
Memory
Elizabeth A. Styles

Introducing Cognitive
Development
Laura M. Taylor

Introducing Neuropsychology,
Second Edition
John Stirling and Rebecca Elliott

Psychology and Culture

Thinking, Feeling, and Behaving in Global Contexts

■ Lisa M. Vaughn

Ψ Psychology Press
Taylor & Francis Group

HOVE AND NEW YORK

First published in 2010
by Psychology Press
27 Church Road, Hove, East Sussex
BN3 2FA

Simultaneously published in the
USA and Canada
by Psychology Press
270 Madison Avenue, New York,
NY 10016

*Psychology Press is an imprint of the
Taylor & Francis Group, an Informa
business*

Copyright © 2010 Psychology Press

Typeset in Sabon by RefineCatch Ltd,
Bungay, Suffolk
Printed and bound in Great Britain by
TJ International Ltd, Padstow,
Cornwall
Cover design by Anú Design

This publication has been produced
with paper manufactured to strict
environmental standards and with
pulp derived from sustainable
forests.

*British Library Cataloguing in
Publication Data*
A catalogue record for this book is
available from the British Library

*Library of Congress Cataloging-in-
Publication Data*
Vaughn, Lisa.
  Psychology and culture : thinking,
feeling and behaving in global
contexts / Lisa M. Vaughn.
    p. cm. – (Psychology focus)
  Includes bibliographical references
and index.
  1. Culture—Psychological aspects.
2. Social psychology.
3. Multiculturalism. 4. Group
identity. I. Title.
  HM891.V38 2010
  306.01—dc22
                              2009035419

ISBN: 978-1-84169-872-4 (hbk)
ISBN: 978-1-84169-873-1 (pbk)

Contents

List of illustrations ix

List of tables xi

1 Introductory concepts 1

2 Identity and culture 21

**3 Human development/
socialization and culture** 45

**4 Basic psychological
processes and culture** 75

**5 Intercultural interactions
and acculturation** 93

6 Relationships, sexuality, and culture 111

7 Health and culture 133

8 Intercultural communication and education 161

9 Work/organizations and culture 183

References 201
Glossary 233
Author Index 245
Subject Index 259

List of illustrations

1.1 Different emphases of 'culture' 3
1.2 Berry et al.'s (2002) six aspects of culture 4
1.3 Nine elements of culture 5
1.4 Functions of culture 6
1.5 Approaches to psychology and culture 9
1.6 Cultural awareness, sensitivity, and competency 11
3.1 Bronfenbrenner's (1979) ecological systems approach 47
4.1 The Mueller–Lyer illusion 82
4.2 The devil's tuning fork illusion 83
4.3 The Ponzo illusion 83
4.4 The horizontal–vertical illusion 84
5.1 Process of psychological acculturation 100
5.2 Intrapersonal, interpersonal, and cultural competence 103
5.3 Stages of culture shock 108
6.1 Sternberg's triangular theory of love (1988) 121

LIST OF ILLUSTRATIONS

7.1   Mandala of health (Hancock & Perkins, 1985)   135

7.2   Six cultural variables (Giger & Davidhizar, 1995)   137

7.3   HEARTS model   155

8.1   Gardner's (2000) multiple intelligences   170

8.2   Campinha-Bacote's (1999) process of cultural competence   177

9.1   Tuckman's (1965) stages of group development   189

9.2   Performance–maintenance leadership theory   190

9.3   Organizational cultural competency   197

List of tables

1.1   Types of research   15
1.2   Differences between 'traditional'
      research and participatory action
      research (PAR)   18
2.1   Summary of minority identity
      development model   26
2.2   Five components/subscales of
      Mulitgroup Ethnic Identity
      Measure (MEIM)   28
2.3   Comparison of Brislin's (1981) coping
      skills and identity negotiation strategies   30
2.4   Characteristics of 'psychological
      engine of adjustment' and multi-
      cultural personality   34
2.5   Summary of gender stereotypes   36
3.1   Changes during adolescence   55
4.1   Six core virtues (Peterson &
      Seligman, 2004)   88
4.2   Results from the 2007 world values
      survey (www.news-medical.net, 2008)   90

LIST OF TABLES

5.1 Berry's (1997, 2001) strategies of
acculturation   98
5.2 Summary of approaches to cultural
competence   106
7.1 Mental health attributions and
treatments   147
7.2 Approaches to cultural competence   152
8.1 Teaching and learning factors affected
by culture   168
8.2 Women's ways of knowing   171
8.3 Intercultural development model   178

Chapter 1

Introductory concepts

- Introduction   2
- What is culture?   2
- Approaches to culture and psychology   4
- Culture and diversity   8
- Cultural concepts   10
- 'Doing' culture   12
- Theoretical and research paradigms   13
- Research methods   14
- And so forth (participatory action research)   16

1

Introduction

PSYCHOLOGY AND CULTURE have a reciprocal relationship of influence. Individual thoughts, feelings, and behaviours influence cultural norms and practices and vice versa. Because the relationship between psychology and culture is multifaceted and dynamic, research and theory consequently take on a variety of forms. Each of these areas, however, contributes to the merging of psychology and culture within a global context.

What is culture?

Culture eludes most of us perhaps in part due to the complexity of the concept and the confusion with which it has been defined. There is lack of consensus about the meaning of culture yet it seems to permeate many aspects of our lives including personal tastes to manners, beliefs, values, world views, and actions. Traditionally, culture has been thought of as national identity however, the scope has broadened to include many aspects of social difference including but not limited to race, ethnicity, gender, social class, religion, and sexuality. Even though much of culture in terms of national identity is tangible and visual (e.g., food, clothing, housing, rituals, etc.), some aspects of culture may not necessarily be 'seen' – socioeconomic status, religion, and sexual orientation.

Broadly, culture can be defined as integrated patterns of learned beliefs and behaviours that are shared among groups and include thoughts, communication styles, ways of interacting, views of roles and relationships, values, practices, and customs (Donini-Lenhoff & Hedrick, 2000; Robins, Fantone, Hermann, Alexander, & Zweifler, 1998) or more simply, 'a total way of life of a people' (Geertz, 1973). Culture can be expanded to include many factors which encompass aspects of daily life and social influences/factors. This means we are all 'culturally different' given different family backgrounds, religions, occupations, disability, gender, socioeconomic status, sexual orientation, etc. Beyond race and ethnicity, we all are part of and influenced by multiple cultures. Each of us is a multicultural individual with many sets of cultures in different contexts that may or may not coincide. See Figure 1.1 for different emphases in the definitions of culture.

Culture is complex and multifaceted, pervasive and embedded in many aspects of life and living. Berry and colleagues (Berry, Poortinga, Segall, & Dasen, 2002) outline six general aspects in which culture can be discussed:

(1) Descriptive emphasizes the different activities and behaviours of a culture.
(2) Historical aspects refer to the heritage and traditions associated with a particular cultural group.
(3) Normative signifies the rules and norms of a culture.
(4) Psychological refers to the behavioural aspects of culture like learning and problem solving.
(5) Structural depicts the social and organizational aspects of culture.
(6) Genetic describes the origins of a culture (see Figure 1.2).

Culture is used to reflect many different aspects of life. Another categorization of culture contains nine broad categories: general characteristics, food and clothing, housing and technology, economy and transportation, individual and family activities, community and

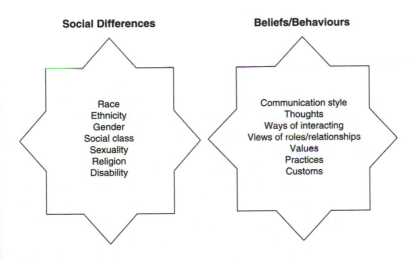

Social Differences

Race
Ethnicity
Gender
Social class
Sexuality
Religion
Disability

Beliefs/Behaviours

Communication style
Thoughts
Ways of interacting
Views of roles/relationships
Values
Practices
Customs

Figure 1.1   **Different emphases of 'culture'**

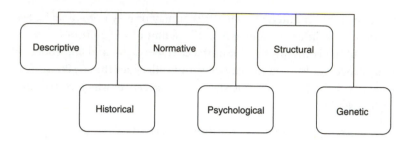

Figure 1.2 **Berry et al.'s (2002) six aspects of culture**

government, welfare, religion and science, and sex and the life cycle (see Figure 1.3).

In defining culture, it is important to remember that 'one size does not fit all' which suggests that cultural behaviour is multidetermined and is likely a product of history, patterns of behaviour associated with economic activity and the influence of philosophical and religious views. Based on culture, people structure their worlds and determine their social interactions. The common characteristics of culture are that it comes from adaptive interactions between humans and environments, has shared elements, and is transmitted across time periods and generations (Triandis, 2007).

Approaches to culture and psychology

Lehman, Chiu and Schaller (2004) suggest four functions of culture in relation to psychology: evolutionary, buffer, epistemic, and resulting from interpersonal interactions. From an evolutionary perspective, culture makes sense because of our need for collective support in order to survive and reproduce and because culture provides an adaptive function via cultural norms, beliefs and practices all of which contribute to efficient organization of societal groups. Another perspective on the function of culture is from terror management theory. According to this theory, culture serves as a protective factor/buffer against existential anxiety about our own mortality. Culture offers mechanisms of 'symbolic immortality' such as naming a baby after oneself so

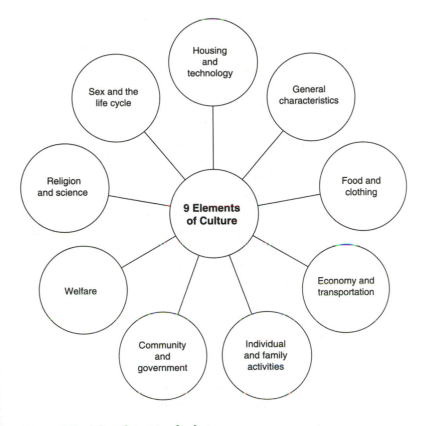

Figure 1.3   Nine elements of culture

that the name lives on, religious beliefs in life after death, and feelings of being a valuable member of and contributor to culture. Culture may serve an epistemic need to validate our perceptions of the world around us. Shared beliefs, expectations and rules that come from culture help fulfill this need. Another perspective on the emergence of culture is that it is an 'unintended byproduct' of interpersonal interaction. Through interaction that involves interpersonal communication, people mutually influence one another toward shared beliefs, behaviours, and norms within a population which results in culture (Lehman et al., 2004) (see Figure 1.4).

The two primary approaches that combine culture and

Figure 1.4 **Functions of culture**

psychology are cultural psychology and cross-cultural psychology. The primary differences between these two perspectives have to do with emphasis. Cultural psychology focuses more on context and culture that is 'inside' the person while cross-cultural psychology emphasizes content and culture 'outside' of the person (Triandis, 2007). Cultural psychology examines variations in human behaviour as it is influenced by sociocultural context and includes both describing the psychological diversity of human behaviour globally and the reasons for such diversity. The discipline of cultural psychology emphasizes cross-cultural interactions, human behaviour and the influence of social and cultural forces (Segall, Dasen, Berry, & Poortinga, 1999), as well as differences and universals across cultures. Cultural psychology, as compared with cross-cultural psychology, is more likely to examine in depth a few cultures and the psychology of individuals within a particular cultural group. In other words, human behaviour is meaningful when considering the sociocultural context of the individuals and how they have internalized that particular culture's qualities (Segall et al., 1999). A relatively recent field, cultural psychology comes from an intellectual tradition of scientific general psychology rooted mainly in Europe but has developed primarily in the United States. In addition to general psychology, cultural psychology has been influenced by many other disciplines including anthropology, physiology, sociology, history, and political science. In research, a cultural psychologist may investigate women's experience of trauma and empowerment in various post-transitional societies (Budryte, Vaughn, & Riegg, 2009) or how fundamental religious principles influence personality traits (Monroe & Kreidie, 1997).

Cross-cultural psychology is more of a 'macro' level approach to culture and psychology. As such, many cross-cultural psychologists are industrial/organizational or political psychologists (Triandis,

2007). Cross-cultural psychology is more about variations in human behaviour influenced by cultural context with data typically collected across many cultures. Cross-cultural psychologists attempt to describe 'the diversity of human behavior in the world' and 'link individual behavior to the cultural environment in which it occurs' (Berry et al., 2002, p. 1). They are also interested in psychologically common or universal thoughts, feelings, and behaviours. Berry and colleagues (2002) define cross-cultural psychology as 'the study: of similarities and differences in individual psychological functioning in various cultural and ethnocultural groups; of the relationships between psychological variables and sociocultural, ecological and biological variables; and of ongoing changes in these variables' (p. 3). In research, cross-cultural psychologists are likely to study attributes of culture that do not change significantly such as high conformity in collectivist cultures (Bond & Smith, 1996) or higher levels of well-being in individualist cultures (Diener, Diener, & Diener, 1995; Triandis, 2007).

Other perspectives of psychology and culture include sociocultural psychology, which is an attempt to unite culture, society and psychology. Sociocultural psychology 'deals with the psychological phenomena that happen because of the sociocultural aspects of human lives in varied social contexts—peace or war, famine or purposeful avoidance of overweight by dieting, poverty, or affluence' (Valsiner & Rosa, 2007, p. 1). Another approach is culture as social-psychological which is a perspective that considers 'culture as a set of social psychological processes' emphasizing the individual in a cultural context (Chiu & Hong, 2006, p. 23). In considering the social psychology of culture, most important is the individual's representation of shared meanings and of generalized others in the culture. Chiu and Hong (2006) suggest that it is explicitly the cultural dimension that makes human cognition and action social.

The approach of indigenous psychologies posits that it is not possible to understand particular groups without a clear understanding of the social, historical, political, ideological, and religious factors that have shaped the people. A growing interest in indigenous psychologies has emerged perhaps due in part to psychologists' recognition that they cannot possibly understand every aspect of every unique culture. Indigenous psychologies are associated exclusively with the cultural group under investigation (Ho, 1998) and are not 'imported' from other regions.

Some psychologists have suggested that the intersection of psychology and culture should be considered global (or international) psychology. Global psychology eliminates boundaries and emphasizes the principles of free market and democracy on the political side and tolerance, freedom, and openness on the cultural and psychological side (Bullock, 2006). The scope of global psychology is worldwide and international psychology signifies across and between nations. Akin to global psychology is the idea of the 'cultural mixtures' approach introduced by Hermans and Kempen (1998). Given that cultures have been transformed and are multifaceted and extremely complex, they argue that studying psychology in cultures defined by geographic location is 'old', static and confining and instead psychologists studying culture should switch to new cultural mixtures including multicultural identities and intersections of cultural changes. Figure 1.5 depicts the various approaches to psychology and culture.

Culture and diversity

Cultural diversity and cultural interactions are some of our biggest challenges in today's global society. Diversity is an overused 'buzzword' to accentuate difference and fails to consider the similarities between cultural groups. To clarify diversity, or cultural difference, definitions of various aspects of cultural difference are provided.

Race has generally been thought of as a distinction of a group of people either based on self-identification or based on similar, heritable physical characteristics (e.g., skin colour, facial features, hair texture, etc.) although many argue that race is really more of a social construct as a result of arbitrary assignment to social categories (Brace, 2005). For example, Black is considered a racial category that encompasses people of African origin. *Ethnicity* indicates cultural heritage of a group of people with common ancestral origin, language, traditions, and often religion and geographic territory. For instance, Hispanic or

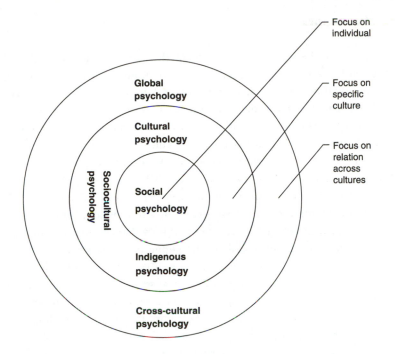

Figure 1.5 **Approaches to psychology and culture**

Latino describes the ethnic group of people of Latin American origin. *Nationality* refers to a person's country of origin; the nation shares a common geographical origin, history, and language and is typically unified as a political entity. Lithuanian is an example of nationality. There are other areas of cultural difference that at first glance may not be considered 'cultural' such as gender, disability, and others. *Gender* refers to the norms and expectations that are culturally assigned to men and women. *Disability* signifies a person with some type of physical impairment and is regarded as a cultural difference if persons with disabilities share ways of thinking and feeling specific to their impairment (Blaine, 2007).

Cultural concepts

As there can be semantic confusion with the word culture itself and the tendency to equate culture as synonymous with race, ethnicity, or nationality, several definitions related to culture are described. *Ethnocentrism* is the belief that your own ethnic or cultural group is better in comparison with others and often results in negative judgements about other ethnic, national and cultural groups. In most cases, ethnocentrism occurs from a position of cultural majority and thus power and privilege (Shiraev & Levy, 2010). *Stereotypes* are overgeneralized beliefs about people from social groups (Allport, 1954). When stereotyping we apply group qualities to individuals from a particular social group that often does not provide accurate information about individual group members. Engaging in stereotyping is a common occurrence because we are 'cognitive misers' who think in simplistic and overgeneralizing ways because we want to conserve our cognitive resources by taking shortcuts and approximations in our thinking (Fiske, 1995) often making errors in attributions about the reason behind other people's behaviours (Forsterling, 2001). With our often limited world views, alternative frames of reference can be a challenge to incorporate, and sometimes, the not-knowing can arouse fear and other unsettling emotions (Ito, Larsen, Smith, & Cacioppo, 1998; Kunda, 1999).

Prejudice is a negative and generally unjustified judgement of another person on the basis of his or her social or cultural group identity (Allport, 1954). Prejudice is unjustified because of the overgeneralizations that are applied to all members of a group. Prejudice can be negative or positive but negative prejudice is the judgement from which disadvantage and discrimination come whereas positive prejudice includes feelings of respect and admiration (Blaine, 2007). Prejudice reflects thoughts and feelings and represents all the 'isms' in society against different groups including sexism, racism, ageism, and ethnocentrism. *Discrimination* is the enacted unjust behaviour resulting from prejudice (e.g., not renting a house to a gay couple because of homosexism). Discrimination differs from prejudice in that it involves action/doing. *Multiculturalism* is the notion that all cultural groups should be recognized as equal and that each cultural group is unique with its own set of shared values, norms and customs which should be respected in their own right (Management of Social Transformations Programme (MOST), 1995).

Other concepts related to culture include etics, emics and various constructs related to cultural competence. *Etics* refer to universal principles across cultures or aspects of behaviour that are consistent across cultures. *Emics* denotes culture-specific principles or aspects of life that differ across cultures. *Cultural competence* is often used synonymously with cultural diversity, cultural sensitivity, and cultural awareness although each term means something a little different (Figure 1.6). *Cultural diversity* as described above is about cultural differences – how people are diverse culturally. *Cultural sensitivity* is the knowledge that both cultural similarities and differences exist. *Cultural awareness* is being conscious of cultural similarities and differences. Cultural competence can be defined at the individual level and at the organizational level. At the individual level, cultural competence requires personal growth through first-hand knowledge, interactions with cultural groups, and an examination of one's own biases. Over time, like the definition of culture, cultural competence has widened in scope to encompass three dimensions: (1) awareness of one's own assumptions, values, and biases; (2) understanding the world view of culturally diverse clients/patients (customers, students); and (3) developing appropriate intervention strategies and techniques (Sue & Sue, 2003). Organizationally, cultural competence is a set of values, behaviours, attitudes, policies, practices that enables staff to work with multicultural populations (Pérez & Luquis, 2008).

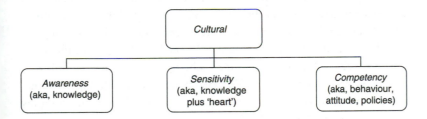

Figure 1.6 **Cultural awareness, sensitivity, and competency**

'Doing' culture

Culture provides a way of seeing the world and in part determines the patterns of behaviour in everyday life. There are many advantages of a culturally heterogeneous global system that include benefits that extend beyond business and societal reasons (Bochner, 2003). Intercultural experiences may enhance creativity and innovation due to an individual synthesizing experiences from different cultures and creatively combining them (Brislin, 1981). However, it is easy amidst such diversity of cultures and our changing world to resort to the 'tried and true' in search of a familiar and seemingly safe and traditional, monocultural identity. The consequences of such behaviour may perpetuate bias and oppression that already exist and increase misunderstanding between individuals, communities, and societies. We all have different intercultural frameworks. When we encounter different norms and values we tend to experience a loss of social support, reference group and social status changes and encounter different attributions of behaviour. It is typical to look for consensual validation from others to confirm that our ideas, values, and behaviours are correct. If someone is perceived as different, then it can undermine such security (Fitness, Fletcher, & Overall, 2007). Lamentably, prejudice and discrimination are common reactions when people are perceived as culturally different and can result in a lowering of self-respect for and learned helplessness in the targets (Horowitz, Davis, Palermo, & Vladeck, 2000; Prochaska & Norcross, 2003).

Without expectations of cultural competence individually and organizationally, we can anticipate that people will remain fragmented and disconnected for significant segments of the globe. As Reynolds (2001) suggests, we need to pay more attention to 'fully accepting the simultaneous nature of individual, universal, and cultural influences' and act accordingly with decisions which 'embrace that complexity' (Matsumoto & Juang, 2008). The examination of psychology within a cultural framework allows for a better understanding of the complex intersections of people and society.

Theoretical and research paradigms

In order to explore the areas of psychology and culture and their inter-section, various theoretical and research paradigms must be considered regarding the variation in culture and behaviour. Absolutism, relativ-ism, and universalism are three orientations from which to approach psychology and culture and the issue of human variation. Absolutism sees cultural phenomena as essentially the same across cultures. The absolutist perspective posits that biological factors underlie psycho-logical differences in behaviour and therefore culture plays a limited role in human differences. Methodologically, research from the abso-lutist orientation can be conducted through comparisons of different cultures given that psychological phenomena share the same meaning across cultures (e.g., a comparison of depression in three cultures). The absolutist perspective coincides nicely with cross-cultural psych-ology. In contrast, relativism approaches human variation as a result of cultural factors. Relativists believe that people should be under-stood relative to the sociocultural context from the perspective of the people involved. When doing research, relativists are not typically interested in similarities across cultures or comparisons across cultures because they believe that behaviour should be examined within the culture, specific to the cultural nuances. The relativist orientation encapsulates cultural psychology and indigenous psychology. Univer-salism adopts the notion basic psychological processes are the same across cultures but that culture influences the different expressions and variations of behaviour. Methodologically, comparisons are made cau-tiously with input and modification from local cultural knowledge (culture-comparative research perspective).

Philosophically, different paradigms offer answers to existence, knowing and methodology within psychology and culture. Lincoln and Guba (2000) outline four paradigms: positivism, post-positivism, critical theory, and constructivism. Positivism is a philosophy which presumes that true knowledge is obtainable and verifiable and results from an objective reality. Post-positivism, according to Lincoln and Guba (2000), is the paradigm most accepted in modern day psych-ology. The post-positivism paradigm assumes that knowledge of real-ity is imperfect and based on conjecture but can be examined through systematic inquiry and critical experimentation. The critical theory paradigm believes that knowledge is subjective and bound by values and sociocultural and historical context. Constructivism reflects the notion that knowledge is relative and reality is socially constructed.

Research methods

The same research methodologies that are used in psychology can be employed to investigate the relationship of psychology and culture in a global context. Quantitative research attempts to measure human behaviour comparatively through empirical means. Typically, statistics are used to determine quantity, amount, intensity, and frequency of the behaviour in question. In contrast, qualitative research is most often conducted in a natural setting and emphasizes enquiry and exploration through analysis of words, views of respondents, and the social construction of experience and meaning. Data collection methods and data analysis techniques differ depending on whether a quantitative or qualitative research approach is used. A mixed methods approach to research that combines both quantitative and qualitative methods has grown in popularity in order to address research questions more holistically.

In part, the research methods for examining aspects of psychology and culture depend on the theoretical approach. For example, in cultural psychology, research methods focus on the 'cultural system' in which the behaviour occurs and the interplay of individuals and the environment relative to the cultural context. This implies that research tools such as ethnography, narrative approaches, longitudinal observations, video recording are used, all of which accentuate the lived experience of people within their cultural contexts versus comparison of data. Other types of research appropriate for use in the intersection of psychology and culture include cross-cultural comparison studies, unpackaging studies, ecological-level studies, psychobiographical research, cross-cultural validation studies, and ethnographies (see Table 1.1 for a description of these types of research).

The same basic concepts of conducting good research still apply when considering research in psychology and culture. However, there

Table 1.1 **Types of research**

Research	Charactertics
Cross-cultural comparison studies	A psychological variable is compared across two or more cultures
Unpackaging studies	Explores why cultural differences occur by exploring other variables to account for differences in addition to the cross-cultural variable(s) of interest
Ecological-level studies	Countries and cultures versus individuals are the unit of analysis
Psychobiographical research	The psychological study of a person's life
Cross-cultural validation studies	Explores whether variable of interest in one culture is applicable to and equivalent in other cultures
Ethnographies	A culture is observed in its natural environment; field study

are additional research issues to consider given the complexity within psychology and culture (Cohen, 2007). Validity can be especially troublesome in research about psychology and culture because the definition and measurement of particular variables may not represent the same constructs in another culture. Related to validity is bias or equivalence of meaning across cultures. Not only does the concept have to signify the same thing in each culture but the theoretical framework, hypotheses, and methods used to compare cultures must have the same meaning in each of the cultures involved. Sample selection poses another challenge for cultural studies in psychology. Homogeneity among a cultural group is often assumed and this is rarely the case. An often hidden barrier to cultural research is the issue of test translation. Given that cross-cultural research generally requires that studies are conducted in more than one language, researchers must establish that the measures and procedures used are linguistically equivalent. Back translation is the most common approach to address linguistic equivalence. It involves the translation of the research protocol into a different language(s) and then having a different person translate it back to the original language and repeated with the goal of semantic equivalence among the protocols (Crystal, 2004).

Political and ethical issues also plague research in psychology and culture. For instance, researchers may not find convergent data across cultures and have to consider how best to interpret the data given that there are likely multiple and overlapping meanings (Cohen, 2007). The issue of within-group and between-group differences can arise when conducting research related to cultures. Historically, much of the research in the field has focused on differences across cultures rather than similarities. Similarities, however, are amidst the differences and vice versa and therefore researchers should be flexible and design research studies that contain both 'integration' and 'differentiation' (Cohen, 2007). Perhaps researchers investigating psychological phenomena related to culture need to be mindful of the Asian saying that, 'all individuals, in many respects, are like no other individuals, like some individuals, and like all other individuals'.

Exploiting cultural groups especially vulnerable populations such as indigenous peoples can be problematic. Even well-intentioned researchers may lose sight of the ultimate effect of research on certain cultural groups who may feel taken advantage of or 'used' only to the benefit of the researcher obtaining data. A native saying reflects this sentiment: 'researchers are like mosquitoes; they suck your blood and leave' (Cochran, et al., 2008). A research approach especially suited for psychology and culture and one that better addresses the issues related to well-being of the participants is the use of participatory action research (Reason & Bradbury, 2008) also referred to as community-based participatory research (Minkler & Wallerstein, 2003). See the And so forth section below for further discussion of this framework of research.

And so forth (participatory action research)

During the last decade, action research in all its multiplicity of meanings has become increasingly important in different social science disciplines, such as psychology, education and interdisciplinary cultural, and international studies. Participatory action research (PAR) can be conceived as an approach to social investigation, an educational process, and a way to take action to address a problem (Hall, 1981). In research, PAR is a collaborative, partnership approach that equitably involves all stakeholders (e.g., community members, organizational representatives, and researchers) in all aspects of the research process (Israel, Schulz, Parker, & Becker, 2001). From the beginning, action research was intended (and it still does) to promote social change. In the words of Ben W. M. Boog (2003), 'action research is designed to improve the researched subjects' capacities to solve problems, develop skills (including professional skills), increase their chances of self-determination, and to have more influence on the functioning and decision-making processes of organizations and institutions in which they act' (p. 426). Such research implies that the objects that are being researched are empowered by their participation in the project. The community then becomes a social and cultural entity of active engagement in the research process (Campbell & Jovchelovitch, 1999). The relationship between the researcher and the researched subjects is based on equality, and the researchers approach the subjects hoping that the latter will benefit from the participation in this project. All participants (including the 'objects' of research) are regarded as equals, although their contributions are nevertheless recognized as different. Advantages of PAR include an increase in the relevance and utilization of the research by everyone involved, a greater likelihood of addressing complex problems because the process is truly collaborative, quality and validity of the research are improved because the process is informed by the people involved, a potential to build trust and partnerships with previously distrustful and culturally different 'subjects', and likely empowerment of community members. See Table 1.2 for a comparison between traditional research approaches and PAR. Freire (1973, 2006) discusses 'conscientization' (or the awakening of critical consciousness) as core in PAR approaches. He believes that people go through a process first from 'intransitive thought' (no control over lives; experience defined by fate so actions cannot change conditions) to 'semi-transitive thought' (fragmented thinking; fail to connect problems to larger societal determinants) to the final stage of 'critical transivity' (achievement of conscientization that involves being empowered

Table 1.2 **Differences between 'traditional' research and participatory action research (PAR)**

Traditional research	PAR
'extractive'	participative
experts	co-investigators
academic	truly translational
journals	applied/action oriented
uninformed 'subjects'	informed 'participants'
isolated	collaborative
tradition-oriented	change-oriented

to think critically and holistically about one's condition and thus act on conditions). Freire believes that the final level of consciousness comes from a social process of learning characterized by dialogical and participatory relationships. Martín-Baró (1994) explains that Freire's concept of conscientization merges with personal consciousness and 'makes manifest the historical dialectic between knowing and doing, between individual growth and community organization, between personal liberation and social transformation' (p. 18).

Community-based participatory research (CBPR) is a PAR approach that has been shown to successfully engage community members in health research initiatives (Minkler & Wallerstein, 2003). The CBPR approach involves community members directly in the design and facilitation of research projects, supporting the notion that communities often already have local knowledge that is crucial to understanding and addressing their own social problems. As a result, through a participatory process, research becomes focused on practical problems of importance to its constituents and provides an outlet to express needs and concerns that can be addressed effectively. By taking successful concrete actions to improve their communities through relevant research initiatives, community members not only identify and help meet the specific needs of their community but also become better connected with that community and build their self-respect and confidence to cope with life situations. CBPR provides a 'voice' for an otherwise marginalized population to realize that they can make a positive difference in their environment (Brydon-Miller, 2003). Researchers have applied CBPR successfully in a variety of settings, including schools and many diverse communities (e.g., Cameron, Manske, Brown, Jolin, Murnaghan, & Lovato, 2007) and to address concerns as varied as bullying in children (Leff, Power, Costigan, & Manz, 2003) and health care utilization among adolescents (Bostok & Freeman, 2003). Particularly compelling are examples of CBPR with minority and/or vulnerable communities with resulting interventions that successfully fulfill a community's unique health needs and at the same time bridge the typical gap between academic researcher priorities and community member concerns. One convincing example with community-built interventions and subsequent positive health outcomes was conducted with Aboriginal peoples in Australia. In order to effectively address alcohol abuse among the Aboriginal peoples, Mardiros (2001) facilitated a CBPR approach that led to community members designing and conducting interventions such as layperson street patrols and the development of an Aboriginal mental health worker position. Such community-built interventions led to health outcomes like the eradication of suicides and suicide attempts and decreases in visits to the emergency room as well as community-level outcomes like increased community pride and empowerment.

Further reading

Blaine, B. (2007). *Understanding the psychology of diversity*. Los Angeles, CA: Sage.

Kim, U., & Berry, J. W. (Eds.). (1993). *Indigenous psychologies: Research and experience in cultural context*. Newbury Park, CA: Sage.

Kitayama, S., & Cohen, D. (Eds.). (2007). *Handbook of cultural psychology*. New York: The Guilford Press.

Lehman, D. R., Chiu, C., & Schaller, M. (2004). Psychology and culture. *Annual Review of Psychology*, 55, 689–714.

Reason, P., & Bradbury, H. (Eds.). (2008). *The SAGE handbook of action research: Participative inquiry and practice* (2nd ed.). Los Angeles, CA: Sage.

Valsiner, J., & Rosa, A. (Eds.). (2007). *The Cambridge handbook of sociocultural psychology*. Cambridge, UK: Cambridge University Press.

Chapter 2

Identity and culture

- Introduction 22
- Culture, self and identity 22
- Personality and culture 32
- Gender and culture 34
- Other aspects of identity and culture 40
- And so forth (is there a terrorist personality?) 41

Introduction

W HO WE ARE as individuals is a cultural construct socialized from a very early age. Culture plays an important role in shaping and maintaining our self-concepts and identity and thus influences our thoughts, feelings, and behaviours. Self-concepts differ across cultural groups. For example, in the Western world, the self is viewed as individualistic and independent and in Asia for example, there is much more of an emphasis on the collective self and interdependence with others (Markus & Kitayama, 1991). The opposite construals of self influence people in these cultures to think, feel, and act differently. Other core elements of the self include gender, religious identity, social class, sexuality, disability, and weight.

Culture, self and identity

Concepts of self

Although there are considerable similarities across cultures regarding sense of self, there are some culture-specific notions about what constitutes identity and the self-concept (how we think about or view ourselves). With regard to cultural variations, one of the most popular distinctions of the self is the collectivism–individualism distinction. In more individualistic cultures, people tend to develop an independent self-concept. Thus, desires, preferences, attributes, and abilities are viewed as distinct and separate from others. In other cultures, the individual is not viewed as separate from the collective and therefore the self-concept develops only within a sociocultural context. Triandis (1989) suggests that early exposure to differing values and beliefs within a cultural context influences the development of the self-concept. For instance, parents in individualistic cultures are more likely to teach their children to be independent and forge a unique, autonomous self whereas in collectivist cultures, parents emphasize the welfare of the collective as more important than the individual. Other researchers have made distinctions between interdependent and independent selves (Markus & Kitayama, 1991) and between the Asian and Western self-concepts (Spiro, 1993). Markus and Kitayama (1991) explain the interdependent self as the collectivist self relying heavily on family, friends, neighbours, and coworkers in determining self-concept. In contrast, the independent self is associated with individualistic characteristics whereby the self is not defined by interrelationships with others. Such a distinction suggests more fluidity and flexibility in the interdependent self because if one's relationships change then the self-concept is likely to change whereas this is not true of the independent self. East Asian cultures tend to view the self-concept as interdependent whereas the self-concept of European Americans is organized around the models of self as independent (Heine, Lehman, Markus, & Kitayama, 1999; Kitayama & Uchida, 2003; Markus & Kitayama, 1991).

Other patterns of the self-concept and identity that demonstrate the influence of culture on the development of the self have been documented in cross-cultural research. In a cross-cultural study about Japanese and US self-concepts, Cousins (1989) reported that Americans used more psychological attributes (traits and dispositions) to describe themselves whereas Japanese subjects included the larger context by mentioning preferences and wishes, social categories and activities when describing themselves. Similarly, Bochner (1994) found that Malaysians, as compared with Australian and British, had fewer personal responses and more group-related responses when describing themselves. In a study comparing self-concepts of Americans and Hindus in India, the Indian subjects were more likely to attribute their actions to contextual factors while the Americans explained their actions as due to personal dispositions. Van den Heuvel and colleagues (1992) asked Moroccan, Turkish, and Dutch children in the Netherlands to describe five things about themselves, about a similar classmate, and about a different classmate. Children from the more collectivist cultures (Morocco and Turkey) used more social statements indicating group memberships, social and interpersonal traits when describing themselves or a similar classmate. Dutch children were more likely to describe themselves or a similar classmate using more psychological attributes such as traits and personal preferences.

Another important aspect of the self-concept is self-esteem, or how we feel about ourselves. Many have claimed that self-esteem is virtually indistinguishable from self-concept, however, this distinction appears to depend on culture. A number of researchers have examined aspects of self-concept and self-esteem and found that the Western cultures are less likely to separate out self-concept and self-esteem whereas in Asian cultures, the distinction between the two aspects of the self is more pronounced (Markus & Kitayama, 1991). Such differences appear to be related to the collectivist–individualistic orientation of the culture. If individuals are independent and responsible for their successes and failures, then emphasizing the positive aspects of the self serves as protection against low self-esteem in contrast to cultures where individual attributes and accomplishments are less important in determining self-esteem (Markus & Kitayama, 1991).

How children are raised also contributes to the development of self-esteem. If children are raised in a warm and accepting atmosphere with consistent rules and expectations, regardless of culture, their self-esteem is likely to be higher. Because of the warmth and acceptance of an extended family with many relatives offering support and nurturance, many African children are thought to have higher self-esteem than children in Western countries who typically have one or two caretakers to foster self-esteem (Olowu, 1990). In Jamaica, children are thought to develop lower self-esteem and self-worth due to family instability and strict authoritarian discipline patterns (Smith & Reynolds, 1992).

Identity development models

Cultural identity refers to 'individuals' psychological membership' in a distinct culture (Matsumoto & Juang, 2008). Likewise, ethnic identity is an important component of one's sociocultural identity (Verkuyten, 2005). Tajfel (1978) describes ethnic identity as part of the self-concept that comes from knowledge of membership in a social group(s) together with the value and emotional significance attached to that membership. Noteworthy are the identity development models that describe the identity development for various cultural categories (Phinney, 2000). These racial/ethnic/cultural identity models provide insight about within-group individual differences and the sociopolitical influences including oppression that affect these groups (Sue & Sue, 2003). In general, the majority of identity models follow similar patterns that begin with a passive or lack of awareness stage and end with an integrated stage which is thought to exist due to oppressed groups sharing similar patterns of adjustment to cultural oppression (Sue & Sue, 2003). See Table 2.1 for a summary of the general stages of a minority identity model (originally developed by Morten and Sue, in Atkinson, 2004). One of the most influential and well-documented identity models is the Cross model of psychological Nigrescence (Cross, 1978) that explains the process of black identity transformation in the USA. The original model delineated a five-stage process in which African Americans move from a white frame of reference to a positive black frame of reference: pre-encounter, encounter, immersion–emersion, internalization, and internalization–commitment. In one example of a study on ethnic identity, Parham and Helms (1985) examined African American youth at various stages (pre-encounter, encounter, immersion, etc.) of establishing individual black identity. They found that those in the encounter stage, or the stage in which they become comfortable with their identity as a black individual, were more present-oriented and inner-directed. By way of contrast those in the pre-encounter stage, or the stage in which they favour white culture and perspectives, were more likely to look externally for identity cues and less likely to be sociable and less likely to be satisfied with themselves as people.

Several Asian American and Latino/Hispanic American identity development models exist (Sue & Sue, 2003). These models identify categories in which an individual maintains their traditional identity, takes on the American identity or combines the two into a meaningful bicultural merged identity. More recent identity models mirror Cross' black identity model with stages ranging from a passive/lack of awareness stage to an integrated identity stage.

Other models of cultural identity development are attempts to combine cultural identity across cultural and racial/ethnic groups – emergence of a 'Third World consciousness' (Sue & Sue, 2003). One such model is a five-stage racial/cultural identity development model (R/CID; Sue & Sue, 2003) developed originally as the minority identity model. The R/CID model proposes five stages through which oppressed

Table 2.1 Summary of the minority identity development model (Atkinson (2004) Counseling American Minorities (6th ed.), reproduced with permission from McGraw-Hill Companies, Inc.)

Stages of minority development model	Attitudes toward self	Attitude toward others of the same minority	Attitude toward others of different minority	Attitude toward dominant group
Stage 1 – conformity	Self-depreciating	Group-depreciating	Discriminatory	Group-appreciating
Stage 2 – dissonance	Conflict between self-depreciation and appreciating	Conflict between group-depreciating and group-appreciating	Conflict between dominant-held views of minority hier-archy and feelings of shared experience	Conflict between group-appreciating and group-depreciating
Stage 3 – resistance and immersion	Self-appreciating	Group-appreciating	Conflict between feelings of empathy for other minority experiences and feelings of culturocentrism	Group-depreciating
Stage 4 – introspection	Concern with basis of self-appreciating	Concern with nature of unequivocal appreciation	Concern with ethnocentric basis for judging others	Concern with the basis of group-depreciation
Stage 5 – synergetic articu-lations and awareness	Self-appreciating	Group-appreciating	Group-appreciating	Selective appreciating

people move as they understand themselves within their own culture, the dominant culture and the tension and oppression between the two cultures: conformity, dissonance, resistance and immersion, introspection, and integrative awareness. The R/CID model begins with the conformity stage (similar to the pre-encounter stage in the Cross model) in which individuals exhibit a preference for the dominant cultural values over their own cultural values. During this stage, individuals identify with the dominant group and use them as their primary reference group (Sue & Sue, 2003). They tend to downplay and feel negative about their own cultural group with low salience as part of their identity. The dissonance stage is marked by an encounter or experience that is inconsistent with culturally held beliefs, attitudes and values from the conformity stage. For instance, a minority individual who is ashamed of their own cultural heritage will encounter someone from their cultural group who is proud of his or her heritage. In this stage, denial begins to occur and there is a questioning of one's beliefs and attitudes held in the conformity stage. Cross (1971) mentions the assassination of Martin Luther King Jr as causing many African Americans to move rapidly from a passive conformity/ pre-encounter stage to a dissonance/encounter stage. In the resistance and immersion stage, a minority person is likely to feel anger, guilt and shame at the oppression and racism that previously they put up with. This stage is marked by an endorsement of minority-held views and a rejection of the dominant values of society and culture. During the introspection stage, the individual devotes more energy toward understanding themselves as part of a minority group and what that means at a deeper level. In contrast to the intense reactivity against dominant culture in the resistance and immersion stage, the introspection stage is more 'pro-active' in defining and discovering the sense of self (Sue & Sue, 2003). The integrative awareness stage includes a sense of security and the ability to appreciate positive aspects of both their own culture and the dominant culture. Individuals in this stage have resolved conflicts experienced in earlier stages and have more of a sense of control and flexibility with the ability to recognize the pros and cons of both cultural groups while still trying to eliminate all forms of oppression (Sue & Sue, 2003).

Cultural identity has been measured in a myriad of ways and

many of the identity models mentioned above have corresponding instruments. However, the measurement of cultural identity usually emphasizes differences across cultural groups. To examine ethnic identity as a 'general phenomenon that is relevant across groups,' Phinney (1992, p. 158) uses a measure called the Multigroup Ethnic Identity Measure (MEIM) composed of various components/subscales (see Table 2.2).

Bicultural and multicultural identity

Given the increasing internationalization and globalization of society with more intercultural marriages and increased communication and interaction among different cultural groups, it is not surprising that bicultural and multicultural identities are becoming more common (Bochner, 2003). Individuals who navigate and have awareness of two or more cultures are considered bicultural or multicultural. In particular, minority groups, especially immigrants and refugees, may be forced to develop a bicultural or multicultural identity as a result of adjusting to a new culture. Because of the need to fit into different cultural contexts, multicultural individuals normally develop multiple

Table 2.2 **Five components/subscales of Multigroup Ethnic Identity Measure (MEIM)**

Subscales	Example items
Self-identification	'In terms of ethnic group, I consider myself to be __.'
Ethnic Behaviors and practices	'I am active in organizations or social groups that include mostly members of my own ethnic group.'
Affirmation and belonging	'I am happy that I am a member of the group I belong to.'
Ethnic identity achievement	'I have spent time trying to find out more about my own ethnic group, such as its history, traditions, and customs.'
Attitudes toward other groups	'I enjoy being around people from ethnic groups other than my own.'

concepts of the self that can be called upon depending on the context. There are a few studies that document the existence of multiple concepts of self within multicultural individuals. In one study with Arab and Jewish Israeli students in Israel, Oyserman (1993) found that individualism was related to private aspects of the self for these students, while collectivism was more apparent in social identities and public aspects of the self. In another study, multiple concepts of self emerged in relation to school persistence and achievement strategies in European Americans and African Americans (Oyserman, Gant & Ager, 1995).

One strategy that immigrants and multicultural individuals may use in multicultural societies is *cultural reaffirmation* or a crystallization of the native culture. For instance, Kosmitzki (1996) studied monocultural and bicultural Germans and Americans and found that the bicultural individuals were more likely to endorse more traditional values associated with their native culture as compared with native monocultural individuals. This same result has been found across other cultural groups (Lee, 1995; Takaki, 1998).

Brislin (1981) offers five coping skills that multicultural individuals typically use:

(1) Non-acceptance – continuing to act according to traditional norms, ignoring cultural differences.

(2) Substitution – behaving in the most acceptable manner by substituting norms from the 'new' culture for traditional norms.

(3) Addition – evaluating the situation and depending on judgement using either non-acceptance or substitution.

(4) Synthesis – combining elements of different cultures.

(5) Resynthesis – integrating ideas from various cultures in an original way, which Brislin notes, is the most culturally competent example of non-ethnocentric attitudes because no one culture is relied upon as the standard.

These coping skills align with the identity negotiation strategies of integration, alternation, synergy, and compartmentalization. Integration involves a blending of two or more cultural identities into one coherent multicultural identity (LaFromboise, Coleman, & Gerton, 1993). Alternation involves switching cultural identities depending on the context, and synergy is the development of a new multicultural identity rather than the sum of individual identities (Anthias, 2001). Compartmentalization occurs when cultural identities are kept separate because the person feels conflicted about meshing the two or more identities or that the identities are in opposition to one another (Benet-Martinez, Leu, & Morris, 2002). See Table 2.3 for a comparison of Brislin's coping skills and identity negotiation strategies.

Some people are able to develop a multicultural identity if they become adept at cultural transitions by learning to easily shift from one set of cultural behaviours and thinking to another cultural set that allows them to move in and out of the dominant culture and the less dominant cultures or that permits feeling comfortable within multicultural situations (Sussman, 2002). This flexibility in shifting from culture to culture using the appropriate cultural lens has been called by

Table 2.3 **Comparison of Brislin's (1981) coping skills and identity negotiation strategies**

Brislin's coping skill	Identity negotiation strategy	What it means
Non-acceptance	—	Rejection of 'new' culture; continuing to act in accordance with traditional culture
Substitution	—	Traditional norms are substituted with norms from 'new' culture
Addition	Alternation	Switching between 'new' and traditional culture, depending upon the context of situation
Synthesis	Integration	'New' and traditional cultures are blended into one multicultural identity
Resynthesis	Synergy	'New' and traditional cultures are combined in an original way
—	Compartmentalization	'New' and traditional cultural identities are kept separate

anthropologists 'cultural frame switching' (LaFromboise et al., 1993) and often results in a more fluid multicultural identity and 'multi-cultural mind' that can be psychologically healthy (Lee, Sobal, & Frongillo, 2003; Sparrow, 2000). One of Sparrow's (2000) multicultural informants from South America said, 'I think of myself not as a uni-fied cultural being but as a communion of different cultural beings. Due to the fact that I have spent time in different cultural environments I have developed several cultural identities that diverge and converge according to the need of the moment' (p. 190). As compared with monocultural individuals, people with multicultural experiences may have more adaptive skills for a variety of intercultural situations. Having a multicultural mind means that individuals have a loose net-work of categories and implicit theories of culture rather than an overall cultural world view and they do not continuously rely on only one cultural meaning system (Hong, Morris, Chiu, & Benet-Martínez, 2000).

Dominant identities and privilege

Dominant identities within any culture are held by those who have more power, prestige, status, and resources than others; which in most cultures means white, wealthy, able-bodied, male, heterosexual, and well-educated. Being dominant in a society carries with it a sense of privilege and opportunity not afforded to those with less dominant status. Most deny their dominance because it is taken for granted given the institutionalized normative features of society that support power and privilege by offering special rights to those in power. The less dominant populations are often invalidated and sometimes even pathologized. Most dominant people think of their lives as the norm and the ideal and take for granted the privilege they have as a result of their dominant identity (McIntosh, 1988). This same normative think-ing that results in denial of privilege may also serve as a barrier to recognizing one's own biases and prejudices about less dominant groups (Sue & Sue, 2003).

Personality and culture

Five factor model of personality

Do people of different cultures have their own unique personality? The five factor model (FFM) of personality suggests that five personality dimensions (extroversion, neuroticism, agreeableness, conscientiousness, and openness) are common to all humans regardless of culture. There is considerable evidence across many cultures to support the universality of these five personality dimensions (McCrae, 2001). One explanation for the universality of the FFM is the evolutionary approach that suggests that these particular traits are naturally selected in order to serve an adaptive function necessary for survival. The universality of the FFM does not in fact negate cultural variability. Culture is believed to engender the behavioural manifestation of personality and facilitate personality expression in thoughts, feelings and behaviours (McCrae, 2001).

Indigenous personalities

Indigenous personalities are personality traits and characteristics found and understood only within the context of a particular culture. Since indigenous personalities are culture-specific, they contrast with the universality of the FFM. Berry and colleagues ((Berry et al., 2002) describe the African model of personality that consists of three layers or aspects of a person housed by the body: (1) the first layer located at the core of the person is based upon a spiritual principle; (2) the second layer involves a psychological vitality principle; (3) the third layer contains a physiological vitality principle.

Another example of an indigenous personality concept is *amae*, a fundamental and distinct feature of the Japanese personality. *Amae* refers to the passive, childlike dependence of one person on another (Doi, 1973). Other indigenous personality dimensions include the Mexican concept of *simpatia* which is the avoidance of conflict (La Roche, 2002); the Indian concept of *hishkarma karma* (Sinha, 1993); and the Korean concept of *cheong* which signifies human affection (Choi, Kim, & Choi, 1993).

Multicultural personality

As a parallel to Goleman's concepts of emotional intelligence and social intelligence (2006) some believe that select individuals possess *cultural intelligence* defined as the capacity to be effective across cultural settings (Earley, 2002; Thomas & Inkson, 2004). Traditionally, examining multicultural effectiveness has been the venue of international business and sojourner success. Matsumoto and colleagues (2001) contend that intercultural adjustment is a phenomenon that affects not just people dealing with new and different cultures but also people who interact with culturally different people in their everyday lives. In particular, minority groups, especially immigrants, indigenous people, refugees, and other marginalized people, may have to manage intercultural adjustment more frequently. A number of personality factors have been identified as contributing to successful multicultural interactions: cultural empathy, open-mindedness, emotional stability, action orientation, adventurousness/curiosity, flexibility, and extraversion (Matsumoto et al., 2001). Van der Zee and Van Oudenhoven (2001) designed the Multicultural Personality Questionnaire to measure multicultural personality using scales for cultural empathy, open-mindedness, emotional stability, social initiative, and flexibility. In their framework, cultural empathy refers to the ability to empathize with the feelings, thoughts, and behaviours of members from different cultural groups. Open-mindedness refers to open and unprejudiced attitudes toward members belonging to other cultural groups and their different values and norms. Emotional stability is defined as the tendency to remain calm in stressful situations without showing strong emotional reactions in such circumstances. Social initiative is the tendency to actively approach social situations and take initiative. Flexibility is the ability to embrace new and unknown situations and view them as a challenge and not as a threat (Van der Zee & Van Oudenhoven, 2001) (see Table 2.4).

Table 2.4 Characteristics of 'psychological engine of adjustment' and multicultural personality

'Psychological engine of adjustment' (Matsumoto et al., 2001)	Multicultural personality (Van der Zee & Van Oudenhoven, 2001)
Cultural empathy	Empathy
Open-mindedness	Open-mindedness
Emotional stability	Emotional stability
Action orientation	Social initiative
Flexibility	Flexibility
Adventurousness/curiosity	
Extraversion	

Gender and culture

Gender and sex roles

One salient aspect of identity is gender and most cultures view gender as an essential part of structuring ideas about the self and corresponding socially appropriate roles and norms (Okun, Fried, & Okun, 1999). Gender differences arise because of differences in socialization and psychological cultures transmitted to men and women, thus there may be truth to John Gray's notion that men are from Mars and women from Venus because gender does in fact represent different cultures. Gender is different from sex. Sex refers to the biological and physiological differences between males and females (i.e., genitalia, chromosomes) whereas gender refers to patterns of behaviour, roles, and responsibilities that a culture ascribes to and deems appropriate for men and women. In every culture, gender role socialization occurs from a variety of sources including parental expectations, modelling by peers, and media images of males and females, all of which support and maintain gender roles for males and females. In other words, gender is socially constructed based on sex.

Cultures differ in the extent to which gender roles ascribed to men and women are flexible and egalitarian versus rigid and hierarchical.

For instance, the Scandinavian cultures appear to have more egalitarian gender roles such that norms for behaviour, roles, and personal traits at work and at home are not defined solely on gender (Hansen, 1997). In contrast, some Arab and Muslim cultures have a more strict delineation of gender roles with expectations for women to cover their head in public, walk behind their husbands, and generally act in deference to men (Okun et al., 1999). In many patriarchal cultures, males are expected to be the primary financial provider for the family while the female is designated as the primary caretaker and domestic manager. Likewise, the male has the ultimate power and authority within the home (Okun et al., 1999).

Gender stereotypes

Alongside gender roles, there are many gender stereotypes that have developed. Early researchers emphasized the expressive (concern for the welfare of others) characteristics of women and the instrumental (assertive and controlling) characteristics of men (Denmark & Paludi, 2008). Across most cultures, males are expected to be independent, strong, self-reliant, emotionally detached and women are taught that they should be nurturing, dependent, gentle, and emotional (Denmark & Paludi, 2008). A popular study of gender stereotypes across cultures was conducted by Williams and Best (1990) who sampled approximately 3000 people across 30 countries. Using the Adjective Check List, Williams and Best asked respondents to indicate how indicative the adjective was for males and females in the specific culture. Across all 30 countries, there was considerable agreement in the characteristics associated with men and women. After numerous follow-up studies and variations, researchers have concluded that gender stereotypes are stable across the globe (Berry et al., 2002). Globally, men are viewed as strong and active with patterns of dominance, autonomy, aggression, and achievement. In contrast, women across cultures are generally viewed in the opposite manner (Williams & Best, 1982). With regard to societal roles, men are viewed as leaders, financial providers, and heads of household while women are viewed as caregivers who shop, tend the house and provide emotional support (Denmark & Paludi, 2008). Physically, women are expected to be pretty, dainty, graceful, and soft-voiced while men should be athletic, brawny, broad-shouldered, and strong. Women are believed to both experience and express a broader range of emotions while men have a limited repertoire of emotions but express certain ones like anger and pride (Plant, Hyde, Keltner, & Devine, 2000). Overall, other research has confirmed the prevalence of traditional gender stereotypes across many cultures (Rao & Rao, 1985) although some caution is necessary because particular ethnic groups or social classes within a culture may have different gender stereotypes (Denmark & Paludi, 2008). See Table 2.5 for a summary of gender stereotypes.

Gender differences

Although there has been much cross-cultural research in the area of gender differences, three primary areas of gender difference lend themselves to a cultural examination: perceptual/spatial/cognitive abilities, activity level, and aggression. In general, men are believed to excel at abstract thinking and problem solving while women are thought to be more artistic and adept at verbal reasoning (Matsumoto & Juang, 2008).

In many Western societies, males are thought to be better at mathematics and spatial reasoning and females are thought to excel at verbal comprehension tasks. Such generalizations do not hold true across all cultures and it appears that gender differences correspond to the adaptability and necessity of such abilities within a specific culture. For example, there are no gender differences in perceptual/spatial/cognitive abilities in the Inuit culture in Canada perhaps because such

Table 2.5 **Summary of gender stereotypes**

	Men	Women
Societal role	Leaders, providers	Caretakers
Physical appearance	Big, strong, athletic	Dainty, pretty
Experience/expression of emotion	Stoic – show only anger/pride	Experience and express emotions deeply

abilities are thought to be adaptive for both genders and therefore both genders are taught such skills from an early age (Berry, 1966). In a meta-analysis of intelligence in men and women no gender differences in overall intelligence were found but there were differences on various subtests of intelligence (Born, Bleichrodt, & Van der Flier, 1987). In eastern Ecuador where women engage in sewing and needlework that requires spatial representation, males did not excel in spatial abilities (Pontius, 1997).

Regarding activity level, male children are more likely to engage in exploratory behaviour using more gross-motor movements and female children typically engage in limited behaviour using more fine-motor skills (Crawford & Unger, 2004). Across many cultures, boys are encouraged to participate in high-activity behaviours whereas girls are socialized to be quiet and play. Girls generally engage in more verbally interactive and cooperative games whereas boys are more involved in competitive physical activities that test their strength or abilities (Crawford & Unger, 2004). Such an early gendered structure may contribute to girls developing stronger interpersonal skills and boys learn to be demanding and commanding – able to issue direct orders, etc. An example of these early games is found in Yauri, Nigeria. Girls play *sunana bojo ne* (My name is Bojo), which involves singing and dancing with girls taking turns at being a song leader. The song leader, in the middle of the circle with girls dancing around her, falls backward into the circle trusting her friends to catch her. In contrast, boys play a competitive version of ring toss attempting to land a rubber ring around the neck of the bottle (Gardiner & Kosmitzki, 2008).

Another stereotype is that males are more aggressive and dominant and females are more nurturing and passive. This stereotype appears to be consistent across cultures (Brislin, 2000) although there are considerable differences across cultures in the expression of male aggression and female nurturance. Across cultures, girls are more likely to play cooperatively using verbal interaction whereas boys tend to participate in more physical activities that are competitive (Eagley, 1987). In both industrial and non-industrial societies, males account for a disproportionate number of violent crimes (Segall et al., 1999). Some researchers have explained male aggression biologically resulting from the hormone testosterone, which increases during male adolescence, while others have looked to the culture and the environment for explanations (Segall et al., 1999).

Many other gender differences ranging from suicidal behaviour to dream content have been documented across cultures. Such research supports the existence of gender differences culturally across many constructs with the expression and extent of the differences differing in degree and nature depending on the specific culture (Matsumoto & Juang, 2008).

Concepts related to gender

Other cultural concepts related to gender include the expression of different gender roles, gender identity and third genders, gender inequality and gender bias. In some cultures, gender roles are more rigid. For instance, Latino culture has long been marked as a *macho* (Camilleri & Malewska-Peyre, 1997) culture meaning that males are glorified and dominant within the cultural system. There has however been some disagreement on how prevalent *machismo* (regard for masculine ability) truly is in Latino relationships. Vasquez (1994) suggests that perhaps there is a stronger adherence to traditional gender roles but that does not require pathologizing a Latino family that otherwise may be healthy and functioning. Gloria and Segura-Herrera (2004) suggest that *machismo* can have both positive and negative meanings depending on the expression however, traditionally *machismo* has had a negative connotation. At one end of the continuum macho Latinos 'promote strict gender roles, drink large amounts of alcohol, are sexually ready and available, are extremely authoritarian, [and] dominate women psychologically or physically. In contrast, the positive aspects of machismo refer to Latinos who support and protect their families, provide structure to family relationships, and are responsible to their family, friends, and community' (p. 293). According to Burgos-Ocasio (1996) and Gloria and Segura-Herrera (2004), the concept of *marianismo* (sanctification of women/reverence of the Virgin Mary) is the ideal applied to girls and the concept of *machismo* is highly encouraged for boys during childhood socialization.

In contrast, psychological *androgyny*, or the possession and expression of both masculine and feminine characteristics historically was thought to be more psychologically healthy and contribute to greater functioning and well-being (Bem, 1995). Traditionally, many cultures have thought of gender as dichotomous – one is either male or female. The notion of androgyny is that gender is not considered as opposite ends of the same spectrum but rather as separate spectrums – instead of simply male OR female, you can be or have both at once (or neither). Thus, Bem believed that masculinity and femininity can be combined in various ways according to preferences, needs, and nature. Bem reconceptualized her notions of androgyny and called for a 'dismantling of gender polarization' and an explosion of the categories of gender and other dichotomous categorizations like sexuality into more of a continuum rather than an either/or dichotomy (Bem, 1995).

Culture plays a role in sexual and gender identity. Some cultures recognize a third gender or third sex to describe a person who is neither man or woman or who is a combination of man and woman – today, typically referred to as transgendered. For example, in New Guinea, there are three terms for sex: male, female, and the colloquial term, *Turnim man*, which signifies an alternative sexual category for ambiguous sexuality or an intersexed person (Crawford & Unger, 2004). Similar categorizations exist to describe the Hijras of India and Pakistan, the Sworn virgins of the Balkans, intersexed people in the Dominican Republic and others. The term 'third' is usually understood to mean 'other' in terms of an intermediate gender/sex between men and women, being both genders/sexes (such as feeling like a man in the body of a woman), being neither, crossing or swapping genders, or another category altogether independent of male and female. Another example of a third gender are the two-spirit people, or *Berdache*, from many Native American and Canadian First Nations indigenous groups. *Berdache* display mixed gender roles. Traditionally, the role of *berdache* included wearing clothing and doing work of both male and female genders. Today, the term connotes both masculine and feminine spirits living in the same body (Crawford & Unger, 2004).

Gender role inequality differs culturally with the general pattern being that men have more power and status than women (Denmark & Paludi, 2008). In the history of psychology, gender bias has plagued much of the research and theory regarding the non-inclusion of women in psychological textbooks and research. Many of the early theories and research in psychology are based on men and many of the early female psychology researchers and theorists were neglected or blatantly ignored in terms of their important roles (Denmark & Paludi, 2008). Culturally, markers of gender inequality include female illiteracy, gender/earning ratio with women earning less than men, and prevalence of abuse against women (wife abuse, genital mutilation of girls, female infanticide, acid throwing, female elder abuse, honour killings, etc.)

Female genital mutilation (FGM; specifically clitordiction and infibulations sometimes referred to as female circumcision) has received much attention in the media. FGM is still practised in many parts of Africa and the Middle East (Caldwell, Orubuloye, & Caldwell, 1997). Such practices range from the removal of the foreskin of the clitoris to the removal of the clitoris and the labia with the two sides of the vulva sewn together (most often performed with unsterilized equipment and without anaesthesia). Despite global outrage at these practices, the continuation of such practices is often driven by tradition, rite of passage, and older female relatives who perform FGM even if parents of today do not believe in circumcising their daughters (Denmark & Paludi, 2008).

Other aspects of identity and culture

There are numerous other categories of sociocultural difference that define oneself and one's identity. Globally, religious differences are a major contributor to defining self-concept and determine practices and rituals in everyday life for many religious denominations. Social class or socioeconomic status (SES) refers to a 'culture' that encompasses educational attainment, income, and by extension, occupational status. Across the globe, poverty remains pervasive. In 2005, The World Bank estimated that a quarter of the population of the developing world lived below the international poverty line of $1.25/day considering 2005 prices (Chen & Ravallion, 2008). Because of the generational aspects and relation to other cultural categories (i.e. race, ethnicity), some view SES and poverty as the key disadvantages in society trumping other categories such as gender and race/ethnicity (Payne, DeVol, & Smith, 2006). Sexuality is a cultural difference typically signifying gay males or lesbians although bisexuality, transgender, and queer perspectives are increasingly being incorporated into psychology with emphasis on the LGBTQ (lesbian, gay, bisexual, transgendered and queer) movements (Clarke & Peel, 2007). Of issue with these labels is whether they constitute a particular identity or whether they refer only to sexual activities (e.g., homosexual sex). Disability and weight are two categories of cultural difference that are often left out of discussions of culture. People who have conditions that interfere with daily activities, have difficulty seeing, hearing or speaking, and/or are confined to a wheelchair are considered to be disabled (Blaine, 2007). Appearance related factors differentiate people especially in terms of body size and shape. Weight in terms of obesity is a highly stigmatized condition and typically results in poor health outcomes and discrimination in many areas of life (Blaine, 2007).

And so forth (is there a terrorist personality?)

Why do people become terrorists? Are some more likely to be terrorists because of certain personality attributes? These questions are difficult to answer because the face of terrorism has changed. Globalization in terms of travel and information sharing has increased the likelihood of conspirators coming together, the growth of religious fundamentalism, and the accessibility and proliferation of weapons of mass destruction all have contributed to the transformation of terrorism into a more serious and dangerous threat to the security of our world (Victoroff, 2005). The demographics of international terrorists have also shifted. In the 1960s and 1970s, international terrorists tended to be well-educated and relatively sophisticated university students and middle-class male and female revolutionaries from urban cultural centres (Miller, 2006). Into the 1980s and currently, international terrorists are more likely to be less educated, unemployed males of Middle Eastern descent who have been inculcated with extreme religious and political doctrines (Miller, 2006). Because of these changes, it is unlikely that there is a singular terrorist mind or personality but instead complex and plural terrorist minds and personalities.

Two main approaches have guided the research about terrorists although most scholars agree that terrorism can not be identified through one unified lens but rather an investigation of interdisciplinary and multiple intersections. One set of approaches emphasize the political, social, religious, governmental, and economic circumstances of the terrorist and the other approaches explore the characteristics of individuals and groups that become terrorists (Smith, 2008). All of these psychological theories are in essence inconclusive, subjective, and have not been tested adequately. Most scholars working in political psychology agree that there is not one terrorist personality but that terrorist behaviour is determined by a complex interplay of many factors including innate, biological, early development, cognitive, temperament, group, and environment (Victoroff, 2005). Thus, we can conclude that terrorists are heterogeneous but that being a terrorist at some level involves a significant social identity whereby the individual him or herself undergoes depersonalization and the ingroup identity becomes salient with other outgroups viewed as distant and deserving of derogation and hostility (Smith, 2008). Accepting that there is no unitary terrorist personality, terrorism can be viewed as a subcategory of human aggression with certain generalizations applicable to the 'typical' terrorist. In general, terrorists feel strongly about a particular ideological issue, have a deeply felt personal stake in the issue (e.g., perceived oppression, need for vengeance, expression of aggression, etc.), possess low cognitive flexibility or tolerance for ambiguity, and are able to suppress the morality associated with harming innocent people (Victoroff, 2005).

Further reading

Denmark, F. L., & Paludi, M. A. (Eds.). (2008). *Psychology of women: A handbook of issues and theories* (2nd ed.). Westport, CT: Praeger.

Markus, H., & Kitayama, S. (1991). Culture and the self: Implications for cognition, emotion, and motivation. *Psychological Review, 98,* 224–253.

Oyserman, D. (1993). The lens of personhood: Viewing the self and others in a multicultural society. *Journal of Personality and Social Psychology*, 65(5), 993–1009.

Phinney, J. S. (1992). The multigroup ethnic identity measure: A new scale for use with diverse groups. *Journal of Adolescent Research*, 7(2), 156–176.

Sparrow, L. M. (2000). Beyond multicultural man: Complexities of identity. *International Journal of Intercultural Relations*, 24, 173–201.

Verkuyten, M. (2005). *The social psychology of ethnic identity*. New York: Psychology Press.

Victoroff, J. (2005). The mind of the terrorist: A review and critique of psychological approaches. *Journal of Conflict Resolution*, 49(1), 3–42.

Weinreich, P., & Saunderson, W. (2003). *Analysing identity: Cross-cultural, societal, and clinical contexts*. New York: Routledge.

Chapter 3

Human development/ socialization and culture

■ Introduction 46

■ Theoretical foundations 46

■ Attachment and developmental processes 48

■ Childrearing and parenting 57

■ Socializing agents 66

■ And so forth (social relations and culture) 71

Introduction

SOCIALIZATION STARTS BEFORE birth and spans a lifetime. Through socialization, humans learn the values and behaviours of their particular culture as they develop and pass through various life stages. Human development is viewed as the actual physical, psychological, social, and behavioural changes that occur across the lifespan. Although cultural groups may disagree about the exact timing, length, and categories, most scholars agree that humans pass through common developmental stages starting with the prenatal period and moving through infancy, childhood, adolescence, and into adulthood. Nevertheless, culturally and even across different families from the same cultural group, customs and practices at each of these developmental stages differ. Two main socialization orientations have been suggested. In most Western countries, self-regulation and autonomy are emphasized, while in many non-Western countries, social interdependency is more common (Berry et al., 2002).

Theoretical foundations

The age-old debate about nature versus nurture especially comes alive with discussions about development and socialization and is replete with various theories about the process of development. For example, biological factors play an important role in maturational theories and evolutionary theories whereas the environment is emphasized in traditional learning theories (e.g., Skinner, 1953). Other theories emphasize the interaction between the individual and the environment such as Piaget's cognitive development theory (1972), and still others view the role of the sociocultural environment as essential to understanding development (Bronfenbrenner, 1979; Vygotsky, 1978). Urie Bronfenbrenner, renowned developmental psychologist, developed an ecological systems approach (1979) in which he posited that changes or conflicts in one layer will affect all other layers. Bronfenbrenner's ecological approach examines the relative impact that environments have on a child's development. The model itself is comprised of four different 'layers' of environment (see Figure 3.1). In this ecological

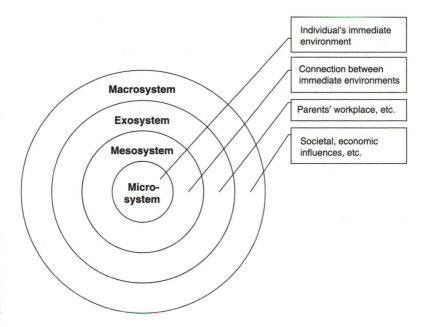

Figure 3.1   Bronfenbrenner's (1979) ecological systems approach

model, societal and cultural influences, values, and traditions lie on the outermost sphere (the *macrosystem*), depicting the largest and most remote level of influence on an individual. Social and cultural ecological factors include peer, familial, cultural, economic, and societal influences. Moving inward, the next layer is the *exosystem* which includes environments that the child does not experience directly, such as a parent's workplace, but that nonetheless have an indirect effect on the child's development. The next layer is the *mesosystem* which includes the connections between immediate environments (e.g., connections between neighbourhood and church). The inner-most layer is the *microsystem* which is an individual's immediate environment including relationships and interactions (e.g., family). According to Bronfenbrenner, each system contains roles, norms, and rules that are powerful shapers of development (1979).

Other important frameworks and theories of development include Erikson's life stage that offers a psychosocial developmental theory encompassing the whole lifespan, Bandura's social learning theory (1977) that highlights the importance of role models and observational learning in the socialization process, Kohlberg's (1976) theory of moral development and Gilligan's (1982) challenge to Kohlberg's theory regarding gender bias. Each of these theories of socialization and development provides important insights about how cultural differences in adults come to exist.

Attachment and developmental processes

Prenatal period

Across cultures the prenatal period or the time between conception and birth is 38 weeks. During pregnancy, the child is exposed to favourable and unfavourable conditions based on the environment in which the mother finds herself. Prenatal care is not always available to or sought out by mothers during pregnancy (Lia-Hoagberg et al., 1990). Nutrition and activity level of the expectant mothers can have a direct effect on the birth weight of the infants. Some common cultural trends in pregnancy are that in most countries, male children are more desired than female children (Hortacsu, Bastug, & Muhammetberdiev, 2001) and teen pregnancies tend to be more common in rural populations as compared with urban populations (Barber, 2001). Mothers may decide to terminate their pregnancies through abortion with some 50 million abortions performed in the world each year (Shiraev & Levy, 2010). Nineteen million unsafe and illegal abortions are estimated to have taken place worldwide in the year 2000 with 98% of these abortions occurring in developing countries. Also in 2000 there was an estimated 60,000 maternal deaths due to such unsafe procedures (Åhman, Dolea, & Shah, 2000).

Attitudes toward pregnancy are different across cultures. In most individualist countries, childbirth is more of a private event whereas in many traditional collectivist countries, childbirth is much more family-centred marked by active participation and guidance from family (Shiraev & Levy, 2010). In Russia, for example, pregnancy is commonly kept a secret until it is obvious that the woman is showing her pregnancy. Husbands do not attend the birth and even if they wanted to they are not permitted to enter birthing clinics (de Munck & Korotayev, 2007). Other customs during the birth include burying the placenta after birth in some African countries, avoidance of the cold by the mother in Vietnam, and in Russia, not letting the baby be seen by strangers for at least one month for fear of the 'evil eye' (Aizenmann, 2002).

The choice to have children is accompanied by sociocultural demands and ideologies. In most cultures, there are cheaper, safer birth control methods and increasing varieties of reproductive technology available (Okun et al., 1999). In some cultures, couples are strongly encouraged to have as many children as possible in order to grow the population (e.g., Israel). In other countries like China, couples are permitted to have one child because of overpopulation concerns.

Infancy

The environmental and social conditions for newborn children affect the care they receive, the child's health and development of personality. Directly related to the socioeconomic and political conditions of each nation, infant mortality rates are different across countries. For instance, infant mortality in Angola and Mozambique is 182.3 and 107.8 deaths per 1000 live births respectively compared to 6.3 in the United States, 2.8 in Japan, and 2.8 in Sweden (US Census Bureau, 2008). Touch and massage of babies can play a direct role in the motor development of the infant. For example, babies born in many parts of Africa and the West Indies are likely to receive extensive massage while babies born in the Western world are often taken away from the mothers and placed in cribs (Hopkins, 1977). Different cultures approach and have different laws and time frames regarding maternity leave and family leave before the birth and during the infant's first year of life.

In a study conducted by McGill University's Institute for Health and Social Policy, the United States was one of the five countries out of the 173 studied that does not require employees to offer paid maternity leave to workers (Heymann, Earle, & Hayes, 2007). The majority of these countries offer 14 weeks of paid maternity leave whereas the majority of even the most family-friendly companies in the USA offer six weeks or less of maternity leave (Institute for Women's Policy Research, 2007). Other major findings of the McGill study were that in comparison to other high-income countries and many middle- and low-income countries, the USA has weaker workplace policies regarding paid sick days and support for breastfeeding. Approximately 127 countries in the McGill study provide at least a week of paid sick days every year, a protection unheard of the United States. In addition, 137 countries require employers to provide paid annual leave, which is not guaranteed in the USA. In the USA, the Family and Medical Leave Act of 1993 permits workers to take up to 12 weeks unpaid leave to care for family or address medical needs. The USA also falls behind regarding working women's right to breastfeed with no protections for women who want to breastfeed. The McGill study found that more than 107 countries give women the right to breastfeed and at least 73 pay women for the breastfeeding breaks (Heymann et al., 2007).

Existing from birth, temperament is a biologically based way of being in the world and interacting with the environment. The most common temperaments are easy, difficult, and slow-to-warm-up (Thomas & Chess, 1977). An infant with an easy temperament is generally adaptable, regular, positive, and responsive to caregivers and the environment. In contrast, a baby with a difficult temperament is more intense, sporadic, withdrawing, and irritable – usually crying often. Slow-to-warm-up infants need time to make transitions. They generally have low activity levels and withdraw from new people and experiences until there is repeated exposure – only then do they 'warm-up'. Cross-culturally, there are differences in temperament. In one study conducted in the 1970s, Chinese American babies were calmer than European American or African American babies. Subsequently, other studies have found differences in infant temperaments comparing Japanese and Anglo infants, Navajo and European American infants, and Puerto Rican infants and European American and African American infants. Examination of temperament across cultures suggests that temperament can be an adaptive function for the child in order to survive and an indicator of what a culture values in terms of being and behaving (Lewis, 1989). Likewise, it is thought that the caregiver and cultural responses to a baby's temperament can affect the child's personality and the later establishment of attachment patterns.

Attachment patterns between the infant and mother are established early in infancy. These mother–child attachment behaviours are thought to be universal (Ainsworth, 1982) and the importance of such bonding was established in early classic work with rhesus monkeys raised in isolation (Harlow & Harlow, 1962). Attachment patterns of babies typically fall into three categories: (1) avoidant – do not pay much attention to their parent; (2) ambivalent – uncertain in response to caregivers and oscillate between staying very close to parents and then shunning them; and (3) secure – sensitive, warm and responsive, not threatened by a stranger in the parents' presence (Ainsworth, 1982). Some researchers report that the anxious–avoidant type is higher in West European countries while the anxious-and-resistant type is more common in non-Western countries like Israel and Japan. Although a securely attached infant is generally preferred in many different cultures, there are some exceptions. For example, some attachment styles are not reported in certain cultures (e.g., no avoidant infants in the Dogon of Mali), some regard avoidant attachment as the ideal (e.g., Germans who view a securely attached child as spoiled), and others display a high prevalence of anxious ambivalent attachments (e.g., Israeli children raised on a kibbutz; Matsumoto & Juang, 2008).

Another issue of importance during infancy is breastfeeding and infant feeding in general. Breastfeeding is a complex and variable process that is mediated by sociocultural practices and beliefs. Due to immunological, psychological, and economic benefits, the World Health Organization (WHO) recommends exclusive breastfeeding for the first six months of life and the American Academy of Pediatrics recommends that infants be fed breast milk throughout the first year of life (Gartner et al., 2005). Despite these mandates, some cultures still have less than desirable breastfeeding rates. Reasons for lower breastfeeding rates include lack of family support, dependence on governmental assistance that provides free infant formula, insufficient breastfeeding education, returning to work early in the postpartum period, and perceived societal norms (Beal, Kuhlthau, & Perrin, 2003).

Globally, the benefits of breastfeeding for children are numerous and include optimal growth, health, and development, decrease in a wide range of infectious diseases, reduction in infant mortality rates, possible decreases in sudden infant death syndrome in the first year of life, demonstrated reduction of diabetes, lymphoma, leukemia, Hodgkin disease, overweight and obesity, and enhanced neurodevelopment. There are also noted benefits of breastfeeding for mothers and the community. Mothers who breastfeed have decreased postpartum bleeding, earlier return to weight before pregnancy, and decreased risk of breast cancer and ovarian cancer. The community can benefit from breastfeeding with reduced health care costs and reduced costs for public health programmes related to infant feeding, less employee absenteeism, decrease in environmental burden due to the disposal of formula cans and bottles, and increased time for other family and community interests due to decreased infant illness (Gartner et al., 2005).

Every culture has specific and nuanced beliefs regarding breastfeeding. For instance, in Hindu communities, breastfeeding is almost universal and continues beyond infancy. Breastfeeding is supported by Hindu cultural and religious ceremonies and grandmothers tend to heavily influence the practice of breastfeeding (Laroia & Sharma, 2006). Turkish mothers forced to migrate from their villages to the slums of Diyarbakir in Turkey believe that breastfeeding is generally positive but colostrum is perceived negatively. In this group of mothers, no woman exclusively fed her infant by breastfeeding and some 40% of mothers had started solid foods before the infant was four months old. These mothers also believed that working under the sun decreased the quality of the breast milk (Ergenekon-Ozelci, Elmaci, Ertem, & Saka, 2006).

Language and linguistic differences emerge during infancy when neonates are surrounded by a complex system of sounds that represents a particular language. Sound distinctions are made very early on that may explain some linguistic differences when learning a foreign language. For instance, the 'B' and 'V' are very difficult for Spanish speakers to distinguish when learning English. English speakers tend to have a difficult time with the hard German 'R' and the 'KH' in Hebrew. Linguists suggest that Danish contains many nuanced sounds and therefore is extremely difficult for non-Danish people to learn because they weren't exposed to the sounds as an infant (Shiraev & Levy,

2010). One area of language with great similarities is the special patterns of speech that parents use when talking to a young baby (Fernald, 1992). Typically the intonation patterns are higher in pitch with larger variations in pitch – sometimes called 'motherese' even though fathers do it as well. Cross-culturally these tonal patterns and communicative interaction appear to be more similar than different. There are variations across cultures however in the styles of speech used by mothers. Bornstein et al. (1992) found that as compared with mothers in Argentina, France and the USA who used more 'information-salient' speech, Japanese mothers are more likely to use 'affect-salient' speech (i.e., more incomplete utterances, song, and nonsense expressions).

Childhood

Childhood is a time of discovery when growth, learning and development continues to accelerate at a rapid pace. Many of the eating patterns, sleeping patterns, play patterns, and elements of social identity are established during childhood. Eating habits and early food preferences of adults can normally be linked with early feeding practices (Schulze, Harwood, & Schoelmerich, 2001). Because of the biological nature of hunger, there are many cross-cultural similarities in eating preferences. We all learn to salivate in response to appealing foods and our preferences for sweet and salty tastes are genetic and universal. In most cultures, children eat bread and many varieties of fruits and vegetables; however, there are food restrictions in some cultures. For example, Muslim and some Jewish children do not eat pork, Hindu children are forbidden to eat beef, and most Europeans and Americans do not eat dog meat (Shiraev & Levy, 2010).

Regulation of sleeping patterns typically starts before the childhood years in most cultures. Super and colleagues (1996) studied young children and parents in the Netherlands and the USA regarding sleeping patterns. The Dutch parents placed a high value on regularity in sleeping patterns for their children and believed that such regularity was crucial for a child's growth and development and to prevent the child from becoming fussy. The US parents however believed that children will acquire regular sleeping patterns as they grow older but it is not something that can be controlled. These findings coincided with amount of sleep and activity level during the day with Dutch children getting more sleep and being in a state of 'quiet arousal' when awake while US children were more often in an awake state of 'active alertness'. Super and his research team suggest that such cultural parental expectations link with cultural views of how children should develop (e.g., greater independence in the Dutch children because they are expected to keep themselves busy and learn to organize their own behaviour without assistance). Regarding play, some functions like cooperation, sharing, and competition are universal across cultures and in terms of social identity, children can identify themselves by ethnicity, nationality and social class between the second and fourth grades (aged 7–10) (Dawson, Prewitt, & Dawson, 1977).

Adolescence

Although there is some disagreement about the exact ages of adolescence and given that some cultures do not recognize adolescence as a discreet period, in general, most cultures concur that adolescence is a time between childhood and adulthood in which biological, cognitive, and social transitions occur (Gibbon, 2000). In addition, adolescents, depending on their specific context, may also experience changes related to schools, home, hardship, migration, violence, and even trauma (Gibbon, 2000). Biologically, adolescence is marked by rapid physical changes in weight and height with girls maturing as much as two years earlier than boys across cultures. Cognitively, adolescents move from the more concrete thinking of childhood and into more abstract, formal operational thinking (Gibbon, 2000). Socially, the adolescent period is typically a time when a new identity is forged and questions of 'who am I' and roles of adulthood are common. Biologically, puberty occurs universally despite somewhat different time tables. Cognitive and social changes during adolescence appear to be more culture specific and dependent upon sociocultural context. For instance, the adoption of Piagetian formal operational thinking has been linked to formal education (Segall et al., 1999). Table 3.1 provides a summary of changes that occur during adolescence.

Within developmental psychology, there has been much debate about whether adolescence is a biologically or socially determined

Table 3.1 **Changes during adolescence**

Type	Change	Context
Biological	Rapid physical changes in weight and height	Universal
Cognitive	Development of abstract, formal operational thinking	Culture-specific
Social	Identity-formation begins	Culture-specific

developmental stage. Across cultures, adolescence appears to be a time for learning new social roles with accompanying tensions, however, adolescence as a 'period of storm and stress' seems to be in existence only in the Western world in the twentieth century (Schlegel & Barry, 1991). Depending on a society's expectations regarding adolescents moving into adult roles, the period of adolescence may vary in length. For example, in rural India, there is not as much time spent on adolescence as in many Western countries because children have to fulfill adult roles at an early age (Saraswathi, 1999).

Several cross-cultural reviews of adolescence indicate the importance of the cultural, economic and political context within which adolescence occurs (Gibbon, 2000; Steinberg & Morris, 2001). In one landmark study on adolescent self-image in ten different countries (Australia, Bangladesh, Hungary, Israel, Italy, Japan, Taiwan, Turkey, West Germany, and USA), adolescents reported healthy relationships with their families, positive self-image, and good coping skills (Offer, Ostrov, Howard, & Atkinson, 1988). Magen (1998) studied adolescent happiness in Israeli Arabs, Israeli Jewish, and US adolescents and found high levels of well-being with numerous moments of joy recounted by the adolescents especially from interpersonal encounters and helping others. Even when adolescents live in difficult or dangerous situations, they fare remarkably well exhibiting resilience, coping skills, and self-esteem.

Adulthood

Across cultures, adulthood is expected to be a stage of maturity, responsibility, and accountability. Some cognitive and psychological

5 5

functions decline with age but socialization continues through adulthood. Two models, persistence and openness, have been used to explain the process (Renshon, 1989). According to the persistence model, attitudes and behaviours learned early in life will be maintained and unchanged throughout adulthood (e.g., child in a religious family remains religious in adulthood). The other model, openness, posits the opposite and is characterized by flexibility and transformation in which people have to change attitudes and behaviours due to changing situations through adulthood. Thus, who one is socialized to be as a child does not necessarily indicate who a person will be in adulthood.

During adulthood, a sense of identity is developed that cannot be understood outside of the cultural context. In some traditional cultures, for example, adults fall into accepted roles and expectations with little variation in ideology and religious beliefs (Camilleri & Malewska-Peyre, 1997). In other Western industrialized societies, social roles tend to be more open and adults can choose to belong to a wide diversity of subgroups. Later adulthood is marked by different perceptions of ageing across cultures with elderly people occupying a high status in collectivist cultures whereas elderly people may be more likely to be rejected and isolated in individualist societies. In many countries, the stage of late adulthood officially begins with retirement from a person's job. Later adulthood can include being a grandparent. Most research about grandparenthood suggests that grandparents have a positive effect on their grandchildren's affective and cognitive development and serve as a major support system during divorce and family breakdown. In addition, most grandparents have reported that they enjoy and find grandparenting easier than parenting (Glass Jr & Huneycutt, 2002).

Physical declines are common as people age. For example, the skin becomes less elastic, bones become more brittle, muscles atrophy, and the cardiovascular system becomes less efficient. Psychologically, some functions decline as well. Hearing and visual impairments are common. Declines in memory and reaction time are common. Most agree that individual and cultural attitude about ageing plays a key role in how adults view ageing. In the arts and other fields, for instance, late-age creativity and incredible accomplishment are common across cultures. Goethe, a famous German poet, completed his Faust at

80 years of age. Mother Teresa remained active in her charity work until she died at the age of 87. In addition, the last works of Shakespeare, Rembrandt, Verdi, Beethoven, and Tolstoy, all suggest that late adulthood may bring freedom to express oneself without a feeling of heavy societal constraints (Shiraev & Levy, 2010).

Childrearing and parenting

A child's socialization and development depends on interactions with others within a sociocultural context. Culture provides a 'developmental niche' in which children grow and change (Harkness & Super, 2002). This niche includes three primary components: (1) the social and cultural environment for parents and children; (2) the culturally based childrearing practices; and (3) the characteristics valued and expected in caregivers.

The social and cultural environment for parents and children

The first component includes the social and cultural environment including the physical and social settings of daily life in which a child and his/her parents live. Many Western cultures idealize nuclear family living while Asian and African countries emphasize extended family arrangements with the presence of multiple generations living together. What constitutes a family differs culturally. Some families have single parents, some families are blended, and there are increasing numbers of internationally adopted children. In part, the family structure determines the company a child keeps with varying numbers of caretakers, parents, siblings, and peers. For instance, in rural areas and small towns as compared with large urban areas, a child may have more siblings and extended relatives living nearby who serve as playmates and caretakers. In one study involving students from Greece, Cyprus, the Netherlands, Great Britain, and Germany, researchers found that wealthy individualist countries (Netherlands, Great Britain, Germany) differed from collectivist countries (Greece and Cyprus) with the collectivist countries being emotionally and geographically closer to extended family members (Georgas, Poortinga, Angleitner,

Goodwin, & Charalambous, 1997). Living spaces differ to accommodate different size families. For instance children in North American middle to upper class families are likely to have their own bedrooms whereas in lower-income families, living, dining and sleeping areas may be shared.

One controversial area related to culture is the 'family bed' and co-sleeping. In many cultures, families sleep together in one bed in the same room (Ball, 2003). Some cultures believe that parent/child togetherness while sleeping promotes the well-being of both parents and children. Some cultural groups share beds and rooms because of economic reasons. Culturally, there are various viewpoints about whether parents should be sexual while sleeping in the same room as their children. For most US and Western mothers, co-sleeping is generally resisted or allowed only in a limited way. Co-sleeping (bed sharing) is a common form of parent–child interaction (Welles-Nystrom, 2005). The most recognized form of co-sleeping occurs between an infant and mother. Families around the world co-sleep for many reasons: it promotes breastfeeding, encourages physical and mental development, decreases parental sleep disturbances, and assists with sleep problems (Welles-Nystrom, 2005). Some cultures such as Japan for example, believe co-sleeping creates an environment for the child that will allow them to become secure, interdependent individuals (Ball, 2003; Welles-Nystrom, 2005). Other cultures like Germany and the USA believe in solitary sleep and encourage autonomy and independence in their children (Valentin, 2005).

For children around the world co-sleeping with parents and, less often, siblings is a common practice. Private bedrooms for children are the exception rather than the rule worldwide (Jenni & O'Connor, 2005). Many studies have addressed the cross-cultural differences among co-sleeping practices. In a comparative study of Japanese and American children Latz, Wolf, and Lozoff (1999) found that the cultural values in each society were reflected in their sleep practices. The Japanese valued interdependence and viewed co-sleeping as beneficial to child development. Caucasian–Americans valued more independence and autonomy and preferred solitary sleep (Latz et al., 1999). Another study examined co-sleeping practices in urban Hispanic–American families. Results showed that co-sleeping was more common in the Hispanic population than the non-Hispanic white population. However, additional factors such as socioeconomic status, household composition, child birth order, and couple status played a role in the decision to co-sleep. For example, co-sleeping was especially common with Hispanic–American single parents living in multiple households with only or firstborn children no younger than 13 months (Schachter, Fuchs, Bijur, & Stone, 1989). Co-sleeping rates were also high in the urban African–American population (Brenner, Simons-Morton, Bhaskar, Revenis, Das & Clemens, 2003).

From an international perspective, co-sleeping with infants did not usually occur with Italian parents (Giannotti, Cortesi, Sebastiani, & Vagnoni, 2005). However, co-sleeping with toddlers was common and increased significantly as the children reached school-age; then the trend decreased as the children reached early adolescence (Giannotti et al., 2005). In the German culture, child sleep practices were not considered except as they related directly to safety (e.g., exposures to environmental risks, infant mortality) (Valentin, 2005). Germans valued self-reliance and autonomy in child development and children were encouraged to sleep alone with minimal assistance. Co-sleeping with children was considered spoiling and any parent who practiced co-sleeping was made to feel guilty by family and friends (Valentin, 2005). A study examining Swedish co-sleeping practices (Welles-Nystrom, 2005) found Swedish parents to be very open to co-sleeping and they viewed it as essential to child development. Fathers' participation in co-sleeping was highly valued and parents believed that providing a safe, nurturing environment would help the child become more secure and independent in the future (Welles-Nystrom, 2005). It is important to note that there are many definitions of co-sleeping in these studies (i.e. bed-sharing, room-sharing, etc.). However, they each express the importance of cultural beliefs in early parent–child interaction.

In addition, overall quality of life in general considering violence, poverty, hunger, and oppression change how these developmental stages and socialization are experienced. According to the World Health Organization and other international groups, there is an extremely high rate of malnutrition of children under the age of five in developing countries and this is intimately tied to socioeconomic status (Van de Poel, Hosseinpoor, Speybroeck, Van Ourti, & Vega,

2008). Socioeconomic status and poverty have profound effects on children's development. The effects of poverty contribute to deficiencies in cognitive outcomes, school achievement, emotional or behavioural outcomes, and other areas like teenage pregnancy, increased child abuse and neglect, increased violent crimes, and fear of neighbourhoods (Brooks, 2004). In addition, cultural attitudes and practices have a strong influence on developmental events. For example, the onset of menarche and menstruation for girls is treated differently depending on the social and cultural environment. Many cultures have some type of ritual to publicize that a girl has reached menarche while other cultures (like the United States), consider such topics taboo (Crawford & Unger, 2004).

The culturally based childrearing practices

The second component of the developmental niche emphasizes the customs of child care and childrearing practices that are regulated by culture. This component includes type of learning, eating and sleeping arrangements, dependence versus independence training, initiation rites, and expectations about play and work. Learning can be formal (in school learning common in Western societies) or informal (apprenticeship models where certain families teach children their particular skill). Eating and sleeping schedules vary with many Western cultures having three meals a day at specified times and five to six smaller meals at unscheduled times customary in some Asian cultures. Sleeping arrangements with regard to where and with whom vary cross-culturally. Play and work are different across cultures. Play is often used by adults to teach children about the importance of cooperation and negotiation while stimulating coordination and developing gross and fine motor skills, encouraging imagination, and fostering interpersonal relationships (Gardiner & Kosmitzki, 2008). In most cultures significant life events such as birthdays, initiation rituals, weddings, graduations, job promotions, birth of children and grandchildren, and retirement mark distinct periods of developmental transitions. There are 'rites of passage' marking progression from childhood to adolescence in some cultures. Significant physiological changes such as losing teeth, first words, pubertal changes, first intercourse, grey hair in older age, etc. also act as indicators of movement from one developmental phase to the next.

In a classic study conducted in the 1950s, Barry and colleagues (1957) identified six central dimensions of childrearing believed to be common across cultures:

(1) Obedience training (degree to which children are trained to obey adults).

(2) Responsibility training (degree to which children are trained to take responsibility for subsistence or household tasks).

(3) Nurturance training (degree to which children are trained to care for younger siblings and other dependent people).

(4) Achievement training (degree to which children are trained to strive toward standards of excellence in performance).

(5) Self-reliance (degree to which children are trained to take care of themselves and to be independent of assistant from others in supplying their own needs or wants).

(6) General independence training (degree to which children are trained toward freedom from control, domination, and supervision).

Extensions of this work reduced the six dimensions down to two clusters and one dimension in which cultures ranged from compliance training to assertion training. Narrow socialization is marked by obedience and conformity and is thought to lead to a restricted range of individual differences and broad socialization is comprised of independence and self-expression leading to a broad range of individual differences.

The characteristics valued and expected in caregivers

The third component of the developmental niche includes the cultural parenting styles, value systems, developmental expectations, and parental belief systems. Parenting involves parenting style, goals and beliefs for children, specific behaviours to achieve goals. There are numerous cultural influences on parenting. Two common models of parenting across cultural and social groups are the independent and interdependent models (Brooks, 2004). In the independent model, parents facilitate children to become self-sustaining, productive adults who enter relationships with other adults by choice. The child receives nurturance in order to develop autonomy, competence, and a freely chosen identity which they carry into adulthood. In contrast, the inter-dependent model emphasizes parents who help their children grow into socially responsible adults who take their place in a strong net-work of social relationships, often with a larger extended family, which places certain obligations and expectations on the adult. In this model, parents tend to indulge younger children but as they grow older, they are expected to internalize and respect the rules of parents and other authorities. Parents and relatives are highly respected and obeyed and the collective needs of the family and larger cultural group are more important than individual needs.

Europeans and Americans tend to embrace the independent model of parent–child relationships while other cultural groups such as many Asian societies focus more on respect for elders and tradition, family and extended family obligations, early indulgence of children with firm expectations, and a strong reliance on spiritual values, thus the interdependent model of parent–child relationships. In every cul-ture, parents develop ideas about parenting including how to discipline, communicate with children, seek advice and much more. In one study about childrearing philosophies across five different cultures (three were industrial and two were agrarian), researchers observed mother–child interactions. Noteworthy was that Gusii mothers in Kenya, as compared with middle-class mothers in Boston, Massachusetts, were more likely to hold and have physical contact with their 9–10 month old infants but look at and talk with the infants less often. This finding supports the importance of cultural context and belief systems in child-rearing. The Gusii infant mortality rate is high and thus their holding and soothing increases rates of infant survival. In addition, they believe that infants do not understand language until they are approximately two years of age and that direct eye contact with others should be avoided so they don't look at or talk to their babies. In contrast, the US mothers believe that language skills and independence training (sleep-ing and playing alone) should be developed early both of which reflect the American value system (Gardiner & Kosmitzki, 2008).

In a study examining childrearing values of Estonian and Finnish parents (Viste & Ahtonen, 2007), researchers found that both cultures assign the most value to characteristics related to benevolence, self-direction, and being trustworthy. Estonians were more likely to value smartness and politeness while the Finnish valued hedonism. Compared with Estonian parents, Finnish parents tend to stress benevolence, hedonism, and bad habits rather than conformity and achievement. The Finnish childrearing values are more homogeneous; and the values held by a mother and father from the same family reveal more similarities. In contrast, Estonian mothers place greater emphasis on benevolence and conformity compared with Estonian fathers. These findings suggest that differences in childrearing values depend on the cultural context.

The authoritarian style of parenting that is based on strictness, control and behavioural sanctions is positively correlated with collectivistic traditions and other societal factors like political authoritarianism, lack of education, social instability, and educational traditions (Rudy & Grusec, 2001). Traditionally, mothers in most cultures have been the primary caretakers of their children and the tasks of birthing and nurturing have been assigned to the mother. In contrast, the father has generally been assigned the role of supporter and family controller. More recently, the roles of mother and father have evolved across most cultures and more research has been conducted on the shift and changing roles of both mothers and fathers into parenthood. However, in most cross-cultural studies about parental involvement, the same pattern still exists – that mothers spend more time and engage in more activities with their children compared with fathers. In addition, there is increasingly more diversity among parents not only with differing social and cultural backgrounds but also with regard to single parents, adolescent, low-income, grandparents as parents, and minority parents (Gardiner & Kosmitzki, 2008). All of these parents, regardless of culture, have different rewards and challenges of being in the parental role.

In many societies, people choose to have children without being married or being a single parent becomes a necessity, thus one-parent families are becoming more common globally. Traditionally, single-parent families have been more common in Western societies but there continues to be a large increase in one-parent families with the major-ity headed by women (approximately 90%). In the 1970s, of the Western countries, Sweden had the highest rates of single-parent fam-ilies but now the United States has the largest percentage. One-parent families occur for several reasons including divorce/separation of two-parent families, births outside of marriage, deaths of spouses, and single people who decide to have children. Some parents may choose to remain single because of lack of suitable partners. For example, in the former Soviet Union, the ratio of women to men is much higher because males are more likely to have died from war, alcoholism, and accidents. In other countries, a common explanation is that one-parent families are able to manage because of support from the state (for example in Sweden, unmarried and divorced mothers receive signifi-cant social supports, maternity leave, and educational leave (Ember, Ember, & Peregrine, 2006)).

Another family form that is making a come-back at least in the United States is the multigenerational family (three or more gener-ations living together). According to the 2000 Census, there are almost four million US multigenerational households which represent about 4% of all households and this number continues to rise. The majority of these households include the grandparent living with their children and their grandchildren in the house of the grandparent. In about a third of these households, the grandparent lives in the home of his/her children (or son- or daughter-in-law) and his/her grandchildren. A very small per cent of these households are comprised of grandparents and great-grandparents as well as children and grandchildren of the grandparents (Generations United, 2006).

Some of the reasons for the rise in multigenerational households include financial factors such as high housing costs, high cost of living, expense of child care/elder care, unemployment, parents returning to school, and parents working to save money to become independent. Cultural reasons such as immigration, value systems, importance of ritual and celebration of holidays and events, and desire to stay con-nected with cultural group all are reported reasons for multigenera-tional households. Other reasons include individual beliefs that child care and elder care are family responsibilities, that age-integration within communities is important, and a conviction to be involved and connected with offspring and elders. Situational factors such as the inability to live alone after being widowed, divorce that requires moving to parent's home with children, illness requiring regular care and assistance, single parenting, housing shortages, and extended lifespan also pre-empt multigenerational households (Generations United, 2006). In the future, multigenerational families are expected to become more commonplace and continue to increase. By 2010 in the United States, it is expected that more children will know their great-grandparents, people in their 60s will be caring for 80 to 90-year-old parents, more children will grow up with support of older relatives and there will be an increase in four-generational households (Generations United, 2006).

Grandparenting in general is a relatively new phenomenon as of the last 100 years because of increased life expectancy and good health. Grandparents parenting grandchildren has increased generally due to crisis situations involving drugs, divorce, desertion, and death (Glass Jr & Huneycutt, 2002). The number of grandparents raising their grandchildren is thought to be on the rise due to high teen pregnancy rates, incarcerated parents with some 80% having dependent children, more women using drugs, and parental deaths from AIDS.

Increasing numbers of lesbian women and gay males are exploring parenting options (McCann & Delmonte, 2005) and taking on parenthood through donor insemination, surrogacy, fostering, and adoption. Although there appears to be no definitive research pointing one way or another, gay parenting has been a contentious issue for many because of the presumed damaging effects that gay parents can have on their children. Concerns have been raised regarding whether the child will become homosexual, whether the child will be bullied, whether the child will have appropriate opposite sex role models, and more (McCann & Delmonte, 2005).

International adoption (sometimes referred to as transnational adoption) is becoming more common in the United States and European countries. Although still on a relatively small scale, international adoption represents a significant shift from historical adoption practices and constitutes an entirely different family structure (Conn, 2008). In the USA, approximately 17,500 internationally adopted children enter the country each year with most children coming from

Guatemala (4123), China (3909), and Russia (1861) followed by countries ranging from Ethiopia and South Korea to Haiti and Poland (Intercountry Adoption, 2008).

Socializing agents

The process of socialization occurs not in a vacuum but in a larger sociocultural context. Across the developmental stages, variation depends on a culture's approach to parenting and raising children, family structure, quality of life in general, educational opportunities, health care accessibility, religious customs and beliefs, and views on relationships (peer groups, friendship, intimate relationships, marriage). Technological advancements and socioeconomic improvements may have an effect on the composition of the family. For instance, globalization including technological advances and international migration has increased the opportunity for interactions among different types of people and has contributed to rapid changes in the structure and function of the family and socialization of children. Agents of socialization include our families, peer groups, and educational and religious institutions.

Families

A family is a group of people who consider themselves related through kinship while a household is defined as people who share a living space and may or may not be related (Miller, 2008). Most households consist of members who are related through kinship, although an increasing number do not. For instance, a group of friends sharing living quarters or a single person living alone constitute a household. Young adults in the USA or the UK usually live away from home when they go to the university. In more complex societies, family members tend to live apart from one another while in more simple societies, the family and the household are impossible to differentiate (Ember et al., 2006). Across most societies, a primary function of families is the socialization and protection of children so that the children can obtain the cultural behaviour, beliefs, and values necessary for survival. The nature of the family inevitably shifts and is a reflection of the social and cultural changes in economics, education, and political systems (Georgas, Berry, van de Vijver, Kagitçibasi, & Poortinga, 2006).

All societies have families although family form and households vary from society to society. The nuclear household, still commonly referred to as the nuclear family, is composed of one adult couple, either married or 'partners', with or without children. Most people belong to at least two different nuclear families during their lifetime. Anthropologists distinguish between the family of orientation, which is the family to which one is born and grows up, and the family of procreation, which is the family formed when one marries and has children of their own. Nuclear family organization is widespread cross-culturally and varies in significance from culture to culture but it is not universal. For instance, in the classic Nayar group, the nuclear family is rare or nonexistent (Kottak, 2008). In contrast, in North America, the nuclear family is the only well-defined kin group and remains somewhat of a cultural ideal (Ember et al., 2006). Such a family structure is thought to arise from industrialism, which contributes to geographic mobility and isolation from extended family members. Generally determined by their jobs, many North American married couples live far away from their parents (neolocality) and establish households and nuclear families of their own (Ember et al., 2006).

An extended household is a domestic group that contains more than one adult married couple related either through the father–son line (patrilineal extended household), the mother–daughter line (matrilineal extended household), or through sisters and brothers (collateral extended household). Extended families are the prevailing form in more than half of the world's societies (Ember et al., 2006). For example, in former Yugoslavia, extended family households, called *zadruga*, consisted of several nuclear families living together. The *zadruga* was headed by a male household head and his wife considered to be the senior woman. Also included were married sons and their wives and children and unmarried sons and daughters. Each nuclear family had their own sleeping quarters, however, many items were freely shared among members in the *zadruga* (e.g., clothes, items from the bride's trousseau, and other possessions). The Nayar, a caste of southern India, provide another example of extended households. The Nayar lived in matrilineal extended family compounds called *tarawads* (residential complexes with several buildings headed by a senior woman and her brother). The *tarawads* were home to the woman's siblings, her sisters' children, and other relatives of matrilineal descent. These compounds were responsible for child care and the home of retired Nayar men who were military warriors (Ember et al., 2006).

Expanded family households (those that include non-nuclear relatives) also exist in some cultures. For example, in lower socio-economic class families of North America, expanded family households are more common than in middle-class families. If an expanded family household consists of three or more generations then it is considered an extended family household. Collateral households, another type of expanded family, include siblings and their spouses and children (Ember et al., 2006). Polygamous married people are considered complex households in which one spouse lives with or near multiple partners and their children. Descent groups including lineages and clans of people claiming common ancestry may reside in several villages but rarely come together for social activities. These descent groups are common in non-industrial food producing societies (Kottak, 2008).

Peer groups

Peer groups appear to play a much larger role in Western cultures, perhaps as a result of extended schooling. In contrast, school stops earlier in more traditional cultures, which gives children less access to peer groups and more access to vertical relationships with elders and extended relatives. In more industrialized societies, young people spend more time with their same-aged peers and thus peers provide a stronger socializing agent in comparison with less industrialized countries. Bronfenbrenner examined the role of peer groups in the Soviet Union and the USA and found greater distance between peer group and adult values in the USA and a more unified single set of peer–parent values in the Soviet Union. He suggested that this meant that adolescents would be more likely to be influenced by peer pressure in more politically and socially pluralistic societies like the United States (Chen, French, & Schneider, 2006). Others suggest that parental belief systems across cultures play an important role in shaping perspectives on peer relationships. For instance, in Japan, peers are viewed as a source of support and socialization whereas in the USA peer pressure is seen as a negative influence (Gardiner & Kosmitzki, 2008). Margaret Mead (1978) described three different types of cultures each with variable levels of peer influence on the socialization of young people: (1) postfigurative cultures where elders are responsible for transferring knowledge to children; (2) cofigurative cultures where adults continue to socialize children but peers play an important role; and (3) prefigurative cultures where change happens so rapidly that young people may be teaching adults. Peer socialization may also be influenced by type of schooling – in the USA for example, schools are stratified according to age whereas in other cultures, schools may contain multi-age groups. Such differences in stratification coupled with the values of the specific culture regarding peer group offer variable opportunities for peers to interact.

Education

A society's educational system offers important socialization to children and such socialization is based on what the culture finds valuable. For example, in traditional Islamic societies, religious leaders and poets were highly respected. In part this value had to do with the ultimate goals of the educational system which were to transmit faith, general knowledge and a deep appreciation for poetry and literature. In contrast, many Western educational systems have emphasized the scientific method with a focus on logical, rational scientific and mathematics training. In comparison with more individualistic cultures that value high-level, abstract thinking, many group-oriented and collectivistic cultures emphasize relational thinking as the desired end-point of formal education so that people can successfully engage in interpersonal situations.

The parent and family view of education varies across cultures. Some cultures take a more active role in the extracurricular educational activities of their children after school and on the weekends. For example, in one study of Asian American families, those with high achieving students, as compared with European American families, were more likely to supplement their children's school learning with after-school and extracurricular programmes (Sy & Schulenburg, 2005). Most likely due to the value placed on individualism or collectivism, some cultures emphasize the equality of all children (e.g., China and Japan) while others are more likely to recognize individual differences (e.g., USA). Some cultures consider effort more important than ability. Many American parents and teachers believe that innate ability is more important than effort whereas Japanese and Chinese parents and teachers consider effort far more important than ability (Yan & Gaier, 1994).

Religion

Religion plays a major role in the socialization and development of children and families. Religion and its importance and pervasiveness vary across cultures. Regardless of religious system, religion can offer guidance and spiritual solace. Most religions also recognize important ceremonies and rites of passage in daily life including baptism, bar/bas mitzvahs, fasting, and naming ceremonies. Many orthodox and fundamentalist religions across cultures have a strong influence on the structure of family and community and direct many aspects of daily living. For instance, Islam has specific rules about family interactions and how people interact outside of the family with same-gender and opposite gender. Orthodox Jews likewise have prescriptive rules that govern time of Sabbath, food, and dress. Southern Baptists in the United States have prohibitions against dancing, playing cards, and drinking alcohol. Many of these religions have a set hierarchy with God first, then husbands and wives last. In contrast, less restrictive religions are not as prescriptive (Blaine, 2007).

Western and Asian religions emphasize almost opposite constructs. Western religions place more emphasis on the individual with membership in a congregation while Asian religions promote the collective whole with religious observance within the family and community. In recent years, Western cultures have become more interested in Asian and Native American spirituality and their emphasis on the whole person with an amalgamation of mind, body, and spirit. Many of the Eastern cultural practices such as yoga, meditation along with acupuncture have become more acceptable and sought out in mainstream Western health care (Okun et al., 1999).

And so forth (social relations and culture)

Social support offers people a mechanism to cope with stressful life events and to connect with close others during times of need. Social support networks act as a buffer mitigating the adverse health effects of physical and mental stress (Seeman, 1996). Wills (1991) defines social support as the perception that one is loved and cared for, esteemed and valued, and part of a social network of mutual assistance. Few studies have considered cultural differences when it comes to the role of social support and patterns of social relationships. However, if the cultural differences in expectations and norms about relationships between a person and the social network are considered, it makes sense that how and whether individuals use social support would be different across cultures. In more independent cultures like North America and Western Europe for example, individuals are expected to be unique and to act according to their own volitions while in more interdependent cultures such as East Asia, individuals are encouraged to emphasize their social relationships and maintain harmony within a group (Markus & Kitayama, 1991). A study conducted by Kim and colleagues examined social support of Asians and Asian Americans (Kim, Sherman, & Taylor, 2008). In this study, Asians and Asian Americans, as compared with European Americans, were more reluctant to ask for support from close others (extended family, friends, etc.). This finding along with other similar findings suggests that social support is culturally mediated and must be viewed within the context of cultural beliefs about social relationships and the norms and concerns of a given culture.

Social support has been shown to reduce psychological distress during difficult times and has a variety of health benefits including resilience to life-threatening diseases. Social support can act to prevent illness, speed recovery from illness, and reduce the risk of death from serious disease (Kim et al., 2008). If social support is defined as the 'explicit seeking and receiving of support', it appears that people from collectivistic cultures are less likely to utilize social support than people from individualistic cultures (p. 522). In general, social support is an important correlate of psychological well-being and plays an important role in the initiation and maintenance of happiness. Having close others around acting as 'cheerleaders' helps people to move forward with intentions (Linley & Joseph, 2004). For example, groups such as Alcoholics Anonymous and Weight Watchers are based on social support and mentors during abstinence attempts.

Social capital is an expansion of social support and refers to connections within and between social networks and the corresponding collective value that such networks provide (Portes, 1998; Putnam, 2000). According to Putnam (2000), social capital requires deep connection amidst trust and reciprocity in a community or between individuals that plays an important role in building and maintaining democracy. Putnam (2000) identifies two types of social capital – bridging (between groups) and bonding (within groups). Bridging social capital links one social group to external assets and bonding social capital reinforces internal solidarity (Putnam, 2000). Social capital has been used to better understand the lives of ethnic immigrants in various societies and in studies of labour market activities. A Chinese application of social capital examines *guanxi* (a cultural practice of nurturing and networking within social relations) in relation to youth unemployment in mainland China, Taiwan, and Hong Kong (Yan & Lam, 2009). Guanxi has been used in Chinese societies to acquire resources and mobilize social networks toward solving problems such as youth unemployment.

Social network analysis (SNA) is an interesting way to measure aspects of social support and social capital. SNA is a widely published approach to measuring aspects of social and community relationships and provides a map highlighting important relationships between people and their communities. SNA has been used to understand social links in numerous capacities, including drug user networks, friendship cliques in schools, HIV/AIDS and other STD transmission, informal learning within organizations, and longitudinal spread of obesity (Christakis & Fowler, 2007; Cross, Borgatti, & Parker, 2002; Paxton, Schutz, Wertheim, & Muir, 1999; Stanton, Aronson, Borgatti, Galbraith, & Feigelman, 1993; Weeks, Clair, Borgatti, Radda, &

Schensul, 2002). SNA aims to illustrate the structure of social inter-action by representing individuals as 'points' and treating their social relationships as connecting 'lines' (Scott, 1991). Scholars in SNA suggest that who you know has a significant impact on what you come to know (Borgatti & Cross, 2003). Thus, SNA produces a social network diagram of individuals and the social ties that link them together. The key feature of these diagrams lies within the pattern of relationships displayed and the relative position of individuals to each other. Perhaps there is some truth to the Spanish proverb, 'Di me con quien andan, y dire quien eres' that loosely translates to 'Tell me who you walk with, and I will tell you who you are.'

Overall, culture is intimately tied with social support, social capital, and social networks and plays a significant role in shaping social boundaries. As Emirbayer and Goodwin (1994) suggest, 'culture and social relations empirically interpenetrate with and mutually condition one another so thoroughly that it is well-nigh impossible to conceive of the one without the other' (p. 1438).

Further reading

Bronfenbrenner, U. (1979). *The ecology of human development: Experiments by nature and design.* Cambridge, MA: Harvard University Press.

Ferguson, S. J. (2007). *Shifting the Center: Understanding contemporary families* (3rd ed.). Boston, MA: McGraw Hill.

Gardiner, H. W., & Kosmitzki, C. (2008). *Lives across cultures: Cross-cultural human development* (4th ed.). Boston, MA: Allyn & Bacon.

Georgas, J., Berry, J. W., van de Vijver, F. J. R., Kagitçibasi, C., & Poortinga, Y. H. (Eds.). (2006). *Families across cultures: A 30-nation psychological study.* Cambridge, UK: Cambridge University Press.

Gibbon, J. L. (2000). Adolescence in international and cross-cultural perspective: An introduction. *International Journal of Group Tensions*, 29(1/2), 3–16.

Harkness, S., & Super, C. M. (Eds.). (1996). *Parents' cultural belief systems: Their origins, expressions, and consequences.* New York: Guilford.

Kim, H. S., Sherman, D. K., & Taylor, S. E. (2008). Culture and social support. *American Psychologist*, 63(6), 518–526.

Chapter 4

Basic psychological processes and culture

■ Introduction 76

■ Biological bases 76

■ Cognition 78

■ Emotion 80

■ Perception 81

■ Language 85

■ States of consciousness 86

■ And so forth (the science of happiness) 87

Introduction

THERE IS DISAGREEMENT about the influence of culture on basic psychological processes making it difficult to summarize each of these areas in a simple fashion as they relate to culture. Many of the main characteristics of these basic psychological processes appear to be shared across human beings, however, the nuances and manifestations are more responsive to differences in the social, ecological, and cultural contexts. An additional challenge with this type of research is that some areas are political and controversial because of apparent biases regarding morality, intelligence, and behaviours of certain marginalized groups. Today, we view much of this early research as politically motivated and outrageously incorrect. As Guthrie (2004) points out, 'early psychological study was bound hand and foot with anthropological studies of "racial mixing" and with a maddening search for definitions of mulattoes and the implications of race mixtures for behavior' (p. xi). The focus of such phrenology (which was taken seriously and viewed as a science), Guthrie (2004) says, was to establish that non-whites were intellectually inferior to whites via differences measured in skin colour, skulls, skeletons, nerves, noses, ears and lips. Such research was used as a method to get rid of less 'desirable' peoples and limit the proliferation of groups thought to be inferior (e.g., sterilization in the USA, Holocaust, labelling of Southern Europeans as inferior compared with Northern Europeans during increased immigration, racist efforts of psychological tests in World War II, etc.). In general, examining psychological processes across cultural groups is complicated because of the widespread belief that biology causes psychology, the common substitution of race for culture, and general bias in research that occurs as a result of a particular political or personal agenda.

Biological bases

Across cultural groups, people appear to have the same structural anatomy and the same or extremely similar physiological functions. However, some differences emerge in the relative size of the anatomical structures and in the psychological and behavioural expression of physiological function. This reciprocal relationship between biology and psychology is increasingly being recognized in research and more recently has gained increased recognition with the biopsychosocial model, which points to the confluence of biological, psychological, and social factors in human functioning especially in the context of disease and illness (Halligan & Aylward, 2006). Researchers have suggested that early learning experiences, including diet, trauma, type of parenting, and environment, may modify any predisposing physiological factors and ultimately alter brain chemistry. Such evidence suggests that culture and corresponding practices and customs may play an important role in biological composition and vice versa (Matsumoto & Juang, 2008). To further understand how genetics and environment interact, it is helpful to examine three types of gene–environment interactions (Scarr, 1993):

(1) Passive genotype–environment interactions – parents provide both the genes and environment (e.g., musical skill developed both from inherited genes and musical environment provided by parents).

(2) Evocative genotype–environment interaction – inherited characteristics evoke certain responses from the environment (e.g., more musical opportunities are presented to a child who seems to have inherent musical ability).

(3) Active genotype–environment interaction – seek environments that support inherited characteristics (e.g., child asks parents to join a children's choir because of musical ability and interest).

Additional examples that demonstrate the link among psychology, biology, and social factors are the disease process and sports. Psychological research points to differences in some physical disease processes in people of different cultural groups. For instance, Triandis and colleagues (1988) examined eight different cultural groups for the relationship between heart disease and degree of individualism versus collectivism. The most individualistic of the eight groups, the European Americans, had the highest rates of heart disease and were the least individualistic, the Trappist monks, had the lowest rate. These researchers suggested that social support was one of the protective factors contributing to lack of heart disease for groups in this study. As compared with people living in individualistic cultures, people living in collectivistic cultures are more likely to be connected with others and thus suffer less from social isolation making them less susceptible to heart disease. In addition, sports research has documented racial differences in physique, stature, muscle size and length and speed of neural transmission (Matsumoto & Juang, 2008).

Cognition

Intelligence, cognitive test performance, cognitive styles and creativity all are subsumed under the cognitive umbrella. Culturally there are many alternative views of intelligence although intelligence viewed through the lens of Western psychology has mostly been considered a constellation of intellectual abilities emphasizing verbal and analytical tasks (Spearman, 1927). Outside the Western world there is considerable variability in the concept of intelligence as suggested by the absence of even a specific word for intelligence in many languages. As we have come to understand more about cultural differences in intelligence, broader, more encompassing theories of intelligence have been suggested and have potential application across cultures. For example, Gardner's theory of multiple intelligences (Gardner, 2000) highlights the myriad of ways that one can be intelligent including areas beyond traditional definitions of intelligence (see Chapter 8 for further discussion on his theory). Sternberg's theory of intelligence (1986) is based on three types of 'process' intelligence (rather than outcome): contextual, experiential, and componential intelligence. Contextual intelligence is the ability to solve problems in one's environment. Experiential intelligence signifies the ability to develop new ideas and merge unrelated facts. Componential intelligence refers to abstract thinking and processing and the ability to figure out what needs to be done. The expansion of the concepts of intelligence indicates that intelligence in a broad sense is beginning to be viewed more in relation to skills and abilities necessary to accomplish cultural goals (Greenfield, 1997).

Intelligence testing has been controversial in cultural research because the interpretation of the performance of different cultural groups on cognitive tests has varied widely. Some have argued that differences are based on innate competencies making some races/ethnicities more 'intelligent' than others. However, the more common viewpoint is that cognitive processes are embedded in and influenced heavily by culture. In other words, cognitive ability is patterned based on ecological necessity and sociocultural context thus different 'types' of intelligence are expected.

Likewise, cognitive testing has been controversial because of questions about the validity of measures and the interpretation of test scores. From the universalist perspective, there are different levels of competence across cultural groups and performance differences on cognitive tests arise because of differences in how the underlying qualities of intelligence are expressed. Standardized tests typically are not constructed in such a way that they take into account cognitive skills that are shaped by a particular cultural environment. As such, cognitive tests created in one culture will continue to be biased against other cultural groups. In addition, there are many aspects of cognition that are not usually measured by standardized tests (e.g., creativity). Cognitive tests or any other psychological test should follow guidelines for the translation and adaptation of tests developed by the International Test Commission (Hambleton, 1994). The four domains include context (principles of multicultural and multilingual studies), construction (good practices for developing tests), test administration (familiarity with item response format and conditions for administration), and documentation/score interpretation (scores of a population not taken at face value).

Cognitive style is different from intelligence – it is the way that a person uses information to solve problems or simply, his or her thinking style. One of the most popular conceptualizations of cognitive style is Witkin's work regarding field independence and field dependence (Witkin, Dyk, Paterson, Goodenough, & Karp, 1962). People with a field independent style are more likely to rely on cues from within themselves and operate 'on' the environment while being less socially oriented whereas field dependent people rely on cues from the environment and are more adept at social engagement.

Another aspect of cognition relevant to culture is creativity.

The same characteristics of creative people appear to be relatively universal – perseverance, risk taking, tolerance for ambiguity, and ability to 'think outside of the box'. However, creativity is fostered in different ways depending on the culture. For example, in one study of organizations across 30 countries, creative individuals from countries high on Hofstede's dimension of uncertainty avoidance were expected to work through organizational rules and norms. Creative people from collectivistic countries were expected to obtain cross-functional support for their creative efforts (Shane, Venkataraman, & MacMillan, 1995).

Emotion

Emotion accompanies us from birth and involves physiological arousal, subjective evaluation, and behavioural expression. Theories of emotion abound in Western psychology. Ranging from William James' initial notion that emotion occurs as a result of bodily experience that morphed into the James Lange theory of emotion (Lange, 1885/1922) to an alternative theory of emotion described by Cannon and Bard which posited that stimuli create both an emotional and a bodily response simultaneously (Cannon, 1927). The identification, interpretation and displaying of emotions are culturally determined. The French word *formidable* conveys a sense of awesomeness whereas in English it signifies something more intimidating or forbidding (Okun et al., 1999). Are human emotions universal or culture specific or a combination of both? Ekman (1994) and others have found universal similarities in how we display our emotions through facial expressions. Through analysis of facial expressions from a wide range of cultures, Ekman and Friesen (1975) and others have identified six universal emotions (happiness, sadness, surprise, fear, anger, disgust). Later, Ekman (1994) added a seventh emotion of contempt. These researchers have found that across cultures, people can identify another's basic emotion without verbally communicating. Through culture and socialization, we learn display rules about expressing emotion – what is forbidden, what is expected in certain events, what intensity of emotion is appropriate and with whom, etc. For example, in some cultures, expressing grief at a funeral is expected to be loud, emotional with crying and wailing. In other cultures, strong displays of emotion are considered offensive and inappropriate even at a funeral. Matsumoto (1994) suggests that one's cultural self-concept strongly relates to emotional expression. In the Western world, for example, where an independent and individualized notion of the self is emphasized, encouraged emotions include pride, superiority, anger, and frustration. This is in contrast to many non-Western cultures that have the cultural view of an interdependent and collective self thus emotions that encourage social cohesion and positive interrelationships among people like respect, indebtedness, and guilt are encouraged (Okun et al., 1999).

Perception

Perception is the interpretation of sensory experiences. A common saying in psychology is 'one's perception is one's reality' to highlight that our perceptions do not necessarily match the physical and sensory world around us. Perceptions are relative and become distorted easily based on sociocultural factors. For example, what one person perceives as extremely painful may only be interpreted as mildly painful by another, indicating variable thresholds of pain and touch. In part our perceptions differ based on the cultural context and familiarity with certain experiences. Physiologists suggest that perception occurs through activation of association areas in the cortex that integrates prior knowledge with current sensation. Early psychological research on sensation in perception found remarkable similarities in sensory and perceptual processes across nationalities. However, we now know that based on differing cultural practices of socialization and acculturation, people learn to sense certain stimuli and not others and have preferences for and familiarity with particular culture-related images, smells, tastes, and sounds (Shiraev & Levy, 2010).

Culture has an effect on the way the world is seen (perceived). Our experiences with the environment shape our perceptions by creating perceptual sets or perceptual expectations. This in turn creates variation in the speed of processing and the likelihood that certain interpretations will occur in different cultures. Perceptual differences can best be exemplified in cross-cultural differences found in visual perceptions to famous optical illusions like the Mueller–Lyer illusion (two lines with arrowheads pointing outward or inward – see Figure 4.1). Typically, people in the Western world perceive the line with the arrowheads pointing in as longer even though the lines are exactly the same length. This is in contrast to an early study with people from India and New Guinea who did not make the same perceptual error the English people made. Such a finding may indicate that in some cultures, people are more accustomed to seeing rounded and irregular shapes so would not respond to the optical illusion in the same way that the English people did who were used to seeing rectangular, geometric shapes. Other perceptual differences have been found across cultures including differences in the horizontal–vertical illusion, the Ponzo illusion, relative size related to depth perception, and spatial relationships.

Early research conducted in the USA and in Hong Kong on perceptual experience suggests differences in children's perceptions of coins depending on whether they were from poor or wealthy families (Dawson, 1975). Children were asked to adjust the size of a circle of light to correspond to the size of different coins. Children from poorer families tended to overestimate the size of the coins (thought to be related to their need for money), whereas children from wealthier families identified the coins as smaller than they actually were. Such differences in perception of coins suggest that the sociocultural milieu plays a significant role in perception.

Depending on where people live (e.g. crowded urban areas or rural), perception of depth, rates of colour blindness, and hearing loss

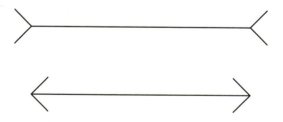

Figure 4.1 **The Mueller–Lyer illusion**

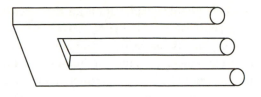

Figure 4.2 **The devil's tuning fork illusion**

can differ. In terms of depth perception, the famous picture of the Devil's tuning fork is often used to demonstrate cultural differences (see Figure 4.2). The Devil's tuning fork is confusing because it is two dimensional but contains confusing depth cues. People who lack familiarity with interpretation of depth cues (e.g. those lacking formal education, those living in extreme poverty, etc.) perceive the picture as two dimensional whereas others seem to have improved depth perception if they have received education and training (Leach, 1975). In a study on the Ponzo illusion (see Figure 4.3) with participants in the USA and Guam, the non-Western and rural participants demonstrated less susceptibility to the illusion as compared with people from Western and urban areas (Brislin, 2000). As compared with individuals with limited landscape views, individuals from open landscapes viewing the horizontal–vertical illusion were more prone to the illusion

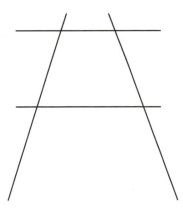

Figure 4.3 **The Ponzo illusion**

(see Figure 4.4). One popular explanation for these perceptual differences is the 'carpentered world' hypothesis (Segall, Campbell, & Herskovits, 1966), which is that people who are raised in an environment shaped by carpenters (rectangular houses and furniture, grid street patterns) are more likely to interpret nonrectangular figures as representations of rectangular figures seen in perspective and a tendency to interpret the lines in a horizontal plane as seeming shorter than the lines that cross the viewer's line of vision: a horizontal–vertical illusion.

Cultural patterns in drawn pictures have also been noted. For example, in many art traditions, there is no linear perspective (e.g., paintings of Ancient Egypt, Crete, India, early Europe, Cezanne, Cubism). Although individuals across the globe can generally detect the same range of colours and generally feel similarly about the feelings provoked by colours, there are some differences in naming and in how colour is perceived. For instance, in some cultures the colours blue and green are not distinguished linguistically. Red has symbolized violence in some cultures and in others like Japan, red is a symbol of vitality (Adams & Osgood, 1973).

Most of the information about cultural differences of sensation and perceptual processes has been directed at vision with significantly less information available regarding the other types of sensations and related perception (e.g., hearing, taste, smell, and touch). In terms of hearing, different cultures attach various meanings to different sounds. Although all people respond to the tastes of sweet, sour, bitter and salty, there is widespread variation in taste preferences across cultures.

Figure 4.4 **The horizontal–vertical illusion**

For example, people living near the equator tend to prefer spicier foods and find food from further north or south to be quite bland. Likewise, there appears to be cross-cultural variation for odour preferences. Regarding touch, cultures differ in their perceptions of pressure, temperature, and pain (Shiraev & Levy, 2010).

Time perception is treated very differently across cultures. In the Western world, time is treated very precisely with 5 minutes meaning 5 minutes whereas in other cultures, time is perceived in a very malleable and flexible way. In many Latin American countries, time is perceived using the *mañana* framework, which means that punctuality is not a consideration, especially if something more important occurs. *Mañana* means 'tomorrow', and indicates that time is perceived in a flexible manner. In many non-Western cultures, time consciousness is simply not a top priority. These ideas about time also mean that the quality of an interaction is more important than how long it lasts. It is fairly common for people from Latin America to arrive late by 30 minutes or more for an appointment or meeting. For them, 4:00 pm can mean any time between 4:00 and 5:00 pm – what is important ultimately is showing up and the quality of the time spent together.

Perception of what is beautiful also differs greatly across the globe. Certain stimuli are perceived as pleasurable and arouse curiosity, appreciation, and joy. Some fads and fashions start at a national level and quickly spread internationally. Other cultures limit the media and thus beauty is often defined for the people without freedom to choose. Perception of music and harmony differs depending on a culture's socialization of musical scales, intervals, and rhythm. What is relaxing and harmonious to the Western listener for example, may be distasteful and arouse dissonance in non-Westerners. It is easy to see how different perceptions could lead quickly to cultural conflicts. Learned patterns of perception acquired in a culture are assumed to be universal and when they are not, basic values and identities are called into question.

Language

Another aspect of culture and basic psychological processes is language. Language and culture are intimately connected. Culture influences the way in which language is used and the structure of language. Language is thought to be a direct reflection of culture, reinforcing our world views and cultural thoughts, values, and behaviours. Some have argued that without understanding the language of a culture, the culture itself cannot be fully understood. An example that reflects this duality is the Spanish use of familiar you (*tu*) versus the formal you (*usted*). Latin American cultures differ in their emphasis on this usage but in general, use of *usted* is expected unless conversing with a close friend. Such a practice reflects the hierarchy, formal nature of interactions, and respect for elders common to Latino cultural groups. Communication differences can be seen cross-culturally in compliments, interpersonal criticism, and apologies.

One of the long debates around culture and language is to what extent language influences culture and vice versa. The Sapir–Whorf hypothesis, also known as linguistic relativity, suggests that speakers of different languages think differently because of the differences in the construction and function of their languages. In other words, a person who speaks more than one language may in fact think differently in each of the languages. Because learning a language well typically occurs within the context of a culture, people learn to have different associations and feelings associated with a particular language. Another debate relative to psychology and language is whether children should learn more than one language. We now know that being multilingual has no negative effects on intelligence and in fact may improve cognitive flexibility (O'Malley & Chamot, 1990).

States of consciousness

Human consciousness and culture are inseparable. Consciousness includes the awareness of one's sensations, perceptions and other mental events and is typically depicted on a continuum with full awareness at one end and loss of consciousness on the other end. In certain circumstances, consciousness can be altered through trances, psychoactive substances, meditation, and hypnosis. Culturally, altered states of consciousness depend on how a culture views the relationship between mind, body, and soul.

Sleep, a nonwaking state of consciousness, varies in terms of patterns and amounts in different cultures. The amount of sleep each person needs appears to be in part a physiological determination and in part a cultural norm. Although the actual content (manifest content) of dreams varies significantly from person to person and culture to culture, dreams are thought to be culturally similar with regard to reflecting our everyday experiences and the latent content, or dream's meaning (Flanagan, 2000). In fact, anxiety is said to be the leading emotion in all dreams regardless of cultures (Hobson, 1999). The role of dreams differs from culture to culture. In particular, some cultures view dreams as a way to share folk wisdom (e.g., Mayan Indians in Central America), others as social understanding related to conflict and problems (e.g., Yolmo Sherpa of Nepal), and like the Iroquois Native Americans, as flights of the soul collecting important information (Desjarlais, 1991; Moss, 1996; Tedlock, 1992).

Altered states of consciousness (ASC) include mystical perceptual and sensory experiences such as meditation, hypnosis, trance, and possession (Ward, 1994). Although being in an altered state of consciousness has historically been contentious because of a potential link with the supernatural, ASC are commonplace globally. Trances are sleeplike states usually induced by singing or music in order to access the unconscious mind. Trances are used for relaxation, healing and inspiration, sometimes accompanied by hallucinations, and can be found as part of many cultural and religious traditions. Possession is another ASC that is depicted as a bodily invasion or capture by one or more spirits. Some cultures and religions describe demonic possessions as a demon taking revenge on a person's psyche perhaps as a form of punishment for some maliciously intended behaviour. Meditation is typically engaged in to expand conscious awareness. Considered therapeutic, cleansing, and liberating by many religious traditions, meditation is described as a deepened state of relaxation or awareness.

And so forth (the science of happiness)

People around the world want to be happy yet happiness eludes most of us. When asked what they most want in life, people in almost every country say happiness is a top priority (Diener & Suh, 2000). What does it take to be happy and who are the happiest people? Happiness research has traditionally been viewed as 'fuzzy' and unscientific however, now under the umbrella of positive psychology (a branch of psychology that studies the strengths of human beings, their lives, and optimal human functioning (Linley & Joseph, 2004)), social science researchers are increasingly certain that happiness does in fact have key determinants, can be measured, and has a substantial explanatory theory. Although there are many definitions for happiness, most happiness researchers simply define happiness as 'the overall enjoyment of your life as a whole' (Linley & Joseph, 2004). Peterson and Seligman (2004) developed the *Character Strengths and Virtues* (CSV) handbook in order to identify and classify the positive psychological traits of human beings. The CSV identifies six core virtues that have been valued throughout history and by the majority of cultures. These six virtues include wisdom and knowledge, courage, humanity, justice, temperance, and transcendence, and when practised are thought to lead to increased happiness See Table 4.1 for definitions of these virtues.

We are often wrong about what makes us happy (Wilson & Gilbert, 2005) and incorrectly work toward things that only last for a short time (e.g., money, possessions) and meanwhile ignore more effective routes to happiness. For instance, in one study of 22 people who won major lotteries compared with matched controls, the lottery winners returned to their baseline of happiness and over time were no happier than the controls and after a few years pass paraplegics are

Table 4.1 **Six core virtues (Peterson & Seligman, 2004)**

Virtue	Characteristics
Wisdom and knowledge	Enjoying and engaging in the pursuit of learning
Courage	Exhibiting bravery and persistence
Humanity	Being kind and sensitive towards others
Justice	Treating people fairly; being a good leader
Temperance	Having self-control; being humble
Transcendence	Being thankful; appreciating beauty; spirituality

only slightly less happy on average than non-paralysed individuals (Seligman, 2002).

So, who *IS* happy? People living in certain cultures, especially those where people enjoy abundance and political freedom, are likely to have an increased satisfaction with life (Diener & Suh, 2000). Certain heritable traits such as extraversion seem to have a strong link with happiness suggesting that at least a portion of happiness is genetically influenced (Linley & Joseph, 2004). People actively involved in faith communities report being very happy as compared with people not involved (Linley & Joseph, 2004). Internationally, social scientists have been studying happiness across nations using the World Values Survey (www.worldvaluessurvey.org/), the World Database of Happiness (Veenhoven, 2009), and the World Map of Happiness (White, 2007). Overall, it appears that happiness is on the rise for people in most countries around the world. Economic growth, democratization and tolerant social norms are thought to have contributed to greater freedom and choices in life, which in turn leads to increased happiness. The 2007 World Values Survey ranked Denmark as the happiest nation in the world and Zimbabwe the unhappiest out of 97 nations surveyed. The United States ranked sixteenth on the list. Iceland, Switzerland, the Netherlands and Canada all fell within the top ten happiest countries in the world. The largest recent increases on the subjective well-being index, measuring both happiness and life satisfaction, occurred in the Ukraine, followed by Moldova, Slovenia, Nigeria, Turkey and Russia (News-Medical.Net, 2008).

Adrian White, a social psychologist at University of Leicester, combined data on happiness from several sources to examine the correlations between poverty, health and education and happiness and produced the 'World Map of Happiness' (2007). Table 4.2 contains the top 20 happiest nations and the three least happiest nations according to this study. White found that happiness is most closely associated with health, followed by wealth and then education. However, there do seem to be some mediators for cultural differences in happiness. For example, personal success, self-expression, pride, and a high sense of self-esteem are important in the United States. In Japan, on the other hand, it comes from fulfilling the expectations of your family, meeting your social responsibilities, self-discipline, cooperation and

Table 4.2 Results from the 2007 world values survey (www.news-medical.net, 2008)

Rank country	*Rank country*
The 20 happiest nations in the world	
1 Denmark	11 Ireland
2 Switzerland	12 Luxembourg
3 Austria	13 Costa Rica
4 Iceland	14 Malta
5 The Bahamas	15 The Netherlands
6 Finland	16 Antigua and Barbuda
7 Sweden	17 Malaysia
8 Bhutan	18 New Zealand
9 Brunei	19 Norway
10 Canada	20 The Seychelles
Other notable results	
23 USA	82 China
35 Germany	90 Japan
41 UK	125 India
62 France	167 Russia
The three least happy countries	
176 Democratic Republic of the Congo	
177 Zimbabwe	
178 Burundi	

friendliness. A culture's notions about wealth, justice and trust, lay beliefs about happiness (e.g., that there are only limited amounts of happiness in life, and specificity of judgement criteria (e.g., winning versus doing well) all contribute to perceptions of happiness (Diener, Oishi, & Lucas, 2002). Lyubomirsky, Sheldon and Schkade (2005) offer an overall map determining happiness: 50% set point from genetics, 10% circumstances, and 40% intentional activity, which suggests that as individuals we can do something about at least 40% of our happiness by engaging in intentional activities that raise levels of happiness.

Further reading

Ekman, P., & Friesen, W. V. (1975). *Unmasking the face*. Englewood Cliffs, NJ: Prentice Hall.

Fiske, S. T. (1995). Social cognition. In A. Tesser (Ed.), *Advanced social psychology*. New York: McGraw-Hill.

Gardner, H. (2000). *Intelligence reframed: Multiple intelligences for the 21st century*. New York: Basic Books.

Lyubomirksy, S., Sheldon, K. M., & Schkade, D. (2005). Pursuing happiness: The architecture of sustainable change. *Review of General Psychology*, 9, 111–131.

Scarr, S. (1993). Biological and cultural diversity: The legacy of Darwin for development. *Child Development*, 64, 1333–1353.

Chapter 5

Intercultural interactions and acculturation

■ Introduction   94

■ Pluralism   94

■ Intercultural opportunities   95

■ Psychological acculturation   95

■ Barriers to intercultural interactions   101

■ Benefits of approaching interactions in a culturally competent manner   102

■ Strategies for successful intercultural interactions   102

■ And so forth (culture shock)   107

Introduction

G IVEN THE GROWTH of culturally plural societies where many cultural groups reside together and share social and political frameworks, achieving greater ease in intercultural interactions is increasingly important. Changing social, linguistic, religious and other cultural differences within countries require greater flexibility in interactions both personally and professionally. Psychological acculturation can affect anyone entering a new cultural situation but most often is applied to immigrant experiences. Despite barriers to intercultural interactions, there also exist many advantages. To maximize the advantages, there are various strategies applicable to intercultural interactions that can contribute to positive outcomes for all involved.

Pluralism

Internationalization, globalization, emigration, and immigration make it imperative that we become comfortable with relationships and interactions within societies. Foreign born and immigrant populations in many countries across the world are growing (Bochner, 2003). The large Southeast and East Asian communities that have been established in Australia, Canada, Britain, and the USA serve as examples of global connectivity and intercultural migration. Such distinctive communities like the large Latino populations in the USA, and African and Caribbean communities in Britain can increase the perception of cultural distance among societal members (Ward, Bochner, & Furnham, 2001). Groups and individuals increasingly have to manage the process of intercultural relations that involves psychological acculturation and specific strategies and coping skills. Berry (1998) distinguishes between two perspectives of plural societies. The 'melting pot' view is the notion that minority/ethnocultural groups become absorbed into mainstream culture. In contrast, the 'mosaic' or multicultural point of view suggests that minority/ethnocultural groups retain their cultural identity and live with some shared norms while allowing different cultural interests to evolve through institutions.

Intercultural opportunities

Crossing cultures does not have to occur in order to encounter intercultural opportunities, as these opportunities present themselves when culturally diverse people interact in multicultural societies – at the workplace and in daily life. Generally, intercultural opportunities are thought to exist when someone is a sojourner to another country. Sojourners are temporary visitors to another country who eventually return to their home country and include students, tourists, business people, humanitarian aid workers/missionaries, and government diplomats (Bochner, 2003). Matsumoto et al. (2001) contend that intercultural adjustment and culture shock are phenomena that affect not only those immersed in new and different cultures but also people who interact with culturally different people in their everyday lives. Minority groups, especially immigrants, indigenous people, refugees, and other marginalized people, may have to manage intercultural adjustment more readily.

Psychological acculturation

Berry et al. (2002) define psychological acculturation as 'changes that an individual experiences as a result of being in contact with other cultures, and as a result of participating in the process of acculturation that his or her cultural or ethnic group is undergoing'. Psychological acculturation can be observed in most cultural interactions, but most often is applied to immigrants coming to a new country. The terms *refugee, asylum seekers* and *immigrants* are often used interchangeably but they are distinct terms. A *refugee*, according to the United Nations (UN) Convention and UN Protocol, is someone fleeing persecution across national borders due to race, religion, nationality, membership in social group, political opinion, torture or war, and who applies for refugee status whereas *asylum seekers* have left their country to look for sanctuary because of persecution or perceived danger in their home country. Once asylum seekers arrive, they are admitted as refugees at the border of a country that has signed the Geneva Convention on Refugees until their claim is adjudicated (Okitikpi & Aymer, 2003).

Refugees and asylum seekers are specific classifications of 'forced migrants' while the term *immigrant* is a broad definition for anyone who leaves his/her country to settle permanently in another country.

While trying to acclimatize to a new culture, almost all immigrants undergo a shared experience dealing with 'unexpected obstacles of poverty, discrimination, language, ambiguous immigration or legal status' (Gloria & Segura-Herrera, 2004). In most situations, immigrants have been parted from family, friends, and are estranged from the inherent security one attains with being a member of a community (Thomas, 1995). Immigrants may also feel burdened by the necessity of learning and/or enhancing non-primary language skills, overcoming bias when seeking employment, living arrangements, schools, etc. – compounded by an overwhelming sense of ineptness in a new and different social environment. These cultural hurdles add to the 'confusion and conflict, anomie, personal disorganization, and a variety of other problems related to social marginality. . . .' (Warheit, Vega, Auth, & Meinhardt, 1985).

Immigrant children endure many of the same hardships as adults when removed from their country of birth. Van Hook and Fix (2000) observe that children of immigrants often are raised in linguistically isolated households, a condition that may undermine familial dynamics by forcing children to become translators and cultural liaisons for their parents. Parents are gradually shifted into the role of subordinates as they become more dependent on their children to act as liasons in cultural interactions. Without help from their parents, children may not fully comprehend all that is related to them and unknowingly give out inaccurate information, such as personal medical information about a family member. Over the last several decades in the United States alone, the percentage of children and youth who are foreign born has been increasingly steadily from 1.2% in 1970 to 3.7% in 1990 (US Department of Health & Human Services, 2008). The fastest-growing group in the USA is first- and second-generation immigrant children under age 15 (Chen & Rankin, 2002). Despite their growing numbers, immigrant children will find it just as difficult to improve their financial and social standing as did their parents. These statistics are juxtaposed to the findings of The National Center for Children in Poverty (NCCP, www.nccp.org/about.html) that reports that in comparison to native-born children in the USA, immigrant children are two to four times as likely to be poor (depending on circumstances – e.g., two parents, both parents working outside of home, etc.) and are at greater risk of living in poverty. Members of immigrant families will often find themselves growing apart from one another in the timeless struggle of old versus new. Children tend to adopt and embrace the ways of their new culture readily, while parents cling to the traditions and familiarities of the past. Immigrant children often become masters of both cultures, easily adapting between both worlds (Suárez-Orozco & Suárez-Orozco, 2001). Immigrant parents may appreciate and accept the necessity of their children becoming acculturated to their new way of life, but often struggle to keep a tenuous hold onto the traditions and beliefs of their own native culture (Suárez-Orozco & Suárez-Orozco, 2001).

While adapting to a new culture might be easier for immigrant children, there are other issues with immigration that can affect their emotional balance. Often with relocation to a new country, the bureaucratic demands of the country's immigration procedures, coupled with additional immigration demands such as obtaining housing, food, and employment outweigh the childrens' need for attention (Aroian, Norris, Patsdaughter, & Tran, 1998). Immigrant children are often the witnesses to the emotional stress of their parents. Consequently, they are affected as well – many of the immigrant children living under conditions of 'parental depression, anxiety and uncertainty were unlikely to be thriving and rediscovering their childhood'; instead the children and their families are faced with a 'continuing sense of dislocation, isolation, fragmentation and fear of the unknown' (Okitikpi & Aymer, 2003, p. 218). Short and Johnston, (1997) compared immigrant mothers who reported experiencing less stress with the immigration process to those mothers who had the opposite experience. It was discovered that the children were less likely to have problems if their mothers reported lower stress levels, than children whose mothers were negatively affected by immigration.

Smart and Smart (1995) define acculturative stress as 'the psychological impact of adaptation to a new culture' with potential effects on physical health and self-esteem (p. 25). Acculturative stress happens as immigrants lose touch with self-identifying constants, values and social institutions of their former homeland. Theorists have suggested that this process of acculturation may lead to higher rates of mental disorders especially with regard to depression, adjustment, and general psychosocial dysfunction all of which result from 'the processes of adaptation, accommodation, and acculturation which involve dynamic and synergistic changes in the immigrants' intrapsychic character, their interpersonal relationships, and their social roles and statuses' (Warheit et al., 1985). Uncertainty about the future along with heightened levels of anxiety may contribute to family dysfunction, strict and authoritarian childrearing practices including harsh disciplinary methods like spanking and possibly severe, physical abuse (Thomas, 1995). Additionally, in households in which both parents work, children may be left unsupervised or neglected. In some cases, sons and daughters are left behind in their native country, creating circumstances which can increase conflicts surrounding relationships, gender roles, and respect issues (Thomas, 1995).

Berry (1997, 2001) postulated that groups and/or individuals may develop one of four strategies toward acculturation. These strategies can be applied to both the dominant and the non-dominant group and are delineated on two dimensions: (1) maintenance of heritage, culture and identity; and (2) relationships sought among groups. According to Berry, the four strategies of ethnocultural groups include integration (maintain one's original culture and have regular interactions with dominant culture), separation (maintain cultural identity and avoid interactions with dominant culture), assimilation (seek out interaction with dominant culture and do not maintain cultural identity), and marginalization (do not maintain cultural identity and little interest in interactions with dominant culture) (see Table 5.1). The

Table 5.1 **Berry's (1997, 2001) strategies of acculturation**

	Original culture is maintained	Original culture is not maintained
No interaction with dominant culture	Separation	Marginalization
Interaction with dominant culture	Integration	Assimilation

acculturation strategies chosen by groups or individuals depend on the sociocultural context of the larger society. For instance, the integration strategy will only work in societies that value cultural diversity and have relatively low levels of prejudice (Berry et al., 2002). The dominant group and larger society play an essential role in how acculturation occurs. Assimilation when desired by the dominant culture is termed 'melting pot' indicating a blending into the dominant group. When separation is demanded by the dominant group, it is 'segregation'. Integration occurs when the dominant society endorses mutual accommodation now widely called 'multiculturalism'. In several studies, Berry's acculturation strategies have been examined in non-dominant acculturating groups. Across these numerous studies, the strategy of integration is generally preferred over the three other strategies and marginalization is the least preferred. However, an exception to this is that some indigenous groups globally and some Turks in Germany and Canada (Berry et al., 2002) prefer separation over integration.

Managing psychological acculturation is complex and difficult due to the complexity of situational and personal factors that contribute to the process. To begin with, there is the society of origin and the society of settlement both of which have unique cultural factors. The cultural characteristics of the individual (developed from the society of origin) and the cultural characteristics present in the society of settlement (including political, economic, and demographic conditions) must be understood in order to estimate cultural distance between the two societies. The 'migration motivation' of the individual needs to be examined in order to understand the individual's degree of reactive (negative, constraining) versus proactive (positive, enabling) factors toward the migration experience (Richmond, 1993). The presence or absence of a multicultural ideology in the society of settlement gives important information about openness to cultural pluralism and thus acceptance of new members. Societies that support cultural pluralism generally provide a better context for immigrants because of multicultural institutions and corresponding resources (i.e., culturally sensitive health care and multicultural education curricula and services) and because of less pressure to assimilate or be excluded (Berry et al., 2002).

Although the process of acculturation is fraught with variability due to moderating factors that occur before or during the process, Berry (1997) has outlined five primary features that affect the process of psychological acculturation. First, there is the stress or demand of dealing with and participating in two different cultures. Second, individuals evaluate the meaning of dealing with the two cultures and depending on the appraisal, the changes that follow will either be relatively easy or more challenging and problematic. Third are the coping skills and strategies used by individuals if the situation is evaluated as problematic. The fourth feature of acculturation is the physiological and emotional reactions to the situation. The last and fifth feature is the long-term adaptation that may or may not be achieved depending on how the other aspects of acculturation have been addressed (see Figure 5.1).

Hong et al. (2000) offer a dynamic constructivist approach to acculturation that emphasizes the process of acculturation rather than

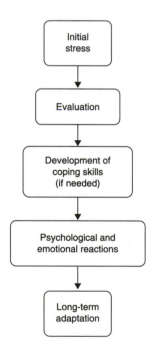

Figure 5.1 **Process of psychological acculturation**

the outcome. The process of acculturation includes the internalization of a new culture that involves frame switching, ongoing negotiation of multicultural identity, and actively choosing the accessibility of cultural constructs. For example, if immigrants want to acculturate quickly, they might surround themselves with symbols and situations consistent with the new culture, or vice versa, if they want to be reminded of home, they may reminisce by priming themselves with stimuli from the home culture.

Barriers to intercultural interactions

Different intercultural frameworks contribute to challenging intercultural interactions with different norms and values. These frameworks include pre-established schemas and scripts that may contribute to distress in interactions (Fiske, 1995). Having the necessary linguistic and cultural knowledge and skills are important in intercultural interactions (Brislin, 2000). People may speak the same language but do not have a 'bicultural' understanding of another's cultural background, which can be problematic (Abreu, Consoli, & Cypers, 2004). Intercultural experiences can precipitate identity conflict due to a constantly changing environment with different challenges and expectations than previously encountered. During intercultural interactions, individuals can feel lonely, alienated, and isolated; which may result in feelings of homesickness and stress or in daily life, a longing for the way things used to be (Cushner & Brislin, 1996). There can be pressure to act as an 'ambassador' for their own cultures and represent positive characteristics for an entire group of people who may or may not be similar to the person (Brislin, 2000). Culture shock is also a common response to intercultural interactions – see *And so forth* in this chapter for more information about the process of culture shock. At a more systemic level, Hong and colleagues (2000) suggest that, 'in part because of the strain of negotiating cultural complexity, a countervailing resurgence of efforts to separate individuals into culturally "pure" groups also exists' (p. 718). This can be problematic because it contributes to simplistic notions that people are easily categorized and if categorized can be interacted with following a recipe or a generalized approach tailored to the one specific cultural group. Because culture is 'carried' through relationships, institutions, and in relation to other cultures and not just at an individual level, it is imperative that we recognize the multiplicity of cultures and individuals within those cultures.

Benefits of approaching interactions in a culturally competent manner

Everyone benefits from cultural competency given that such competence can, for example, decrease disparities in health care (Betancourt, Green, Carrillo, & Park, 2005) and result in greater equity overall. Despite consensus in many fields about the importance of cultural competence, the pursuit of cultural competency has been limited by confusion about the meaning and complexity of culture, an uncertainty as to whether social factors should be included, the lack of systematic approaches, inadequate tools for assessment, and limited research examining the contribution of culturally competent professionals to enhanced outcomes (e.g., productivity, cost reduction, retention, etc.). In the business sector, cultural competence can result in decreased staff turnover, liability (medical errors), and an increase in market share due to reputation for creativity, innovation, and buying power (Hubbard, 2008). Overall, cultural competence contributes to the bottom line with related societal and individual benefits (Haugh, 2005).

Strategies for successful intercultural interactions

There are a variety of challenges and approaches to intercultural interactions in order to achieve the clear benefits of cultural competence. Cultural competency is often viewed synonymously with cultural diversity, cultural sensitivity, and cultural awareness although it is much broader than all of these. Most approaches do not define culture broadly and tend to dismiss important social factors of diverse groups (Green, Betancourt, & Carrillo, 2002). To be successful in intercultural interactions, one must have: (1) awareness of one's own assumptions, values and biases; (2) an understanding of the world view of culturally different people; and (3) appropriate strategies and techniques to use during the interaction (Sue & Sue, 2003). This requires knowledge, skills and awareness about one's strengths intrapersonally, interpersonally, and culturally. Although proposed as a model for intercultural adjustment, Vaughn and Phillips (2009) offer a comprehensive model that can also be useful for intercultural interactions (Figure 5.2). Their model includes three elements that could contribute to successful interactions: (1) intrapersonal competence (knowledge of self); (2) interpersonal competence (knowledge of self and others); and (3) cultural competence (application of knowledge of own and other's cultures). Similar approaches have been more singular, focusing only on knowledge, skills, or attitudes whereas this model offers a holistic approach incorporating various aspects of self and others.

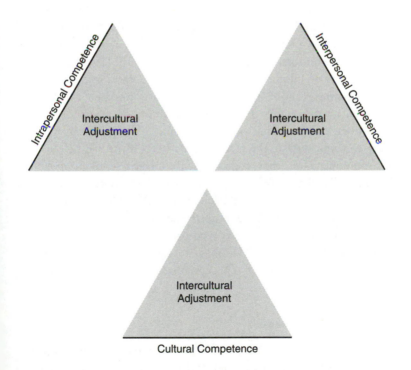

Figure 5.2 **Intrapersonal, interpersonal, and cultural competence**

Intrapersonal competence

Intrapersonal competence requires knowledge of the self, self-awareness, and the ability to engage in reflection. Intrapersonal competence can be challenging due to cognitive traps such as making assumptions about why people are the way they are, being 'cognitive misers' by thinking in simplistic ways because we don't want to 'use up' our scarce mental resources (Fiske, 1995), often making errors in attributions about the reason behind other people's behaviours (Forsterling, 2001). With our often limited world views, alternative frames of reference can be difficult to incorporate, and not-knowing can arouse fear and other unsettling emotions (Ito, Larsen, Smith, & Cacioppo, 1998; Kunda, 1999). Intrapersonal competence requires certain personality characteristics that contribute to successful intercultural interactions: cultural empathy, open-mindedness, emotional stability, action orientation, adventurousness/curiosity, flexibility, and extraversion (Van der Zee & Van Oudenhoven, 2001). Matsumoto and colleagues (2001) propose a 'psychological engine of adjustment' that contributes to notions of intrapersonal competence: (1) emotion regulation: ability to monitor and manage one's emotions, experiences and expressions; (2) openness: ability to incorporate new experiences, emotions, and thoughts; (3) flexibility: ability to incorporate new experiences, schemas, and ways of thinking; and (4) critical thinking: ability to think outside the box. Brislin (1981) identified helpful personality dimensions that coincide with intrapersonal competence: tolerant personality traits, strength of personality, relations with other people, intelligence, task orientation, and potential for benefit to both self and other. Others have argued that cross-cultural skills and effectiveness may be a separate type of 'intelligence' called cultural intelligence (Earley, 2002; Thomas & Inkson, 2004) that can be included in Goleman's (2006) conceptualization of social intelligence.

Interpersonal competence

Culture is translated through parents, family, and community members from birth; which inherently makes cultural experiences interpersonal in nature. To be interpersonally competent, one needs knowledge of self and others and the ability to relate with others who have different experiences. Bochner (2003) empirically confirmed that poor interpersonal skills have adverse effects in intercultural situations. Interpersonally, we prefer people who we perceive as similar to ourselves, which is known as the similarity-attraction hypothesis (Brehm, 1985). This makes interpersonal competence difficult to achieve because we might not put the energy or time into interpersonal relationships with people whom we perceive as different.

Cultural competence

In intercultural interactions, it is not sufficient to be only intrapersonally and interpersonally competent. Culture competence is the ability to apply knowledge of your own and others' cultures. What you do before and after, are as important as what you do during, an intercultural interaction. Initially, it is critical to prepare by obtaining relevant information regarding the intercultural situation and people. Sussman (2002) discusses the importance of post-experience debriefing by considering changes, understanding that distress may occur, and recognizing that others have not necessarily had the same intercultural experience, which may contribute to the person feeling isolated and misunderstood.

Across disciplines there are a wide variety of cultural competence techniques and strategies all of which have similarities but emphasize different dimensions of cultural competence. For ease of application, I have grouped these techniques into four areas (Vaughn, 2009):

(1)   Collaborative approaches to cultural competence include respectful interaction and some type of negotiation between people. The ResCUE Model (Res = Respect; C = Communicate; U = Understand; E = Engage) is an example of a collaborative approach to cultural competency used in health care (Betancourt, Green, & Carrillo, 2007). This model is about respecting the patient, communicating with them about their needs and expectations, understanding where they are coming from in terms of their medical concerns and how that is seated in their cultural values,

and engaging in a collaborative medical plan that is culturally supportive (Betancourt et al., 2007).

(2) Personality approaches to cultural competence include characteristics or competencies of the individual that can be developed. Some of these approaches are mentioned above in the *Intrapersonal competence* section (Matsumoto et al., 2001).

(3) Assessment approaches to cultural competence include ideas, questions, and techniques that can be used with people to better understand their cultural background. Kleinman's medical anthropology questions (Kleinman, 1981) are among the most popular assessment techniques for cultural competency, used in medicine and psychology. Some of the questions are: *What do you call your problem? What name does it have? What do you think caused your problem? What does your sickness do to you? What do you fear most about your disorder? What kind of treatment do you think you should receive?*

(4) Partnership/Empowerment approaches to cultural competence are based on the idea that individuals and communities themselves are the experts about their cultural situations and that partnerships should be co-created toward interventions that meet the needs of the people involved. Using community-based participatory research methodologies is an example of these types of partnership approaches (Reason & Bradbury, 2008).

Table 5.2 contains a summary of the four approaches with examples.

Table 5.2 **Summary of approaches to cultural competence**

Type of approach	Example
Collaborative	ResCUE model
Personality	Development of traits outlined in Matsumoto et al's (2001) 'psychological engine of adjustment'
Assessment	Kleinman's (1981) medical anthropology questions
Partnership/ empowerment	Community-based participatory research

And so forth (culture shock)

Culture shock is a common experience in intercultural interactions. It includes the physical and/or emotional discomfort one experiences when coming to live in another country or a new, unfamiliar, or different place (Sussman, 2002; Ward et al., 2001). Culture shock can also include exhaustion, negative psychological responses, and inappropriate thinking or behaving. Signs and symptoms of culture shock can include sadness, loneliness, melancholy, worry about health, aches, pains, and allergies, insomnia and sleep difficulties, depression, temperament changes, vulnerability, powerlessness, anger, irritability, resentment, withdrawal, idealization of home culture, loss of identity, feeling overwhelmed, problem-solving difficulties, lack of confidence, inadequacy or insecurity, stereotyping of the new culture, obsessional thinking and actions (e.g., overcleanliness), longing for family, feelings of being lost, overlooked, exploited, or even abused (Sussman, 2002; Ward et al., 2001).

Culture shock has been repeatedly studied. Typically conceptualized as stages (Bochner, 2003), there has been some debate about the pattern and order of stages with inconclusive evidence (Sussman, 2002; Ward et al., 2001). Culture shock can be experienced to a greater or lesser degree depending on personal experience with culturally different situations (Bochner, 2003). In addition, not everyone experiences all stages of culture shock and the stages can be experienced out of order. Culture shock typically begins with the honeymoon stage when a person is enthusiastic about the newness of difference (Figure 5.3). The second stage, rejection/crisis, is probably the most difficult stage. It is marked by difficulty and dissatisfaction and may include problems with communication, impatience, anger, and sadness. Regression follows with an emphasis on the home culture and idealistic illusions about the home culture. Next is recovery/understanding during which the person typically reconciles some of the cultural differences and more comfortably adjusts to differences. The final stage is re-entry shock experienced with a return to the 'home culture' (Bochner, 2003). Given the incorporation of ideas, values, and behaviours from the other culture, individuals may not feel comfortable in their own culture and may feel that that some ways of being and doing in the

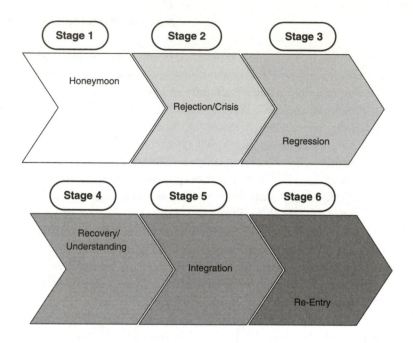

Figure 5.3 **Stages of culture shock**

home culture are not as acceptable as they once may have been (Sussman, 2002).

Further reading

Arends-Tóth, J., & van de Vijver, F. J. R. (2006). Assessment of psychological acculturation. In D. L. Sam & J. W. Berry (Eds.), *The Cambridge handbook of acculturation psychology* (pp. 142–160). Cambridge, UK: Cambridge University Press.

Bennett, J. M., & Bennett, M. J. (2004). *Developing intercultural competence: A reader*. Portland, OR: Intercultural Communication Institute.

Berry, J. W. (2001). A psychology of immigration. *Journal of Social Issues, 57*(3), 615–631.

Matsumoto, D., LeRoux, J., Ratzlaff, C., Tatani, H., Uchida, H., Kim, C., et al. (2001). Development and validation of a measure of intercultural adjustment potential in Japanese sojourners: The Intercultural Adjustment Potential Scale (ICAPS). *International Journal of Intercultural Relations*, 25, 483–510.

Vaughn, L. M., & Phillips, R. (2009). Intercultural Adjustment for Cultural Competency in Shared Context. *Journal of Interdisciplinary Social Sciences*, 3(11), 1–12.

Ward, C. A., Bochner, S., & Furnham, A. (2001). *The psychology of culture shock (2nd ed.)*. Hove, East Sussex: Routledge.

Chapter 6

Relationships, sexuality, and culture

- Introduction   112
- Friendships   112
- Courtship patterns and mate selection   114
- Marriage   117
- Love and marriage   119
- Forms of marriage   122
- Sexuality   125
- Divorce   128
- And so forth (computer mediated relationships)   130

Introduction

R ELATIONSHIPS ARE THE *sine qua non* of life for most of us. We turn to friends for advice and support during times of need. We seek out potential mates for courtship, mating, and possibly marriage. The majority of people across the globe describe their personal relationships as the most important part of their lives and the quality of personal relationships is one of the best predictors of overall life satisfaction (Noller & Feeney, 2006). Close relationships are found across cultures; however, customs in the expression of these relationships vary significantly depending on the culture. Cultures differ regarding what is considered appropriate in attraction and mate selection, in the expression of love and sexuality, and in the forms of marriage and choice to divorce. Overall, relationships cannot be removed from their sociocultural, historical, and political context.

Friendships

The relationship of friendship is found across virtually all cultures and friendship invariably occurs within a cultural context (French, Bae, Pidada, & Lee, 2006). Friendship seems to serve the purpose of socialization and enculturation within society in terms of learning about culturally appropriate negotiation, reciprocity, cooperation, and interpersonal sensitivity. Most research on friendship has been focused on Western, particularly North American, cultures; however, more recently there have been increased studies on friendship in different cultures.

Part of the way that children and later adults learn to approach the friendship relationship may have to do with how they are socialized and thus their culture's value system and the emphasis placed on issues like collectivism and individualism. For example, within Western individualistic cultures, individuals are more likely to personally choose whether or not and with whom to enter into social relationships and such relationships are seen as a social context for the achievement of individual competencies. In contrast, many Asian and Latino collectivistic cultures emphasize affiliative and cooperative activities along with advocating for interpersonal harmony and responsibility within friendships (Chen et al., 2006). In one study, Korean adolescents tended to form smaller exclusive friendship networks than their peers in Indonesia and the United States (Chen et al., 2006). Overall, friendship in the Western world seems to serve the purposes of enhancing self-esteem (Chen, et al., 2006; French et al., 2006) and fulfilling individual psychological needs such as the development of self-identity and enhancement of feelings about self-worth whereas in other cultures, friendship is more about the socialization of cooperative and compliant behaviour with others (Chen et al., 2006). In a recent study examining friendships among children in China, Russia, and former East Germany (similar with regard to former socialist system but with different cultural heritages), Gummerum and Keller (2008) found in general, that there appears to be a universal developmental sequence of friendship reasoning for children in different societies (e.g., stages that begin with friendship formation and include trust, jealousy, and conflict resolution, etc.) but that cultural factors influence the types and expectations of friendships which can be cultivated within particular cultures (e.g., heart-to-heart friendship in China that emphasizes the psychological and intimate aspects of friendship).

Friendships may also serve a regulatory function so that children learn to modify behaviours to fit acceptable peer norms and ultimately cultural norms (Chen et al., 2006). In other contexts, friendships may also serve as a buffer that protects children during adjustment to life events (e.g., immigration, new school, etc.) or during social and economic transitions in some societies (e.g., war, famine, etc.).

Extensive research has examined gender differences in friendships of girls and boys (for reviews, see Maccoby, 1998 and Rose & Rudolph, 2006). Compared with boys, the friendships of girls tend to be more intense, more intimate, and of higher quality. The friendships of boys are generally more focused on activities, less intimate, and more stable compared with those of girls. Girls, compared with boys, emphasize relationships and connection. Girls self-disclose and engage in social conversation. Girls appear to be more sensitive to others' distress and receive more emotional provisions as a result of their friendships. Girls, however, are more sensitive to peer status and face more interpersonal stressors in their friendships and in the larger peer group (Rose & Rudolph, 2006). All of these friendship characteristics for girls may increase the development of close, intimate friendships but also may increase girls' likelihood of experiencing depression and anxiety (Rose & Rudolph, 2006). Boys, in contrast, interact mostly in large structured groups focused on activities and might have one or two mutual relationships in the larger peer group (Maccoby, 1998). In friendships, boys are more involved than girls in rough-and-tumble play and competitive activities emphasizing dominance and self-interest. Compared with girls, boys are more likely to be victims of physical and verbal peer victimization. Overall boys receive less emotional support in friendships than girls (Rose & Rudolph, 2006). For boys, these features of friendship may promote group relationships and provide some protection against internalizing problems but increase boys' propensity for behaviour problems and difficulties developing close relationships (Rose & Rudolph, 2006).

In general friendships occur within a defined sociocultural context with 'cultural blueprints' (French et al., 2006) existing for the expectations and norms of what friendship signifies in terms of who, types of interactions, and degree of emotional connectedness. Cross-cultural studies have found some variation between collectivistic and individualistic culture in terms of friendships with friendships in collectivistic cultures being more intimate and less extensive than those in individualistic cultures (French et al., 2006).

Women's friendships appear to serve a therapeutic function. Women of all ages are more likely than men to have close friends, to confide intimate matters to their friends, to have a varied circle of friends, and to have closer networks of relatives (Crawford & Unger, 2004; Antonucci & Akiyama, 1997). Female friendships have been shown to have 'protective' factors to help maintain physical health, increase psychological adjustment and satisfaction, and contribute to psychological growth in old age.

Courtship patterns and mate selection

There is a plethora of research about what attracts people to potential mates. Proximity has long been linked to attraction and physical attractiveness seems to be a key ingredient in romantic relationships especially for males (Buss, 1985, 1988). Several hypotheses have been proposed about what attracts someone to a partner for a romantic relationship. The matching hypothesis proposes that people who are equal in physical attractiveness select each other as partners (Brehm, 1985; Hendrick & Hendrick, 1983). The similarity hypothesis proposes that people with similar demographics of age, race, religion, social class, education, intelligence, attitudes, and physical attractiveness tend to form intimate relationships (Brehm, 1985; Hendrick & Hendrick, 1983). Another approach is the reciprocity hypothesis that suggests that people like others who are unlike them (Byrne & Murnen, 1988).

How and why individuals are attracted to each other varies significantly across cultures. Despite some of the differences, there are cross-cultural similarities with regard to mate selection. In a well-known study conducted by evolutionary psychologist, David Buss (1989, 1994), more than 10,000 respondents across 37 different cultures responded to questions about factors in choosing mates. In 36 out of 37 cultures, females, as compared with males, rated financial prospects as more important and in 29 of the 36 cultures, they rated ambition and industriousness as more important. In all 37 cultures, females preferred older mates and males preferred younger mates. In 34 of the cultures, males rated good looks as more important than did females and in 23 of the cultures, males rated chastity as more important than females. Buss concluded that his findings represented and supported an evolutionary framework of universal mate selection across cultures whereby females look for cues in potential male mates that signal resource acquisition and males place more value on reproductive capacity. Others have emphasized the cultural differences in Buss' study. As compared with more advanced or modern cultures, trad-itional, less advanced cultures place greater value on chastity, domestic skills (e.g., housekeeping), desire for home and children, and abilities to support the home (Zebrowitz-McArthur, 1988). In China, India, Taiwan, and Iran, chastity was viewed as highly desirable in a prospect-ive mate while in the Netherlands, Sweden and Norway, it was con-sidered irrelevant. Being a *good housekeeper* was highly valued in Estonia and China and of little value in Western Europe and North America. *Refinement/neatness* was highly valued in Nigeria and Iran and less so in Great Britain, Ireland and Australia. Being *religious* was highly valued in Iran, moderately valued in India, and little valued in Western Europe and North America (Buss, 1994). Gender differences were also revealed in the study. Women across cultures place high value on characteristics of men that relate to providing resources – good earning capacity, financial prospects, ambition, industriousness, and social status. Men across the 37 cultures place a high premium on the physical appearance of a potential mate, which according to Buss supports an evolutionary argument because men use physical attractiveness as an indicator that the woman is fertile and has good reproductive capacity (Buss, 1994).

Other similar studies have shown that men across cultures rate physical attractiveness higher than women in terms of preferences in a marital partner (Hatfield & Sprecher, 1995). However, there seem to be more consistencies than differences in descriptions of physical attractiveness. For instance, female attractiveness cross-culturally is connoted by characteristics of kindness, understanding, intelligence, good health, emotional stability, dependability, and a pleasing disposition (Shiraev & Levy, 2010). Attractiveness is usually described in terms of cleanliness, health and feminine plumpness. Although the degree of plumpness varies across cultures, extreme thinness seems to be considered as unattractive and unhealthy (Zebrowitz-McArthur, 1988).

Other theories like the social construction perspective suggest that interpersonal attraction is due to individual and cultural factors instead of evolutionary factors. One study conducted in the USA highlights gender similarities in mate selection with both men and women rating kindness, consideration, honesty and a sense of humour as important traits in mate selection (Goodwin, 1990). A more recent study of American and Israeli students and their perceptions of romantic relationships (Pines, 2001) combines both the evolutionary and social construction theories. Pines (2001) found that more men than women, regardless of culture, reported physical attractiveness as a major part of attraction (evolutionary theory). However, culture was important in other factors of attraction (e.g., compared with Israelis, Americans indicated status, closeness and similarity as key determinants of attraction – social construction theory). In one study that demonstrates different standards of beauty, Daibo and colleagues

(1994) compared judgements of physical attractiveness made by Japanese and Koreans. In Japan, attractiveness ratings were positively correlated with large eyes, small mouths and small chins. In Korea, however, attractiveness ratings were positively correlated with large eyes, small and high noses, and thin and small faces. Koreans were more likely than the Japanese to attach other judgements such as maturity and likeability to judgements of attractiveness (Daibo et al., 1994).

Patterns of courting and flirtation have similarities across many cultures (Aune & Aune, 1994), however there are many exceptions to the rules. Kissing, for example, is a widely acceptable cross-cultural phenomenon but is unknown to some cultures in Africa and South America that would not consider kissing as an aspect of mate selection and reproduction (Fisher, 1992). In Mediterranean cultures, physical affection is displayed by touching as a form of communication and is considered acceptable and appropriate whereas in the United States it may be considered inappropriate with some groups. The expectation of marital fidelity appears to be almost universal although among some Arctic peoples it is customary to offer a host's wife to a guest (Shiraev & Levy, 2010). Men everywhere react more negatively, as compared with women, when their partners share sexual fantasies about having sex with others. Women everywhere are more distressed than men when their partner is kissing someone else (Rathus, Nevid, & Fischer-Rathus, 1993).

Marriage

Marriage is found in virtually all societies and the majority (some 90%) of people in every society get married at least once in their lifetime (Carroll & Wolpe, 1996; Ember et al., 2006). Cultures vary with regard to what is considered appropriate premarital behaviour, whom one marries, how one marries, whether there is a proper marriage ceremony, and length and purpose of the marriage. Each culture defines marriage differently although there are some common criteria across many societies. Marriage is typically defined simply as a 'socially approved sexual and economic union, usually between a woman and a man' (Ember et al., 2006, p. 343) that is generally denoted symbolically in some way, for instance through a ceremony, certificate, or symbols such as rings. Normally, there are reciprocal rights and obligations between the two spouses and their future children (Stephens, 1963). Marriage is typically viewed as a social process where new relationships are set up between the kin of both the husband and the wife. Socially, marriage transforms the status of each participant by altering the relationships among the kin of each party and perpetuates social patterns through the production of offspring (Karp, 1986).

Traditionally, marriage was defined as a union between a man and a woman with children born to the woman being recognized as legitimate offspring to both parents (Royal Anthropological Institute, 1951). Marriage was thought to change the status of a man and a woman, stipulate the degree of sexual access for the married partners, establish the legitimacy of the children born to the wife, and create relationships between the kin of both the wife and husband. Anthropologists have noted the exceptions to this standard definition and have expanded it to reflect broader practices. As such, Miller (2008) offers a working definition of marriage given the complexity of practices that fall under the umbrella of marriage – 'a more or less stable union, usually between two people, who may be, but are not necessarily, co-residential, sexually involved with each other, and procreative with each other' (p. 140).

In some cultures, there are other reasons for marriage. For instance, Hindu religion considers marriage sacred and representative of the marriage between the sun goddess Surya and the moon god Soma. Without a wife, a man is considered spiritually incomplete (Kumari, 1988). Representing the two interacting principles of *yin* (female, passive, weak) and *yang* (male, active, strong), long-term relationships in China are thought to be a spiritual necessity that ensures survival. Still others may marry to gain higher status (Sonko, 1994).

Across societies, many people live in long-term 'common-law' domestic partnerships that are not legally sanctioned. Some people have civil marriages that are licensed and legalized by a justice of the peace while others go through religious marriage ceremonies so they are united from a religious perspective but not a legal one (Kottak, 2008).

Love and marriage

The role of romantic love has been debated historically and cross-culturally. Many argue that romantic love did not become part of marriage until Western Europe and America accepted the idea given the strong influence of the Enlightenment and the individualistic emphasis during the French and American Revolutions (Coontz, 2007). Romantic love may have been more common in cultures where women are dependent on men economically but increasingly, marriage based on romantic love is becoming widespread in many cultures (Levine, Sato, Hashimoto, & Verma, 1995).

There is cultural variation in the extent to which love plays a role in marriage. Marriage for love is a fairly recent development in the Western world and may be related to the individualistic orientation (Coontz, 2005). In many Western cultures, marriage is viewed as the culmination of romantic love represented by the idealistic and somewhat 'fairy-tale' notion that an individual meets his/her soul-mate, who they are destined to meet, fall in love, marry and live 'happily ever after' with the notion that 'love conquers all'. People in collectivistic cultures place less emphasis on romantic love and love commitment in marriage. Historically, people married for political reasons – for instance, to acquire status through influential in-laws, family alliances and increased labour forces, and business mergers. Romantic love was not unknown but it was not considered an essential part of marriage and thus was discouraged on the basis of being a selfish and weak reason to marry. For instance, in ancient India, love before marriage was perceived as irresponsible and antisocial. During the Middle Ages, the French viewed love as a type of insanity only curable through sexual intercourse either with the beloved or someone else (Coontz, 2007).

In contrast, many of the arranged marriages common in Asia, Africa and other parts of the world do not have romantic love as a basis. This 'Eastern ideal' is based on the notion that individuals have several possible mates with whom they could have a successful and enduring marriage. Arranged marriage is still practised in some places like India where arrangements may be made between families during a child's infancy. Such arrangements are typically based on the parents' status and knowledge of other families. Arranged marriages are viewed as more than just a union between two individuals but an alliance between families and even communities (Saraswathi, 1999). However, trends are changing even in countries where arranged marriage has been popular. For example, in Japan, love marriages are replacing the earlier practice of arranged marriages but traditional customs often remain as part of the ceremony.

For thousands of years, the institution of marriage served many economic, political and social functions at the cost of minimizing the needs and wishes of individuals (Coontz, 2005). Especially in the last 200 years, marriage, especially in Europe and America, has become more personal and private with a greater emphasis on the emotional and sexual needs of the couple. With this historical transition came free choice in mate selection as the societal norm and love as the primary reason for marriage. As Coontz (2005) notes, 'marriage has become more joyful, more loving, and more satisfying for many couples than ever before in history. At the same time it has become optional and more brittle. These two strands of change cannot be disentangled' (p. 306). For some this transformation of marriage and love has been appreciated as a liberating option from restrictive social and cultural expectations. For others, the shift has meant a significant loss of rules and protocol for relationships with nothing in its place. Coontz (2005) suggests historical factors that have supported single living and personal autonomy. Factors include the belief that women have just as much sexual desire as men, less societal/governmental regulation of personal behaviour and conformity, reliable birth control that became readily available in the 1960s relieving women from fears of unwanted pregnancy, increasing economic independence of women, and more time and labour saving devices, which have lessened the demand on women to do housekeeping. With such factors, the need to marry or remain unhappily married decreases. Examining the role of love in marriage provides a unique lens that reveals many aspects of culture, economics, interpersonal, and emotional beliefs and values (Padilla, Hirsch, Muñoz-Laboy, Sember, & Parker, 2007).

A popular theory of love is Sternberg's triangular theory of love (1988) which includes three factors: (1) intimacy – closeness and sharing; (2) passion – sexual feelings and romance; and (3) commitment

– shared achievements and the intention to remain in the relationship despite difficulties. Sternberg posits that seven different kinds of love can exist in a relationship depending on the presence or absence of the three factors. When all three factors are present, he says this relationship represents *consummate love*. For example, *infatuation* is passion alone and *empty love* is commitment alone. *Romantic love* is a combination of passion and intimacy without commitment (e.g. a summer romance) and *companionate love* is a combination of intimacy and commitment (see Figure 6.1).

Cross-culturally, there are different attitudes about love and romance. For example, Levine and colleagues (1995) asked students in different countries to rate the importance of love for the establishment and maintenance of marriage. Overall, individualistic countries, countries with high gross domestic products, countries with high marriage and divorce rates, and countries with low fertility rates were more likely to rate love as essential to the establishment of marriage. Rates of divorce were related to the belief that the loss of love was reasonable grounds for divorce. In another study, cultural differences related to communicating love were examined among young adults from the United States and East Asia (China, Japan and South Korea). Researchers found caring, trust, honesty, and respect were important to Americans and East Asians in friendship love. Friends in both the

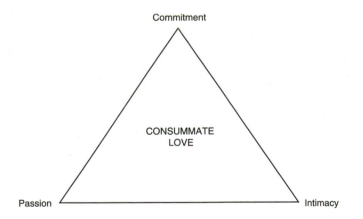

Figure 6.1 **Sternberg's triangular theory of love (1988)**

USA and East Asia communicate love through acts of support, sharing common experiences and open discussion. Trust was essential for love in marriage for both groups. For the Americans, love in marriage was viewed as essential and unconditional whereas for East Asians, love in marriage was expressed through caring. Both the American and East Asian students expressed love in marriage through support, physical intimacy, and verbal expressions of love (e.g., 'I love you,' 'I miss you'). Americans expressed love in the activities of sports, preparing food, and shopping and East Asians in talking and preparing food (Kline, Horton, & Zhang, 2008).

Forms of marriage

Monogamy is the marriage between two people (opposite gender if heterosexual and same gender if homosexual). Heterosexual monogamy is the most frequent form of marriage across cultures and constitutes the only legal form of marriage in many countries (Miller, 2008). Serial monogamy appears to be a common form of monogamy among North Americans where people may have more than one spouse in their lifetimes but never legally at the same time (Kottak, 2008).

Some societies recognize various kinds of same-sex marriages (Kottak, 2008). Same-sex marriages are legal in Denmark, Norway, Holland, South Africa, Ontario Canada and Massachusetts USA. Other places like the UK recognize civil partnerships (Directgov, 2009), which gives legal recognition to the relationship of same-sex couples. Civil partners are treated equally to married couples in a variety of legal matters (see www.direct.gov.uk). There is much debate politically and socially regarding the legal status of same-sex marriages (Miller, 2008). Depending on the historical and cultural setting, same-sex marriages have been accepted. In some African cultures, for instance, women may marry other women in order to strengthen her social and economic status among society (Kottak, 2008). Among the Nandi of Kenya, approximately 3% of marriages are female–female marriages. The Nuer of southern Sudan are also reported to have woman–woman marriage. In this type of marriage, a woman with economic means gives gifts to obtain a 'wife' and brings her into the residential compound just as a man would do if he married a woman. The wife's role in a Nuer woman–woman marriage is to produce offspring with a man since the two women do not have a sexual relationship with each other. Her children will belong to the two women who are married (Miller, 2008). In former times, the Cheyenne Indians allowed married men to take *berdaches* (two-spirits/male transvestites) as second wives (Ember et al., 2006).

Individuals of the same sex are permitted to have sexual relations and/or marry in certain cultures. Culturally, most research has focused on homosexual relationships between men. Carpo (1995) reviewed research across many cultures and identified two types of socially acceptable long-term homosexual relationships – mentorship and pathecism. A mentor relationship is a relationship between men of different ages and social status in which the older man socializes the younger man in matters related to war, politics, and religion. The mentor relationship may or may not involve sexual relations. Pathic relationships involve men of similar age and status who form a long-term relationship similar to heterosexual marriage or homosexual marriage (in the countries and states where it is now recognized legally). There are few studies about the prevalence of homosexual relationships across cultures; however, Bolton (1994) concluded from a review of anthropological studies that male homosexual relations exist in 41 to 64% of societies studied. Research on lesbian relationships is even sparser but Bolton suggests that the same societies that are tolerant of male homosexuality are likely to be accepting of female homosexuality as well.

Polygamy is marriage that involves multiple spouses and it is still permitted in many cultures (Miller, 2008). The most common form of plural marriage is polygyny; which is the marriage of one man with more than one woman. Polygyny in many societies serves as an indicator of a man's wealth and prestige – in other words, the more wives he has, the greater status he accrues. In other societies, polygyny is practised because a man has inherited a widow from his brother (levirate). In still others, polygyny is a way to advance politically and economically. For polygyny to work, there has to be some agreement among the wives about their status and household chores. Generally, there is a first wife or a senior wife who is in charge of the household and has some say-so regarding who is taken as another wife. For instance, among the Betsileo of Madagascar, each wife lived in a different village but the senior, first wife called 'Big Wife' lived in the primary village of her husband where he spent most of his time (Kottak, 2008). Other customs like having separate living quarters for co-wives who are not sisters help lessen jealousy among the co-wives. The Tanala of Madagascar require the husband to spend one day with each co-wife in succession and assist with cultivation of that wife's land. If this rule is not followed, a wife can sue for divorce and alimony up to a third of the husband's property. Such a practice gives co-wives greater equality in matters of sex, possessions and economics (Ember et al., 2006).

Marriage between one woman and more than one man (polyandry) is extremely rare although it is still practised in Tibet and parts of the surrounding Himalayan region. In Tibet, fraternal polyandry (brothers jointly marrying a wife) is still practised. Fraternal polyandry is one of the least common forms of marriage globally, however in Tibet, it remains an acceptable and practical form of marriage and family. Practically, the eldest brother is normally the dominant authority. The wife is expected to treat all brothers equally and the sexual aspect of sharing spouses is not viewed as repulsive by males or females. Any offspring are treated similarly and the children consider all the brothers their fathers. The typical explanation given for this type of marriage in Tibet is a materialistic and economically advantageous one. The brothers do not have to divide their property and can therefore have a higher standard of living. Due to changes in social and economic conditions, polyandry may vanish within the next generation (Kottak, 2008).

In the Brazilian community of Arembepe, people can choose among various forms of sexual union including common-law partnerships (not legally sanctioned), civil marriages, and 'holy matrimony' (religious ceremony but not legally sanctioned). This means that some can have multiple spouses at the same time from the different types of unions (Kottak, 2008).

The frequency of interaction with people of different ethnic and cultural backgrounds has increased. As such, intercultural and interracial relationships have become more frequent (Breger & Hill, 1998). Over the past 40 years, there has been a 1000% increase in interracial or intercultural marriages (Lang, 2005). In an ever increasingly complex and globalized society, individuals are coming into contact with a more diverse array of individuals (George & Yancey, 2004). In a recent study with US college students, one-fifth of the students surveyed reported having been in a romantic relationship with a person of another race (Reiter, Krause, & Stirlen, 2005). Technological changes that have increased the ease of travel and communication make experiences with other cultures more likely. There has also been an increase in study abroad programmes in colleges and travelling abroad for global business is also becoming more popular. 'Global nomads' or persons whose parents were diplomats, missionaries, military personnel, academics, or international business executives do not feel like they belong to one culture, and are therefore more likely to seek out an intercultural marriage (Romano, 2008). In Romano's book, *Intercultural Marriage*, ten factors for a successful intercultural marriage were outlined. The top two factors were 'commitment to the relationship' and the 'ability to communicate' (Romano, 2008).

Sexuality

Although sexual behaviour has physiological components related to the motivation to engage in sexual activity across cultures, it is the sociocultural factors that contribute to the laws, customs, values, and norms of what is viewed as acceptable in terms of sexual behaviour and expression. Many cultures view sexual pleasure as natural and acceptable whereas other cultures view sex and the open expression of sexuality as abnormal and sinful. For instance, masturbation is still viewed by some cultures as causing retardation and other serious psychological problems (Allgeier & Allgeier, 2000). Historically and across the world, sexuality has always been shrouded in mystery and mythical beliefs. Women have been viewed as seductive and powerful sexual temptresses who pose danger to men (Allgeier & Allgeier, 2000). In contrast, in contemporary North American culture, men are typically viewed as more sexual than females.

Chastity is viewed by some cultures as crucial to a woman's acceptance societally whereas in others gaining sexual experience is seen as important. Some cultures place great importance on restricting sexuality. For instance, in some parts of Africa and the Middle East, female circumcision (referred to by some as female genital mutilation) is still practised which is thought to keep a girl chaste, clean and safe from sexual desires and will also ensure virginity at marriage and fidelity thereafter (Crawford & Unger, 2004). This practice ranges from clipping the clitoris to cutting away the external part of the female sexual organs and even infibulations (wound and vagina are sewn closed leaving a small hole for urination and menstrual discharge). Although culturally female circumcision remains a rite of passage for some societies, the World Health Organization and the United Nations Children's Fund argue that all forms of female circumcision should be abolished because of the danger to female health. In other nontraditional sex cultures such as Scandinavian countries and other Western European countries, sex does not carry the same mystery, shame, and conflict as it does in more traditional sex cultures (Allgeier & Allgeier, 2000).

Depending on the specific culture, there are different attitudes toward particular types of sexual lifestyles. Homosexuality is tolerated in most Western industrial societies whereas in other cultures, it is seen as a cause for shame or fear of expression. The acceptance of homosexuality in general varies by cultural and historical context. For example, until the 1970s, homosexuality was considered a mental disorder in the *Diagnostic and Statistical Manual* of the American Psychiatric Association. Some more restrictive societies deny homosexuality and thus forbid homosexual practices. Historically in other groups, like the Siwans of North Africa, there are examples of much greater permissiveness regarding homosexuality and all males were expected to engage in homosexual relations. The Etoro of New Guinea are reported to have preferred homosexuality to heterosexuality with specific prohibitions against heterosexuality most of the days during a year. Furthermore, male homosexuality was thought to make crops flourish and strengthen males (Ember et al., 2006).

In many cultures, marriage sanctions sexual relations between partners. In others, sexuality is confined to procreative purposes. Depending on the society, there are different views about procreation. In some societies, it is believed that spirits place babies in women's wombs. Some cultural groups believe that a fetus has to be nourished by continual insemination during pregnancy. The Barí of Venezuela believe that multiple men can create the same fetus (multiple paternity). When the baby is born, the mother names the men she recognizes as fathers and they assist her in raising the child (Kottak, 2008). According to the *Global Study of Sexual Attitudes and Behaviors*, both men and women across 30 countries have sexual problems related to ageing (Laumann, Nicolosi, Glasser, Paik, Gingell, Moreira et al., 2005). For instance, the most common problem for men is erectile dysfunction and for women, lack of interest in sex and inability to experience orgasm (Neto, Mullet, Deschamps, Barros, Benvindo, Camino et al., 2000).

Sexual practices differ as well depending on the society. Some societies are more restrictive concerning sexuality. The regulation of premarital sex and extramarital sex differs depending on the society. For example, Inis Beag, off the coast of Northern Island is a sexually conservative and prohibiting culture. Nudity is prohibited, sexual ignorance is widespread, female orgasm is unknown, marital sex occurs infrequently, and the idea of sexual pleasure is nonexistent (Messenger, 1993). In other societies, like the Melanesian Islands in the South Sea, marital sex is perceived as a normal and natural form of pleasure; however, premarital and extramarital sex are almost equal to the crime of murder (Davenport, 1965). Reportedly, marital intercourse including orgasm is expected to occur two to three times per day in the early years of marriage and later subsides to once a day or less. Premarital masturbation is encouraged for both males and females. The Trobriand Islanders approve of and even encourage premarital sex and provide thorough instruction in various forms of sexual expression for adolescents believing that it is important preparation for later marital activities. The Ila-speaking population of central Africa encourage trial marriage between adolescents so that girls can 'play wife' with the boys of interest before marriage. Reportedly, virginity in this group does not occur after age 10 (Ember et al., 2006). Other cultural groups, like many Muslim societies, 'test' the female's virginity by displaying blood-stained sheets from the wedding night as proof of her premarital chastity. Extramarital sex is fairly common across societies with men in 69% of societies and about 57%

of women engaging in extramarital sex more than occasionally. Most societies have a double standard with regard to women's sexual behaviour and expect that women will not engage in extramarital sex.

One commonality of sex occurring during marriage in almost all societies is privacy. North Americans typically find privacy in their bedrooms whereas others have to locate other private areas or sometimes perform coitus with others present. Night-time is generally the preferred time for coitus in most cultures although there are examples of preferences for daytime sex (e.g., the Rucuyen of Brazil). There are other prohibitions in some cultures restricting sexual activity for example before certain activities like hunting or planting or because of certain events like death, pregnancy, or menstruation (Ember et al., 2006).

Divorce

Many believe that divorce occurs more frequently in the modern USA as compared with other societies. However, anthropologists have reported rates of separation and remarriage among hunting and gathering societies and other groups that are just as high as modern-day industrial societies. For example, the highest rates of divorce ever recorded in the first half of the twentieth century were in Malaysia and Indonesia which surpassed the US record rates of 1981 (Coontz, 2007). Depending on the society, ease of divorce varies. Marriage is much easier to dissolve in societies where marriage is more of an individual affair. In other societies where marriage represents a political and social union between families and communities, divorce is more difficult (Kottak, 2008). Considerable bridewealth and replacement marriages (*levirate* and *sororate*) work to preserve group alliances and thus decrease divorce rates. A wife among the Shoshone Indians could divorce her husband by merely placing her husband's possessions outside the dwelling, which was considered her property. Divorce is official among the Cewa of East Africa when the husband leaves his wife's village taking along his hoe, axe, and sleeping mat (Coontz, 2007). In traditional society of Japan, a woman wanting a divorce had to complete two years of service at a special temple whereas the man could simply write a letter containing three and a half lines in order to divorce his wife. Coontz (2007) posits that the reasons for divorce in any given time period depend upon the reasons for marriage. For example, common reasons for divorce in contemporary society are the loss of love and the lack of individual fulfillment or mutual benefit. Perhaps this is the case because love and romance are viewed as the primary reason for marriage. In Western societies, there is more flexibility with the notion of a failed marriage. Generally, if romance, love, sex, or companionship dies out in a marriage, then couples in contemporary Western society may opt for divorce. However, sometimes for economic reasons, or because of obligations to children, negative public opinion, or simply inertia, couples may maintain 'failed' marriages. Among countries across the globe, the USA has one of the highest rates of divorce although rates have dropped as compared with the 1970s. From historical records of divorce in the United States, there is an increase after wars and a decrease after tough economic times. The high rates of US divorce are thought to be related to the economic independence enjoyed by many women and the cultural ideas of independence and self-actualization which give greater permission for people to abandon marriage if it is not working for them (Kottak, 2008).

Globalization including technological advances and international migration has increased the opportunity for interactions among different types of people and has contributed to rapid changes in the structure and function of marriage and the family. The institution of marriage continues to retain popularity although many of the details of marriage are undergoing transformation. For instance, the Internet has provided new forms of finding a potential partner and courtship. The age of first marriage is rising in most places due in part to increased emphasis on completing education and higher marital aspirations (e.g., owning a house). Marriages between people of different nations and ethnicities are increasingly commonplace, which can lead to pluralistic practices and customs of marriage and family. Coontz claims that marriage 'has been displaced from its pivotal position in personal and social life' (2007, p. 15) with many children being raised in alternative non-nuclear settings. The definition of marriage has changed given that most people today live in a global climate of choice with many options. This makes divorce and other relationship forms like cohabitation viable options for many people across the world.

And so forth (computer mediated relationships)

A relatively new phenomenon is Internet dating and the development of computer mediated relationships (CMR). Since the 1990s, the Internet has become a primary venue for social encounters across the globe offering an expanded world of mate possibilities in a shorter period at less expense (Lawson & Leck, 2006). Although some theorists have lamented the technological isolation and reduction of face-to-face interaction leading to emotional disconnection or superficial attraction that can occur with the Internet (Lawson & Leck, 2006), others have suggested that the Internet can be helpful in promoting romantic relationships because physical attributes and traditional/ constraining gender and relationship roles are downplayed whereas other factors related to emotional intimacy (e.g., rapport, similarity, mutual self-disclosure) are emphasized (Lawson & Leck, 2006).

Whitty and Carr (2006) describe how online relating is different than romantic and sexual relationships offline. Advantages include the opportunity to 'grow' a relationship, a safe space to flirt and experiment with relationship development, and greater freedom for people who are anxious or introverted (Whitty & Carr, 2006). The biggest benefits of Internet dating are the sheer number of potential partners and the freedom of choice among partners (Lawson & Leck, 2006). In fact, in one study examining the dynamics of Internet dating, Internet daters reported being lonely and many said they were seeking comfort after a crisis situation. The majority of the respondents liked the control over the presentation of self on the Internet and the feeling of a safe environment for getting to know someone. Finally respondents reported that Internet dating provided freedom from commitment and stereotypic roles (Lawson & Leck, 2006). Some of the typical dating problems still remain with Internet dating – people still tell lies, trust has to be negotiated, presentation of self must be managed, compatibility continues to be important, and appearance and shyness issues do not completely disappear when dating online. Rejection and emotional pain still can be part of Internet dating as it is with face-to-face dating. There is a dark side of online relationships, including Internet infidelity, Internet addiction, cyber-harassment, cyber-stalking, and misrepresentation of self online (Whitty & Carr, 2006). However, many Internet daters say they are willing to take the risks associated because of the advantages offered by this technology (Lawson & Leck, 2006). Overall, successful relationships online start with people 'living up to their profiles' (Whitty & Carr, 2006).

Further reading

Chen, X., French, D. C., & Schneider, B. H. (2006). *Peer relationships in cultural context*. Cambridge, UK: Cambridge University Press.

Clarke, V., & Peel, E. (Eds.). (2007). *Out in psychology: Lesbian, gay, bisexual, trans and queer perspectives*. Chichester, England: John Wiley & Sons, Ltd.

Coontz, S. (2007). The origins of modern divorce. *Family Process*, 46(1), 7–16.

Coontz, S. (2005). *Marriage, a history: How love conquered marriage*. New York: Penguin Books.

Noller, P., & Feeney, J. A. (Eds.). (2006). *Close relationships: Functions, forms, and processes*. New York: Psychology Press.

Padilla, M. B., Hirsch, J. S., Muñoz-Laboy, M., Sember, R. E., & Parker, R. G. (2007). Introduction: Cross-cultural reflections on an intimate intersection. In M. B. Padilla, J. S. Hirsch, M. Muñoz-Laboy, R. E. Sember & R. G. Parker (Eds.), *Love and globalization: Transformations of intimacy in the contemporary world* (pp. ix–xxi). Nashville, TN: Vanderbilt University Press.

Chapter 7

Health
and culture

■ Introduction   134

■ Models of health and culture   134

■ Cultural health beliefs   136

■ Approaches to health and healing   141

■ Immigrants and health   143

■ Culture and mental health   146

■ Culture-bound syndromes   147

■ Culturally competent treatment/therapy   149

■ And so forth (global health disparities)   157

Introduction

CULTURAL INFLUENCES ON health and health beliefs and practices are well recognized. Shifts have occurred both in the goals and approach of health and the definition of health itself. Rather than simply focusing on curing illness and health problems, societies are now placing more emphasis on prevention of disease and promotion of health (e.g., appropriate diet and exercise). Internationally, this shift came about in part due to the *Alma Ata Declaration* of health for All by the year 2000 (World Health Organization, 1978) and the *Ottawa Charter* (World Health Organization, 1986). Also increasing in importance has been the inclusion of social and behavioural sciences to understand health problems and supplement the biological and medical technology emphases (Aboud, 1998). This has underscored the importance of context via community-based approaches (Peat, 1997) and the important role that sociocultural factors and environmental conditions play in health such as poverty, immigration, shared water sources, etc. The definition of health has been extended to include other aspects of well-being – 'state of complete physical, mental, and social well being, and not merely the absence of disease or infirmity' (World Health Organization, 1978). This definition of health encompasses well-being including quality of life, positive mental health, and the consideration of culturally sensitive approaches to health care as well as indigenous and alternative forms of healing as legitimate forms of treatment.

Models of health and culture

Hancock and Perkins (1985) offer a conceptual model that demonstrates this important link between health and culture. Called the 'mandala of health', this model contains four factors that influence a person's health (human biology, personal behaviour, psychosocial environment, and physical environment). Also influencing health are the family, lifestyle, medical care system, community, biosphere, and culture (Hancock & Perkins, 1985). See Figure 7.1.

Giger and Davidhizar (1995) describe six cultural variables

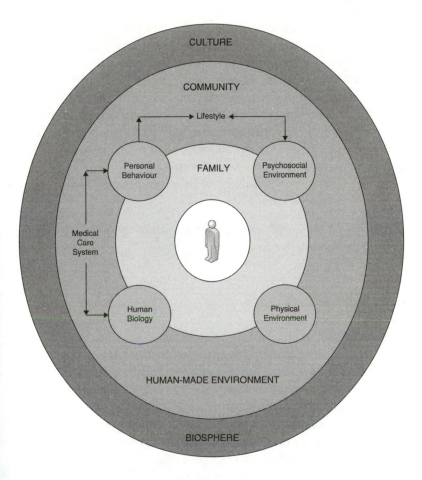

Figure 7.1 **Mandala of health (Hancock & Perkins, 1985)**

that vary among cultural groups and affect health care and health beliefs:

(1) Environmental control relates to traditional health and illness beliefs, folk medicine, and traditional healers all of which can have a direct effect on environmental factors.

(2) Biological variations emphasize physical and genetic differences of people (e.g., smaller stature of some cultural groups).

(3) Social organization is the social environment in which people are

raised and socialized which includes family background, identification with social group organizations, and social barriers like unemployment and poverty which prevent access to quality health care (Spector, 2004).

(4) Communication includes language differences, verbal and non-verbal behaviours and use of silence within cultural groups.

(5) Space refers to the personal space and territoriality people hold with variations in the intimate zone, personal distance, social distance, and public distance (Spector, 2004).

(6) Time orientation and the view of present, past or future varies among cultural groups.

All of these factors can greatly affect how people view health care and prevention (Spector, 2004) (see Figure 7.2).

Cultural health beliefs

Different cultural groups have diverse belief systems with regard to health and healing in comparison with the Western biomedical model of medicine. These belief systems may include different disease models, wellness/illness paradigms (e.g., Chinese medicine and magico-religious thinking), various culturally specific diseases and disorders, feelings about health care providers and seeking Westernized health care, and the use of traditional and indigenous health care practices and approaches. Helman (2001) suggests that people attribute causes of illness to factors within one of four spheres:

(1) Factors within individuals themselves such as bad habits or negative emotional states.

(2) Factors within the natural environment such as pollution and germs.

(3) Factors associated with others or the social world such as interpersonal stress, medical facilities, and actions of others.

(4) Supernatural factors including God, destiny, and indigenous beliefs such as witchcraft or voodoo.

There is support for the finding that Westerners are more likely

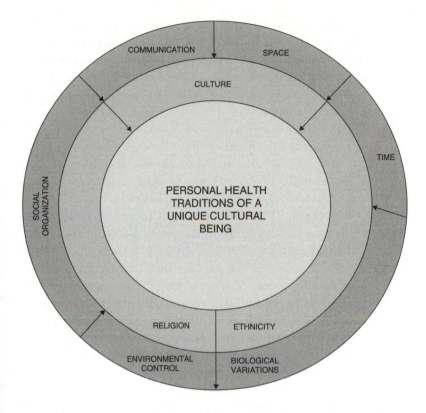

Figure 7.2 **Six cultural variables (Giger & Davidhizar, 1995)**

to attribute the cause of illness to the individual or the natural world whereas individuals from non-industrialized nations are more likely to explain illness as a result of social and supernatural causes (Furnham, Akande, & Baguma, 1999). Jobanputra and Furnham (2005) tested Helman's (2001) model of health beliefs in British Caucasians and British Gujarati Indian immigrants and found general support for the four domains with the Gujarati Indian immigrants being more likely to endorse supernatural explanations of ill health as compared with the British Caucasians. There was no significant difference in the two groups in terms of attributions made to psychological factors, social factors, and the external environment.

Landrine and Klonoff (1994) compared African Americans,

Latinos and Pacific Islanders with white Americans on causal attributions of illness and found that the ethnic minority groups rated supernatural beliefs as significantly more important than white Americans. There was no difference between the groups about illness causation due to interpersonal stress, lifestyle, environment or chance. Another example comes from the examination of health beliefs across three Canadian ethnocultural groups (Chinese, Asian Indian, and AngloCeltic). In comparison with the AngloCeltic group, Chinese and Indian participants had stronger psychosocial beliefs about illness causation and preferred psychosocial oriented treatments; which suggests that culture of origin remains an important influence on health beliefs.

Stainton Rogers (1991) describes eight 'theories' for health and illness: body as machine, body under siege, inequality of access, cultural critique, health promotion, robust individualism, God's power, and willpower. Furnham (1994) explored British lay perceptions on health and recovery from illness and found that strength of religious beliefs tends to predict fatalistic or supernatural health-related beliefs; older people and those with left wing political beliefs were more likely to emphasize external causes and cures for illness; and people who believed in alternative medicine were more likely to endorse controllable or internal causes of health, illness and recovery and less likely to believe in fatalistic or external causes. Overall, the British participants emphasized psychological and behavioural determinants of health and illness. Furnham et al. (1999) also examined health beliefs across the three cultures of Britain, Uganda and South Africa and found that the African participants were more likely to attribute illness to 'evil others' but all of the groups rated interpersonal stress as a potential source of illness. The British participants rated fatalistic factors as extremely unimportant whereas both African groups rated them as marginally important contributors to illness. In other studies, the importance of spiritual factors on health and illness is apparent. For instance, Mulatu (2000) found that Ethiopians attributed mental illness predominantly to cosmic or supernatural causes including curses or spirit possession. Berry and colleagues reported that fate and cosmic influences played a major role in health beliefs in Bangladesh and parts of India whereas personal action and the ability to control problems were more influential in

Canada and the Christian parts of Indonesia (Berry, Dalal, & Pande, 1994).

Many cultures take the ethno-medical approach that seeks to establish internal balance. This belief assumes that good deeds are rewarded and bad deeds are punished by some force or deity. For example, Torsch and Xueqin Ma (2000) found that Asian and Asian American culture are based on the balance between yin and yang. The elder Chinese Americans emphasize that health and illness are functions of behaviour, lifestyle, and emotion. They also believe in holistic healing because of their strong spiritual beliefs (Torsch & Xueqin Ma, 2000).

Focusing on black people primarily of South Africa in an article entitled *Western and African Conceptualizations of Health*, Beverley Chalmers (1996) explains that the African views of health and illness reflect 'a belief in an integrated, interdependent, totality of all things animate and inanimate, past and present' (p. 3). She comments that this holistic and integrated African concept of health is influenced by spirituality, community, and duality as compared with the Western perception of health; which is more focused on rationality and empiricism (Chalmers, 1996). The African conceptualization of health and illness emphasizes balance and harmony among all things so that disequilibrium in any area may manifest in discordance at other levels of functioning (Gelfand, 1981). Africans in general tend to de-emphasize rationality in comparison with the Western world (Chalmers, 1996).

Compared with the West, Africans in general have different values regarding health and illness. For example, obesity is viewed as a health problem in the West whereas it may be viewed as a measure of wealth and prestige in African countries (Jansen, 1983). There may be more emphasis placed on the community, ancestors, alternative healing practices, and on multiple sources of healing regarding African health care decisions (Chalmers, 1996). Africans may attribute illness to a spiritual or social cause as compared with the Western attribution of physiological or scientific causes thus contributing to the practice of a more psychosocial medicine in many African countries with emphasis on the whole person composed of body, mind, and soul (Madge, 1998). Africans regard the human organism 'as a whole which is integrated with the total ecology of the environment and with the interrelated spiritual, magical and mystical forces surrounding him/her' (Cheetham & Griffiths, 1982, p. 954). Health practitioners in Africa are expected not only to have a cure for disease but to offer an explanation as to the reason for the affliction to the specific person whether it is due to something that occurred in daily experience or a spiritual reason. This means that most remedies involve both material (e.g. herbal remedy) and spiritual (e.g., amulets) explanations and techniques. Medicine in the African sense, as compared with the Western concept of medicine, is 'global and is the focal point around which all life-events, illness, disaster, subsistence and the economy devolve' (Cheetham & Griffiths, 1982, p. 954). Chipfakacha (1994) notes that most black Africans are superstitious and therefore believe that disease is due to (1) magic and evil spirits; (2) conditions for which causes have been empirically determined; and (3) psychological phenomena. Thus, for many Africans the cause of disease relates to conflict and tension between good/evil and harmony/disharmony (Chipfakacha, 1994).

In the United States, African Americans may be likely to attribute illness externally to destiny or the will of God (Gregg & Curry, 1994). They may also rely on social networks within their families and communities for illness-related support (Atkinson, 2004; Snowden, 2001) and believe in the healing power of prayer (Klonoff & Landrine, 1996). In almost all aspects of life, Latinos tend to value family needs (including extended family members) over individual needs (Marín & Marín, 1991) and may present medically with certain culture-bound syndromes such as *ataques de nervios* (Guarnaccia, De La Cancela, & Carrillo, 1989) and acculturation-related health problems such as stress or loss of support network (Gloria & Segura-Herrera, 2004). Murguía and colleagues (Murguía, Zea, Reisen, & Peterson, 2000) found that US acculturated Latino adults were less likely to make equity attributions – that is, they are less likely to attribute health outcomes to reward or punishment by an outside source (e.g. 'God is punishing him' or 'She got better because she is a good person'). Of those Latinos who do make equity attributions, they were more likely to delay seeking health care when sick and to use ethnomedical approaches to health care such as *santeros*, *hierbistas*, and folk remedies. As compared with ethnic minorities, Anglo Americans are likely to value and access better quality health care (Saha, Komaromy, Koepsell, & Bindman, 1999; Smedley, Stith, & Nelson, 2003), have greater trust in the provider (Doescher, Saver, Franks, & Fiscella, 2000; Moseley, Clark, Gebremariam, Sternthal, & Kemper, 2006), and hold more traditional Western health beliefs such as individual responsibility for health and illness (Landrine & Klonoff, 1992, 1994) and more 'empirical' explanations of illness (Furnham et al., 1999). Because of the emphasis on micro-level and natural causes of illness, many white Americans may believe that illness can be treated without reference to family, community or deities (Landrine & Klonoff, 1992).

Approaches to health and healing

The Western biomedical model views disease as originating inside the body due to a specific, identifiable 'medical' cause or pathogen (viral, bacterial, etc.). Psychologically, the biomedical model posits that abnormal behaviour comes from within the person whether innate or learned (Annandale, 1998). In the traditional biomedical model, the pathogens need to be eradicated so that the person is without disease and only then are they considered healthy. Although health care professions are aware that patients' cultural background plays a major role in immigrant families' health beliefs, little research has been conducted assessing the experiences of immigrants in their interactions with Western medicine. It is important to recognize that immigrants are familiar with and have faith in the medical beliefs and practices from their culture and that these beliefs are significantly different from those of Western medicine. For example, some Asian cultures believe in the yin and yang principle in which there is a balance between opposite forces (e.g. positive and negative, light and dark, hot and cold) that reflect the difference between health and illness. Others believe that illnesses are caused by spirits or ghosts. Some Asian immigrants believe in certain medical practices that cause bruising of the skin (e.g. coin rubbing – *cao gio*). Western clinicians may mistake this as signs of abuse or of haematological diseases (Lessard & Ku, 2003). Without prior knowledge of these practices, physicians may misdiagnose and/or offer incorrect treatment methods to their patients.

Central American immigrants' health beliefs and practices are largely influenced by religious tradition, and, they may use spiritual folk healers and folk remedies that ultimately have an impact on their health.

In contrast to Western allopathic medicine, there has been an increasing interest and training in osteopathic medicine in North America and Europe (Grossoehme, Ragsdale, Dixon, Berz, & Zimmer, 2009). In 1874, Andrew Taylor Still, an American physician, developed a system of medicine where the musculoskeletal system was the key element of health and medicine was viewed from a wellness perspective. Osteopathy according to Still is composed of four principles: (1) the body is a unit; (2) the body possesses self-regulatory mechanisms; (3) structure and function are interrelated; and (4) rational therapy is based upon an understanding of these. In osteopathic medicine, it is considered to be the physician's work to correct structural dysfunction in order to return the body to its normal, healthy state (Ward, 2003).

Integrative medicine is a growing field that seeks to combine best practice from both conventional and complementary and alternative medicine (CAM). Leaders in the field of integrative medicine consider their practice to be healing oriented incorporating aspects of the whole person (mind, body, and spirit) and lifestyle. The focus of integrative medicine is on utilizing the body's own natural healing ability, incorporating the individual's health beliefs, attitudes and culture into treatment decisions that may include both conventional and complementary and alternative medicine practices (Willms & St Pierre-Hansen, 2008).

Two well-known cultural systems of medicine and healing considered to be alternative by Western standards of medicine are Chinese Medicine and Ayurvedic Medicine. Traditional Chinese Medicine (TCM) is based on the concept that the human body has interconnected systems/channels (*meridians*) that need to stay balanced in order to maintain health. TCM healing practices include herbal medicine, acupuncture, dietary therapy, and Shiatsu massage. Qigong (breathing and meditation practice) is also closely associated with TCM (Holland, 2000).

Ayurvedic Medicine is native to India. The Ayurvedic system is based on the idea that every human contains a unique combination of *Doshas* (the three substances of wind/spirit/air, bile, and phlegm) that must be balanced for health. In addition, healthy metabolism, digestion, and excretion are thought to be vital functions of the body. Similar to TCM, Ayurvedic Medicine also uses herbs, massage, meditation and Yoga as healing practices (Chopra, 2003).

The Western world has become more interested in alternative healing 'practices' such as acupuncture, homeopathy, herbal medicines, and spiritual healing (Eisenberg, Davis, Ettner, Appel, Wilkey, Van Rompay et al., 1998). Depending on the model of health and cultural health beliefs, there are a variety of possibilities for the treatment approach.

Immigrants and health

Health care of immigrants can present challenges. Certain infectious diseases may exist that are endemic to the patient's country of origin. Immigration itself can cause illness and disease due to disrupted family and social networks and financial barriers and discrimination that prevent the establishment of a healthy lifestyle. There are many reasons that may have contributed to immigrants leaving their countries – violence, economic hardships, or natural disasters all of which cause extreme stress and perhaps physical injury (Bigby, 2003). Immigrants frequently work in low-paying jobs, face poverty, lack health insurance, have limited access to health care and social services, and have communication difficulties due to language differences (Bigby, 2003).

Accessing health care services can be problematic for immigrant families. Language and cultural barriers (including lack of culturally competent health care providers), distance to care, cost of treatments, lack of transportation, perceptions of lack of respect, discrimination or racism, and a complex Western health care system all contribute to reduced access to health care (Bernal, 1996). Immigrant families from collectivist countries in which kinship is a strong value may view the role of caregiver (when a family member is ill) as expected and a way of showing gratitude and love (Srivastava, 2007) – this may cause families to not seek professional health care. Mir and Tovey (2002) note that some immigrant families may not seek health care because they lack awareness of the health care services offered or they may find the services culturally inappropriate or insensitive.

Compared with the US born population, foreign born immigrants are twice as likely to lack health insurance (Thamer, Richard, Casebeer, & Ray, 1997). Recent immigrants have less contact in general and less timely contact with the health care system (Leclere, Jensen, & Biddlecom, 1994) and are more likely to have infectious diseases as compared with US natives (Institute of Medicine, 1998; Liu, Shilkret, Tranotti, Freund, & Finelli, 1998) especially tuberculosis, Hepatitis B, and parasitic infections (Centers for Disease Control and Prevention, 1991; Gavagan & Brodyaga, 1998; Institute of Medicine, 1998). Immigrant children may have infectious diseases that Western paediatricians are not used to diagnosing and treating and they may be not be immunized adequately. What is more, the psychosocial factors of immigration may impose unique stressors on immigrant children such as disparities in social, economic, and professional status from country of origin, ongoing mental health issues due to relocation and potential atrocities experienced in home country, adaptation issues with school, peer groups, etc., and lack of a larger social support network of family and friends from country of origin (Committee on Community Health Services, 2005). As compared with US born children, immigrant children may experience more dental problems and be more at risk for nutrition problems that result in growth deficiencies (Committee on Community Health Services, 2005). In addition, as immigrant children become adolescents, there is an increase in risk behaviours especially the longer children reside in the United States. For example, by third or later generations, immigrant adolescents are engaging in risky behaviours that approach or exceed those of white adolescents (Institute of Medicine, 1998).

Much of the health-related information about immigrants globally paints a bleak picture; however, interestingly, immigrants in the USA are generally better off on measures of health risk factors, chronic conditions, and mortality as compared to US natives (Fennelly, 2006). Recent immigrants to Westernized countries such as the USA seem to have a health advantage in certain areas – what has come to be known as the 'healthy migrant' phenomenon. Counter-intuitive because of the poor health conditions of many immigrants' countries of origin, over time, this health advantage disappears dramatically and moves to health disparity. Length of time in the United States is positively correlated with increases in low birth weight infants, adolescent risk behaviours (alcohol/drug abuse, teen pregnancy, etc.), cancer, anxiety and depression, and general mortality (Fennelly, 2006). Noh and Kaspar (2003) offer insight about why this change occurs for immigrant families as compared with native born residents: 'The more "they" become like "us", immigrants and immigrant children fail to maintain their initial health advantages … The process is poorly understood, but may be the result of the adoption of our poor health behaviors and life styles, leaving behind resources (social networks, cultural practices, employment in their field of training, etc.) and ways in which the settlement process wears down hardiness and resilience' (p. 25).

One causal factor affecting the health disparities of immigrants in the USA is poverty. Martin and Midgley (2003) found that 16% of foreign born people and 11% of US born people were living below the poverty line in 2002. Poverty can seriously contribute to health risks and barriers to care. One consequence of poverty is substandard housing; which contributes to stress and illness and can be even worse for immigrants because of language barriers, large family sizes, and lack of awareness about housing rights. Changes to an unhealthy American diet that has been linked to obesity, diabetes, and cancer (Li & Pawlish, 1998) and increased use of tobacco, alcohol and drugs all contribute to an increase in immigrant health problems the longer they reside in the United States.

Siegel, Horan, and Teferra (2001) completed a study examining health status, health behaviours, and health care access and utilization among African born residents of the metropolitan Washington, DC area. Compared to the general local and regional population, they found that of the African immigrants who participated in the study 29% were uninsured and 24% lacked a usual, appropriate source of primary care. The majority of the African immigrants in the study were in good health; 15% had infectious diseases. However, African born residents were at risk regarding access to health care and some faced critical barriers to access. As a result, use of preventive and dental services was considerably lower than in the general population. The main reasons offered for not making health care visits were lack of perceived need (79%) and lack of insurance/ability to pay (21%).

Culture and mental health

Psychological disorders are found in all cultures and some disorders like schizophrenia and depression are thought to be universal. Schizophrenia is one of the most widely studied and most commonly occurring disorders globally (Jablensky, et al., 1992). It is thought to be recognized across cultures with a common core of symptoms including social and emotional withdrawal, bizarre delusions, and flat affect with the expression mediated by different cultural experiences. The *Diagnostic and Statistical Manual* of the American Psychiatric Association (DSM) has been the Western standard for classifying abnormal behaviour (e.g., DSM-IV-TR, American Psychiatric Association, 2000). Culturally, diagnosing abnormal behaviour has been somewhat controversial because what is considered abnormal or normal is thought to be culturally determined

Hales (1996) examined traditional West African beliefs about mental illness by doing content analysis of Liberian students' writing assignments. Although specific to Liberia located on the west coast of Africa, her study highlights some important beliefs about mental illness that are likely to apply to other cultures. Hales asked 14 Liberian students to write short papers about their experience with someone they believed to be mentally ill and to interview a grandparent, older relative or village elder about their beliefs about mental illness. She identified three major categories about the causes of mental illness:

(1) *punishment for wrongdoing* – wrongdoings can include minor (e.g., eating a taboo food) or major violations (e.g., murder) and the degree of mental illness is associated with the seriousness of the wrongdoing. Wrongdoings can include offending ancestral spirits or God.

(2) *Being 'witched' by another person* – this occurs when a person 'witches' or 'puts medicine on' another individual for some

perceived wrongdoing (e.g., a husband puts a mental illness or a 'sign' on his wife because of adultery).

(3) *An illness 'passed down' through the family* – inherited mental illness that is believed to be passed via the mother during birth or a whole family can inherit mental illness if an ancestor has been extremely offensive to the spirits.

The elders were interviewed by the students regarding treatments for mental illness. The elders offered three possibilities: (1) confession of wrongdoing; (2) removal of a spirit or the 'thrown sign' through indigenous medicine; and (3) prevention of 'down the line'/inherited illness. If mental illness is believed to be the result of wrongdoing, the person first must confess to the wrongdoing, then along with his/her family make sacrifices to the person or spirit who received the wrongdoing, and finally participate in some type of cleansing ritual. To remove an evil spirit or sign, either sacrifices are made to the spirit or a person's body is made uncomfortable for the spirit so it will flee (e.g., beating is a common method used to drive out an evil spirit). Purification ceremonies and herbal treatments for purification are also used to drive out bad spirits. If a mental illness is thought to be inherited, it is usually seen as incurable although there are some extreme ceremonies and rituals that may be attempted (Hales, 1996). See Table 7.1 for a summary of perceived causes of illness and corresponding treatments.

Culture-bound syndromes

There are some physical and mental illnesses that are unique to particular cultures and are influenced directly by cultural belief systems

Table 7.1 Mental health attributions and treatments

Perceived causes of illness	Appropriate treatment
Punishment for wrongdoing	Confession of wrongdoing
Being 'witched'	Removal of spirit through indigenous medicine
Inherited illness	Largely incurable; some extreme rituals

and other cultural factors. Since 1994, the DSM (*Diagnostic and Statistical Manual* of the American Psychiatric Association) added culture-bound syndromes that were defined as troubling patterns of behaviour/experience that may not fall into one of the traditional Western DSM diagnostic categories. Culture-bound syndromes are considered within the specific culture to be illnesses, or at a minimum afflictions, and the majority have local names. For example, *dhat* is a disorder that affects Indian males and involves an intense fear that losing semen will result in the depletion of vital energy. *Dhat* is thought to occur through intoxicants, eating heated foods, having a fiery constitution, and sexual excesses and can cause fatigue, weakness, body aches, depression to the point of suicidal feelings, anxiety, and loss of appetite (Dhikav, Aggarwal, Gupta, Jadhavi, & Singh, 2008). In Latin America, *susto* (magical fright) and *mal de ojo* (evil eye) are common afflictions. *Susto* is thought to occur when the soul leaves the body after a frightful episode. Symptoms include sleep disturbance, easy startling, palpitations, anxiety, involuntary muscle tics, and other depressive symptoms. *Mal de ojo* is a hex caused by an admiring glance/gaze from a more powerful/stronger person and usually affects children. The symptoms of evil eye are fussiness, refusal to eat or sleep, fever, and seizures (Loue, 1998). Prevention includes wearing special amulets and shielding babies from direct eye contact. Treatment for evil eye can include physical contact from the perpetrator on the head or prayers and rituals conducted using eggs (Spector, 2004).

Another disorder which crosses physical and mental boundaries are eating disorders. Health professionals continue to see a rise in eating disorders especially in highly industrialized societies (Hsu & Zimmer, 2009). Although in some cultures, being stout and plump is associated with good health and prosperity and historically, certain time periods have celebrated more voluptuous women (e.g., Renaissance paintings), being thin and fit as a cultural ideal for women has increased in popularity (Adams, Katz, Beauchamp, Cohen, & Zavis, 1993; Crawford & Unger, 2004). In the Western world, especially with young women, there is a cultural notion of the thin ideal and overall, it is clear that culture has a definite influence on attitudes toward body size, body shape, and eating behaviours (Adams, et al., 1993).

Somatization, or physical ailments due to stress or emotional distress, is common especially in collectivistic societies perhaps because people avoid expressing psychological complaints to families and friends. In other words, a person suffering from depression or anxiety might use somatization as a culturally sanctioned way to signal distress (Draguns, 1990). Recognizing that there are culture-bound syndromes and that the expression and formation differs culturally paves the way for practising culturally sensitive medicine and psychotherapy. Otherwise, misdiagnosis can occur when ethnic and cultural differences are not taken into account.

Culturally competent treatment/therapy

One aspect of health care is how a society organizes the health system in terms of public or private access to care. In some countries, access to health care is mediated by socioeconomic access with only the wealthy receiving quality care. In other countries, health care is widely accessible by all regardless of income level or insurance status. Many aspects of culture can affect successful and effective treatment approaches including religion and spirituality, social support networks, beliefs and attitudes about causes and treatments, socioeconomic status, and language barriers. There seems to be no one perfect programme that is culturally relevant for all involved, but approaching treatment and healing from a culturally competent perspective should be paramount.

There is an undeniable need for culturally competent health care services in order to address the health needs of our growing, pluralistic population, eliminate existing health disparities for minorities, mend a fragmented system of care where some receive better services than others, and meet the required cultural competency standards of accreditation bodies within health professions and medical training. Within health care, the idea of cultural competency comes mostly from a medical anthropology background whereby the universality/relativity of distress and disease is considered. Kleinman (1981) described medicine as a cultural system that requires careful cultural analysis to determine disease and illness (e.g., what is considered illness in one culture may be considered idiosyncratic or even divine in another). Traditionally, the focus of cultural sensitivity initiatives in health care was international in scope targeting immigrants and refugees with limited English proficiency and 'buy-in' to Western norms. This approach became somewhat problematic in that providers were stereotyping and not recognizing the unique experiences and perspectives of the various immigrant and refugee groups.

Cultural issues have increasingly become incorporated into health care as there has been increased recognition of the intimate tie between cultural beliefs and health beliefs. Perceptions of good and bad health and the causes of illness are formed in a cultural context – what is acceptable in one culture may not be in another. For example being overweight is viewed as acceptable in some cultures – it may even be seen as a sign of health and wealth. Many health care institutions and community sites have incorporated linguistic competence into their services and have employed skilled interpreters to manage linguistic diversity in their patients. However, being linguistically competent is not the same as being culturally competent. For example, although a site may have interpreters available for patients, the site may still impose a Western values-based health care and environment (e.g., certain feeding practices and dietary mandates, lack of religious accommodation such as non-denominational spaces for prayer, particular grieving expectations, non-recognition of extended family members or 'tribal' connections as immediate family, etc.).

Training in cultural competency is typically categorized by models/approaches that address attitudes, knowledge, and skills (Betancourt, 2003). There has been no standard approach to teaching health care professionals how best to care for a multicultural patient/ family population. The attitudinal approach emphasizes respect, sensitivity, and awareness of the cultural differences of the patient. This approach typically includes self-reflection on one's own culture, biases, stereotypical thinking, and appreciation for diversity (Betancourt, 2003). The attitudinal approach is helpful in that the same attributes coincide with effective community strategies and professionalism that providers should be using with all patients regardless of cultural background. Although the attitudinal approach is a 'feel good' approach that celebrates diversity, the pitfall of this approach is that attitudes do not necessarily translate into behaviours. The other risk with the attitudinal approach is that it can become much more of an 'Epcot center approach' (Vaughn, 2009) focused on food, dances, and positive customs that do not have the same depth as other approaches and can minimize more serious issues like health disparities experienced by minorities.

The knowledge approach emphasizes the multicultural differences of various groups whereby each cultural group is examined for their attitudes, values, attributes, beliefs, and behaviours. Commonly, lists of health-seeking behaviours are categorized for the prototypical 'Latino' patient or key practice points for working with 'Hmong' patients. With the array of cultural differences and multiple factors affecting health, it is difficult to teach a set of 'unifying facts about any particular group' (Betancourt, 2003). A disadvantage of this approach, which has often been the basis for the diversity training approach used by many medical centres and hospitals, is that the uniqueness of individual patients/families is overlooked, people are oversimplified into stereotypical boxes, and the fluidity and intermixing of culture is lost. As Gilbert notes, people want to be given 'dependable cultural recipes' that delineate exactly what a cultural group will or won't do in a specific circumstance (Gilbert & Galanti, 2005). This can be detrimental because although there are core cultural concepts and belief systems, they are only generalities or possibilities and it can be problematic to apply them in a 'one size fits all' approach. Betancourt (2003) points out that it can be helpful, however, to use the knowledge-based approach when learning about trends in the surrounding community in which one practices or when the knowledge is based on evidence (e.g., differential ethnopharmacologic effects on different populations and potential effects on health of cultural practices such as observance of Ramadan by Muslims who have diabetes).

The skills-based behavioural approach traditionally focuses on general communication skills and interviewing techniques that can be generalized across various cultural groups with models that help clinicians to understand patients' explanatory models, social context factors, communication styles, decision-making preferences, family dynamics, beliefs about healing, and effects of prejudice, discrimination, acculturation, mistrust, etc. The emphasis is on the individual patient/family rather than generalizations that fit groups of individuals.

This approach has probably become the most popular as it seems to have clinical applicability for either diverse groups or targeted populations. This approach is also pertinent because social and cultural factors influence illness, adherence, and compliance differently with particular individuals and circumstances. The skills-based approach essentially views the patient/family as the teacher regardless of cultural background (Betancourt, 2003). Table 7.2 contains a summary of these approaches to cultural competence.

In health care, the most commonly cited approaches are a combination of group specific information with enhancements to communication and assessment skills. Some of the more popular models include the L-E-A-R-N model (Berlin & Fowkes, 1983), Kleinman's tool (1981), cultural assessments (Isaacs & Benjamin, 1991; Miller, 1982), and the ETHNIC framework (Levin, Like, & Gottlieb, 2000). Green, Betancourt, and Carillo (2002) recommend a social context review of systems to examine the factors of social stressors, support networks, changes in environment, life control and literacy to understand the depth and breadth of cultural differences. Mostly from

Table 7.2 **Approaches to cultural competence**

Approach	Description	Advantages	Disadvantages
Attitudinal approach	Self-reflection on one's own culture, appreciation for diversity	Celebrates differences in culture	Does not necessarily prescribe culturally competent behaviour
Knowledge approach	Certain cultural groups are assigned general characteristics in order for health care providers to effectively meet their needs	Can be useful when looking at trends in a certain area	Risk oversimplifying cultures, overlooking individual differences
Skills-based behavioural approach	Focus on characteristics of individual, rather than culture at large	Patients are assessed on an individual basis – no generalization	

international business and sojourner work, Brislin (2000) uses critical incidents in order to provoke thinking as participants reason through different responses. Many of the techniques/strategies share similarities but concentrate on different aspects/dimensions of cultural competence. Given the array of models, four main categories of culturally competent approaches to health and healing are suggested: (1) collaborative; (2) personality; (3) assessment techniques; and (4) partnership/empowerment strategies (Vaughn, 2009).

Other nontraditional approaches to health care include the exploration of life domains (Arends-Tóth & van de Vijver, 2006). These life domains include language, social affiliation, daily living habits, media, education, work, intimate relations, childrearing, celebrations and events, identity, values, religion/spirituality, and health practices. By examining these life domains, health care providers can better understand a family's acculturation level and their world view; which will assist in future health care provision.

As health care providers often lack time to do a thorough cultural assessment or to go to the depth that may be necessary with immigrant families and children, other intermediaries such as cultural brokers and lay health workers that allow for more time commitment and training enhanced interaction should be considered. *Cultural brokers* in the health care context are patient advocates who act as liaisons, bridging, linking, or mediating between the health care provider and the patient whose cultural backgrounds differ in order to negotiate and facilitate a successful health outcome (National Center for Cultural Competence (NCCP), 2004). 'A cultural broker program has the potential to enhance the capacity of individuals and organizations to deliver health care services to culturally and linguistically diverse populations, specifically those that are underserved, living in poverty, and vulnerable' (National Center for Cultural Competence (NCCP), 2004).

Lay health workers (LHW)/promoters, sometimes referred to as *Promotores* when working with Latinos and by many other names (see Glossary), provide public health services to those who have typically been denied equitable and adequate health care in many different cultures and countries. LHW typically come from the communities in which they work and they engage in health promotion and education and service delivery within a limited scope of practice. 'Lay health workers are effective because they use their cultural knowledge and social networks to create change' (Lam, et al., 2003, p. 516). There is good evidence that these type of models work because they are culturally appropriate and integrated into communities (Lewin et al., 2005). By working in partnership with parents, children and community leaders, health care providers are more likely to ensure the optimal health of immigrant children. In fact, Chipfakacha (1994) says that the only way primary health care can be successful is by having community participation as a prerequisite.

Psychological therapy is based on the Western model of the self. Cross-culturally psychological therapies have included prolonged sleep, rest, social isolation (Morita therapy in Japan), altered states of consciousness (dream, meditation, psychedelic drugs), dissociative states in religions or cults (e.g., Zar cult practices in the Middle East), and use of dreams as a tool for understanding, meditation, and mystical experiences. Buddhist psychology offers a positive therapeutic approach that emphasizes the development of human potential (Daya, 2000). Principles in counselling include changing client self-thoughts (first-order change) and how the client relates to his/her environment (second-order change). Meditation is often suggested within Buddhist psychology as a strategy to focus on the present moment rather than past experiences. In general, recommendations have been made for enhanced culturally competent therapy. They include flexibility in therapeutic approach, utilization of cultural assets, exploration of available coping avenues, working on both the individual and cultural levels, establishing quick credibility with the client, giving, and in general, 'rolling with the punches' (Whaley & Davis, 2007).

As globalization continues to increase, other international approaches to therapy should be considered especially ones that consider trauma and violence at a cultural level. One model based on a developmental perspective is the HEARTS Model (Hanscom, 2001). The HEARTS model is not linear and should be adjusted according to client's needs. The steps include: **H** (listening to *history*) – providing the opportunity for client to safely communicate their story, compassionate connection necessary keeping in mind the honour of a survivor's willingness to relay his/her story to you; **E** (focusing on *emotions and* reactions) – focusing on the emotions experienced throughout their experience, allowing a survivor to put words to his/her feelings about what took place, increasing 'feeling vocabulary'; **A** (*a*sking questions about symptoms) – discussing behaviours and physical symptoms; **R** (explaining the *r*easons for symptoms) – helping survivor make sense of symptoms, discussing physical and psychological symptoms as related to experience of trauma, normalizing; helping establish sense of control, symptoms as method employed by body for protection; **T** (*t*eaching relaxation and coping strategies) – increasing sense of mastery and reducing symptoms, imagery and focused breathing, identifying coping skills used during times of trauma and stress; **S** (helping with *s*elf-change) – identifying ways in which a survivor is the same and different after trauma, positive changes (see Figure 7.3).

Folklore therapy or the use of Spanish *dichos/refranes* (sayings or folklore) may be helpful to mental health practitioners working with Spanish-speaking clients. Dichos/refranes are proverbs and sayings that use folk wisdom to convey helpful information (Zuñiga, 1991). Dichos therapy groups and individual therapies have been used successfully by

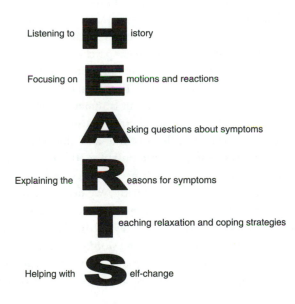

Listening to **H**istory

Focusing on **E**motions and reactions

Asking questions about symptoms

Explaining the **R**easons for symptoms

Teaching relaxation and coping strategies

Helping with **S**elf-change

Figure 7.3 **HEARTS model**

some therapists (Aviera, 1996). Dichos can draw clients in because of their 'cultural and familial relevance, vivid imagery, and the flexibility with which they can be used' (Aviera, 1996).

Ubuntu therapy (Van Dyk & Nefale, 2005) comes from the South African philosophy of Ubuntu that contains three dimensions: (1) psychotheological; (2) intrapsychic; and (3) interpersonal/'humanness' – (e.g., there is a Zulu saying 'umuntu ngu muntu nga bantu' that means 'I am because we are', which emphasizes the critical importance of positive connections with others). The psychothelogical dimension views God as creator who breathed life into all people. The intrapsychic dimension signifies the human essence enabling a person to become *abantu* (humanized being). The interpersonal dimension emphasizes relationships with others (kindness, good character, generosity, hard work, discipline, honour, respect, ability to live in harmony with others). The overall goal of Ubuntu therapy is to address conflicts within these three dimensions as related to Ubuntu values. The therapeutic process consists of hearing the client's story and determining at what level their conflict exists and at what level to address the problem. Therapeutic techniques include eclectic approaches and art.

Many survivors of trauma have extremely important stories to tell but often do not because they are never asked. In addition, few survivors of human rights abuses seek psychotherapy, because not every culture endorses psychological exploration, and because psychiatric care is often highly stigmatized. Testimonial therapy bridges the gap between the clinical – talking about traumatic experiences (which is therapeutic) – and the political. Therapists using this approach collect 'testimonials' through collaboration and documentation. The intended outcome is to use the testimonial for education and to advocate for justice while seeing oneself as an 'empowered spokesperson rather than as a voiceless victim' (Lustig, Weine, Saxe, & Beardslee, 2004). Using this approach, the survivor has control over the story telling (how much is shared, how it is revealed). The transcript is created and the client has the final say in the wording and the distribution. Assuming control over the story is a major step in the healing process because clients may feel they have lost any sense of control as a result of the traumatic experience.

Such alternative models to health and healing bring a fresh

perspective because they do not rely on traditional methods of addressing cultural challenges that tend to focus either on improving the cultural competence of the provider such as through training or improving the patient such as through culturally relevant informational materials. Making either party to the health care transaction more competent is laudable but addresses only the individual competency of persons and does not address the interaction between family and provider or the systemic competency of the organization. As such more creative and comprehensive approaches are required that do not rely on the traditional approaches of changing the persons involved but instead focus on the system as a whole.

And so forth (global health disparities)

Health disparities and commiserate lack of health equity are stark realities faced by families and children globally. In general, there has been widening disparities in health and human rights worldwide and simultaneously patient populations are becoming increasingly more vulnerable – advancing age, growing diversity, higher burden of chronic illness, and socioeconomic decline (Ezzati, Friedman, Kulkarni, & Murray, 2008). The 'big problems' in global health have been defined as HIV/AIDS, malnutrition, lack of access to medical care, and lack of adequate resources (Vamus, Klausner, Zerhouni, Acharya, Daar, & Singer, 2003). The goals in global health identified by the Bill & Melinda Gates Foundation and the National Institutes of Health (Grand Challenges in Global Health, 2008) are:

(1) Improve vaccines.
(2) Create new vaccines.
(3) Control insect vectors.
(4) Improve nutrition.
(5) Limit drug resistance.
(6) Cure infection.
(7) Measure health status. (Go to http://www.grandchallenges.org/Pages/BrowseByGoal.aspx for details of the 14 grand challenges linked to these 7 goals.)

For instance, according to the United Nations World Water Development Report, 1.1 billion people do not have access to clean water and 2.4 billion lack adequate sanitation facilities (United Nations, 2009). Food deprivation, food insecurity and malnutrition are commonplace worldwide. Some 170 million children in poor countries are underweight with over 5 million dying each year as a result of undernourishment and deficiencies in essential vitamins and minerals (Food and Agriculture Organization of the United Nations, 2004). Every year, more than 20 million low birth weight babies are born in the developing world (Food and Agriculture Organization of the United Nations, 2004). More than three-quarters of all child deaths are caused by neonatal disorders and treatable infectious diseases, including diarrhoea, pneumonia, malaria, and measles with more than half of these deaths traceable to the increased vulnerability of children who are undernourished and underweight (Black, Morris, & Bryce, 2003). Worldwide, undernutrition is the underlying cause of death for at least 30% of all children below age five. Inadequate breastfeeding, inappropriate food, lack of access to highly nutritious foods, and common childhood diseases that affect a child's ability to eat or absorb the necessary nutrients from food contribute to almost 20 million children being severely malnourished (World Health Organization, 2004).

Globally, the poorest countries tend to experience higher rates of communicable disease compared with more developed countries. For example, sub-Saharan Africa is the worst-affected region in the world by the AIDS epidemic. In this region, some 1.9 million adults and children became infected with HIV during 2007, which resulted in 22 million people living with HIV/AIDS and the death of approximately 1.5 million people by the end of 2007 (UNAIDS, 2008). These deaths are thought to be the result of lack of access to adequate health services due to weak health care systems and shortages of human resources (World Health Organization, 2004). The region of sub-Saharan Africa accounts for 67% of the worldwide HIV population but contains just over 10% of the world's population. Approximately 95% of people living with HIV live in the developing world (UNAIDS, 2008).

Regarding mental health, disorders such as depression are among the top 20 causes of disability globally. Depression affects approximately 120 million people worldwide with projections for an increase. Less than 25% of those affected by depression have access to adequate treatment and health care (World Health Organization, 2004).

Overall, this information makes apparent that people in developed countries are more likely to die from chronic diseases – many of which can be attributed to modifiable risk factors – whereas people in developing countries around the world are suffering from conditions that could be helped if they had appropriate care and treatment. In the USA, researchers have found that racial and ethnic minorities receive differential and less optimal technical health care than white Americans across diseases and care settings that is not due to lack of insurance or socioeconomic factors alone (Devi, 2008; Smedley, Stith, & Nelson, 2003). Furthermore, as compared to white patient populations, racial/ethnic minority patients utilize health care services less frequently, report being less satisfied with their care, have less access to care, and use fewer health care resources (Mead, Cartwright-Smith, Jones, Ramos, Woods, & Siegel, 2008). Racial/ ethnic minorities consistently have higher rates of infant mortality, disease burden, and premature death rates (Devi, 2008), are in poorer overall health, and are more likely to be uninsured (Mead et al., 2008) than white Americans. Socioeconomic, racial, and ethnic disparities in health care have been documented for black Americans who are less likely to see specialists or receive preventive care, receive less intensive hospital care including fewer cardiovascular procedures, lung resections, kidney and bone marrow transplants, and peripheral vascular procedures, receive less aggressive treatment of prostrate cancer and fewer antiretroviral medications for HIV infection, and have poorer quality of care in general (Fiscella, Franks, Gold, & Clancy, 2000). There is less research on other ethnic minority groups in the USA although there is some evidence that Hispanics and Asian Americans are affected by these same disparities as well.

Further reading

Betancourt, J. R. (2003). Cross-cultural medical education: Conceptual approaches and frameworks for evaluation. *Academic Medicine*, 78(6), 560–569.

Bigby, J. (2003). *Cross-cultural medicine*. Philadelphia, PA: American College of Physicians.

Chen, J., & Rankin, S. H. (2002). Using the resiliency model to deliver culturally sensitive care to Chinese families. *Journal of Pediatric Nursing*, 17, 157–166.

Spector, R. E. (2004). *Cultural diversity in health & illness* (6th ed.). Upper Saddle River, NJ: Prentice Hall.

Vaughn, L. M. (2009). Familes and cultural compentency: Where are we? *Family & Community Health*, 32(3), 247–256.

Whaley, A. L., & Davis, K. E. (2007). Cultural competence and evidence-based practice in mental health services. *American Psychologist*, 62(6), 563–574.

Chapter 8

Intercultural communication and education

- Introduction   162
- Communication and verbal language   162
- Nonverbal communication   164
- Intercultural communication in general   165
- Culture and education   166
- Teaching and learning across cultures   167
- Diverse forms of learning   169
- Multicultural education   171
- Cultural competence and education   177
- And so forth (indigenous knowing)   178

Introduction

WITH INCREASED TRAVEL, study, business, and socializing across cultures, more multinational corporations, universities with study abroad and teacher/student exchange programmes, there is more opportunity for intercultural communication. Every intercultural encounter requires at least an attempt of communication and communication provides the basis for most aspects of everyday life including education, work, and relationships. Communication also plays an important role in passing on cultural values from one generation to the next and in our understanding of culture and cultural influences on behaviour. Both verbal and nonverbal communication are essential elements in successfully transmitting and receiving messages within communicative interactions. Communicating with people from different ethnic, racial, religious, socioeconomic, and national backgrounds can be challenging and complex because of the myriad of factors involved and the assumptions about what is meant. Communication involves more than verbal language although communication via verbal language is unique to human beings. Being proficient in verbal language is essential to effective communication although communication also involves personal space and distance when talking, degree of physical touching, appropriate and inappropriate topics, and nonverbal communication including tone of voice, facial expressions, body movements and eye contact. Communication and processes like education can only be understood by considering people and events in their sociocultural context.

Communication and verbal language

Mastery of verbal language is an important part of successful communication. Culture and language are inseparable since both have a reciprocal relationship with each other. Many believe that a culture cannot be understood without understanding its language and vice versa. As mentioned in Chapter 4, linguistic relativity or the Sapir–Whorf hypothesis, suggests that speakers of different languages think differently because of the different nature, structure, and function of their language(s). One of the classic examples of linguistic relativity and this hypothesis is the multiple words Eskimos have to describe various types of snow in contrast to other cultures who simply communicate all types of snow as a singular idea. There have been challenges to the Sapir–Whorf hypothesis questioning its validity (Pinker, 1995).

Okun et al. (1999) identify a variety of conversational traits that influence communication including formality, intimacy, directness, acknowledgement and tolerance of conflict, and involvement. People use different degrees of formality and informality when addressing others and in the intent of their communication. In some cultures, people almost always use formal titles when addressing others (e.g., Doctor, Mr, Ms) unless they are friends or family. Informality in its extreme form includes the use of pet names or nicknames for familiar friends and relatives. In more formal cultures, people present themselves more seriously and the content of the conversation follows an acceptable and somewhat rigid cultural protocol whereas in more informal cultures, there is greater likelihood of spontaneous humour and joking. The degree of informality and intimacy in a culture also gives some idea about the extent to which it is typical to reveal personal and sensitive information. For example, discussing sexually related matters may be more appropriate in some Scandinavian or European cultures but in more conservative cultures such as in Latin America it may be considered as highly offensive. Directness is a conversational trait that varies across cultures. Some expect that listeners will understand hidden messages whereas other cultures expect straightforward talk about what one is thinking and feeling at the moment.

Culture strongly affects the acceptance of conflict. Some cultures tolerate and expect conflict in everyday interactions with arguments, insults, and negative feelings all viewed as acceptable (e.g., bargaining in market settings in Arab cultures) whereas others try to avoid conflict and confrontation and expect that individuals will agree at least publicly. Another conversational trait is the degree of involvement or enthusiasm when communicating. High involvement communicators talk at the same time, elaborating and adding onto another's incomplete statement and take part in conversations that typically don't have much silence whereas low involvement communicators take turns talking, don't interrupt, and typically are more comfortable with silences in the conversation. Communication style in the Western world is more direct, to the point, and emphasizes clarity whereas in Eastern cultures, communication tends to be more subtle, indirect, and typically mediated via a third party (Abdullah, 1996).

An aspect of culture that influences communication and education is whether a culture is high context or low context. High-context cultures are ones where little needs to be stated directly – information is gleaned from the context, situation, or culture. This is more typical in many areas of Africa, Asia, and Latin America where the group is valued over the individual. In high-context cultures, it is assumed that the majority share the same world views, traditions, and history and therefore communication will be understood without being explicit or direct. In contrast, low-context cultures like North America and Britain use more explicit verbal communication since the context and culture rarely alters the information (Samovar & Porter, 2004). Politeness is a culturally determined aspect of speech – what is considered polite in some cultures is considered offensive in others (Okun et al., 1999).

Nonverbal communication

Individuals from Western cultures are generally better at decoding the meaning of words and the verbal communication versus more elusive nonverbal communication that includes emotions, posture, gestures, pace of speaking, voice level, and timing (Okun et al., 1999). Many have suggested that nonverbal communication reveals the true intentions during interpersonal communication – what you say verbally doesn't matter if your nonverbals say something else. High-context cultures tend to use many nonverbal cues and vague descriptions while assuming a collective history and shared meanings. In contrast, low-context cultures generally use few nonverbal cues but rather explicit descriptions and meanings while ignoring common history.

Facial gestures convey different meanings in different cultures. For example, smiling has different connotations ranging from happiness (USA) to nervousness (Japan). Japanese people may smile or giggle when they want to say 'no' rather than being rude by verbally disagreeing (Okun et al., 1999). Eye contact is a powerful nonverbal communicator that has cultural significance. Direct eye contact can be interpreted in many ways. If it is a continuous stare, then it may be perceived as an act of defiance, a challenge, or an invitation to conflict. Many cultures forbid direct eye contact with people of status or power (e.g., rulers, holy images, etc.). In Muslim cultures, it is considered inappropriate for women to directly look at males who are not family members. In Western culture, direct eye contact can be interpreted as an invitation to sex. Touch is a nonverbal communicator that ranges from expressions of love and intimacy to assault. Rules for touching in some cultures are implicit and vary from context to context; which can lead to confusion and ambiguity (Okun et al., 1999).

Distance between people or proxemics is a form of nonverbal communication with four zones: (1) intimate distance; (2) personal distance; (3) social distance; and (4) public distance. These zones are determined by culture and can contribute to misunderstandings. For example, people, regardless of culture, generally have more flexibility with distance in intimate relationships (Okun et al., 1999). In most cultures, women tend to stand closer together and when talking, face each other directly compared with mixed groups or men. One's posture is also a nonverbal form of communication. For instance, an open bodied posture with arms and legs uncrossed and open is considered more masculine and persuasive in Western culture (Okun et al., 1999).

Intercultural communication in general

Part of the reason that intercultural communication is so complex is due to the perceptions and phenomenology we all start from or the 'intentional worlds' (the construction of meaning from objects, people, and processes with whom and with which they interact) from which we operate (Shweder, 1991). Each person is speaking from and through previous attitudes, beliefs, expectations, norms, socialization and life experience, meaning systems, and cultural world views. For example, pork is dinner for a Christian and sinful for a Muslim or Jew; dog is dinner to a Korean but a pet for Americans (Okun et al., 1999). Other elements influence communication across cultures. Gender differences comprise a significant portion of the communication literature and indicate that men and women use substantially different strategies when communicating (Tannen, 1990). Another aspect that influences intercultural communication is the negotiated public image or 'face' that people present to others. Maintaining face across cultures varies widely and is based on various notions of being courteous, humourous, respectful, deferential, etc. (Okun et al., 1999). The depth of relationship and type of relationship affects intercultural communication. Business relationships with all of their particular cultural protocol (gift giving, time usage, deference to authority, appropriate attire, modes of address, work schedules, etc.) vary from more intimate or personal relationships in terms of cultural norms, expectations, values, forms of address, time, and ways of showing respect. Overall, intercultural communication is dynamic, unpredictable, nonlinear and can be compared with improvisational music that includes 'harmony and discord in an evolving pattern' with underlying repetitive themes of respect and understanding (Okun et al., 1999, p. 29).

Culture and education

Our responses to ethnic, gender, and cultural diversity in learning situations are personal, complicated, confusing, and dynamic. Culture wields a large effect on human behaviour within the context of teaching and learning and can make intercultural interactions in this context challenging. To address cultural difference with learners, different models and strategies that incorporate sociocultural factors, emotional judgement, and learning styles must be employed. Models of multicultural education and partnership approaches can be particularly effective when considering the cultural aspects of education.

In almost every culture, educational systems are strong socializing agents and there is an intimate link between culture and education across many areas: language, school systems, parental and familial values, teaching styles and teacher–student relationships, different ways of learning, attitudes and appraisals of students.

School reflects what the culture believes is important to learn. The content that is taught in schools tends to mirror the culture's view on intelligence and expected competencies for adulthood. The environmental setting for education also varies across cultures. In some cultures, there is a formal education system with identifiable structures, processes, and expected roles – with teachers who are formally educated to teach students, typically in a school building. In other cultures, education may take place in small group settings led by elders in the community and in other cultures, parents may be responsible for educating their children in a less formal setting (Matsumoto & Juang, 2008). Differences exist globally in how long children spend in school and whether they go year round or not.

Teaching and learning across cultures

In order that teaching and learning practices are culturally competent, there are numerous factors to be considered. An important part of learning is the aspects of social organization (peer, collaborative). A culture's sociolinguistic practice will affect the teaching and learning situation (e.g., questioning, wait time, non-assertiveness, inclusiveness). Cognitive styles (sensory presentation, context of learning) and learning styles of students (dependent, independent, participatory, competitive, collaborative, avoidant) have to be taken into account. Finally, motivation is a key factor in teaching and learning situations (affiliation versus achievement, value of family/peers, framework for recognition). Depending on the culture and the specific topic, learning can be: formal–explicit rules and facts usually from schools; informal–implied rules and behaviours and exceptions to rules passed on from generation to generation and peer to peer; and technical – details, skills, implementation of rules of specific topics in specific situations (Okun et al., 1999) (see Table 8.1).

How people teach varies culturally. In some cultures, didactic teaching is expected and encouraged with teachers lecturing to students in order that students may listen and receive information. In some cultures, teachers are viewed as leaders or facilitators of the learning process so that students can discover principles and concepts. Some teachers use praise to reinforce students whereas teachers in other cultures focus on student mistakes. In cultures that have formal

Table 8.1 Teaching and learning factors affected by culture

Factor to be considered	Possible characteristics
Social organization of student body	Composed of peers, collaborative
Sociolinguistic practice of culture	Inclusiveness, non-assertiveness
Cognitive style/learning style of students	Dependent, independent, participatory, competitive, collaborative, avoidant
Motivation	Value of achievement/affiliation
Teaching style	Formal, informal

classrooms, there are different approaches to inclusion of different types of students (e.g., those with learning disabilities, physical handicaps, or special talents) with some treating all students equally and incorporating them into the same classroom and others with separate classes and/or teaching mechanisms. There is inconclusive evidence about whether people from various cultures share similar expectations of teacher and student roles. In one study, there were cultural differences in student and teacher role expectations for ten cultural groups (Indonesian, Chinese, Korean, Japanese, Persian, Arabic, Hispanic, Thai, American, Other Asian) in a second-language learning context (McCargar, 1993). In high-context cultures, modelling is used as the primary method of teaching and it is assumed that learners use their intuition by imitating their teachers and learning by experience. Direct instruction is used in low-context cultures and students are expected to absorb facts with little reliance on imagination or their intuition (Okun et al., 1999).

The parent and family view of education varies across cultures. Some cultures take a more active role in the extracurricular educational activities of their children after school and at the weekend. For example, Yao (1985) found that Asian American families of high achieving students, as compared with European American families, were more likely to supplement their children's school learning with after-school and extracurricular programmes. Likely due to the value placed on individualism or collectivism, some cultures emphasize the equality of all children (e.g., China and Japan) whereas others are more likely to recognize individual differences (e.g., USA). Some cultures consider effort more important than ability. Many American parents and teachers believe that innate ability is more important than effort whereas Japanese and Chinese parents and teachers consider effort far more important than ability (Yan & Gaier, 1994). Mastering language offers a unique perspective of cultural aspects of education. Learning language, like culture, involves a complex process with many types of learning involved including the stated rules of the particular culture, the implied rules and behaviours, and how to implement the grammatical rules and when to speak about certain topics (Okun et al., 1999).

All of these ideologies impact formal education with differences in the amount of time spent on individualized instruction versus whole group instruction. These beliefs also impact later causal attributions of the children in college successes and failures. For instance, Yan and Gaier (1994) found that as compared with Asian students, American college students were more likely to believe their academic success was due to ability and effort but their failures were not as linked to effort.

Diverse forms of learning

People learn differently and 'culture' impacts how people learn to learn. Gardner (2000) proposes that the traditional idea of intelligence based on IQ tests is far too limited. He expanded intelligence to include eight types of intelligence, which accounts for a broader range of human potential: (1) linguistic intelligence (word smart); (2) logical-mathematical intelligence (number/reasoning smart); (3) spatial intelligence (picture smart); (4) bodily-kinesthetic intelligence (body smart); (5) musical intelligence (music smart); (6) interpersonal intelligence (people smart); (7) intrapersonal intelligence (self smart); and (8) naturalist intelligence (nature smart) (see Figure 8.1). Gardner's concept of multiple intelligences (2000) allows for different possibilities of learning especially when a traditional approach is not working. Each type of intelligence has a corresponding methodology. For instance, using words corresponds to linguistic intelligence or using

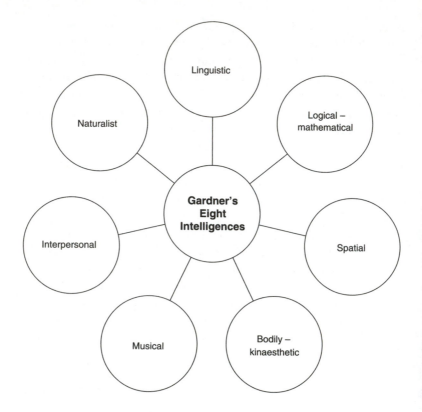

Figure 8.1 Gardner's (2000) multiple intelligences

self-reflection goes with intrapersonal intelligence. The use of numbers, pictures, music, physical experiences, social experiences, and natural world experiences are all alternatives to facilitating learning. Gardner says that schools in the Western world generally do not operate from such a philosophy and instead emphasize linguistic and logical mathematical intelligence. He suggests that teachers should be trained in nontraditional ways of incorporating music, cooperative learning, art, multimedia, field trips, self-reflection and more.

In *Women's Ways of Knowing*, Belenky and colleagues (1997) identified five ways of knowing from which women interact with and approach the world as well as ideas about education and learning (see Table 8.2). Although Belenky's work has suffered much criticism

Table 8.2 **Women's ways of knowing**

Ways of knowing	*Characteristics*
Silence	Complete dependence on authority, no creation of knowledge
Received knowledge	Knowledge gleaned from listening to others
Subjective knowledge	Knowledge viewed as personal, private and based on intuition
Procedural knowledge	Knowledge gleaned from using reason versus feeling
Constructed knowledge	Individual opinions integrated with outside world

regarding its replicability and choice of research methodology, the work nevertheless suggests that gendered learning does in fact represent diverse ways of knowing and that women and men may approach learning differently.

Educational thought and practice often get lumped into schooling thus education becomes equated to formal classes and learning. Formal learning is distinguishable from informal learning that occurs in everyday life – other sources of knowledge come from religion, family, and cultural customs and traditions. In a comparison of Western and African systems of thought, Jegede (1999) suggests that Western learning is very much individual in nature with knowledge 'documented' and in African culture, learning is more community oriented with oral traditions predominating as the manner in which knowledge is transmitted. The *And so forth* section of this chapter contains information about various indigenous ways of knowing.

Multicultural education

In plural societies regarding education, there is always a question of whose culture is being transmitted via whose language, whose values, knowledge and beliefs. In most schools across the globe, the dominant culture's interests predominate and determine what is taught and learned through formal education. The key components of multicultural education are the educational system itself, the teacher, and the learner. Traditionally the system and the teacher share the same dominant culture and the learner does not.

McLeod (1984) identified three types of multicultural schooling: ethnic specific, problem oriented and intercultural. Ethnic specific schools, at least partially convey one culture's history, values, language, and religion generally to preserve that particular culture or provide alternatives to learners who may otherwise go without a voice (e.g., historically black colleges and universities in the USA). Problem-oriented education is targeted toward specific groups who are struggling with particular issues such as a secondary language acquisition or disadvantages due to poverty. Intercultural schools emphasize intercultural knowledge and competence in tandem with the social and emotional aspects of interacting with culturally different people. Intercultural schooling is the closest to the ideal of multicultural education because it contains both cultural maintenance and participation. Without both, groups can become encapsulated in their own cultures or forced into assimilation.

Multicultural education must accomodate sociocultural conditions, including changing demographics, globalization of society, and evolving technology, which shape contemporary learning (Merriam, Caffarella, & Baumgartner, 2007). With regard to the changing demographics, we have more adults than youth, more older adults, we are more highly educated people, and there is increasing cultural and racial/ethnic diversity. Although the changes and diversity bring new possibilities for global interaction and expanding learning modalities, they also may have a 'splintering' and 'fragmenting' effect on society where minorities and marginalized people may have less access to educational resources and may experience oppression from the dominant groups (Merriam et al., 2007). Within such a framework, education cannot be separated from its political nature. Every teacher has opinions, ideologies, and values that are transmitted whether they are aware of it or not. Critical theory and social change education offer important insights for education and learning concerning the political realm including sociocultural issues, globalization, oppression, and power within society.

Critical theory originated from the Frankfurt School. The

Frankfurt School is an informal name given to members of the Institute for Social Research (*Institut für Sozialforschung*) at the University of Frankfurt in Germany. The designees of the Frankfurt School were considered neo-Marxist and therefore ardently anti-capitalist. The School emphasized social theory, sociocultural research, and philosophy and became known for critical theory that focused on radical social change and was the antithesis of 'traditional theory' in the positivistic and scientific notions. The emphasis of critical theory in general is the analysis and critique of power and oppression in society. At its root, critical theory aims for human emancipation from any circumstances that cause enslavement. Critical theory emerged as a critique of capitalism and emphasizes social inequality, the dominance of a single ideology, and the potential impact of critical thought in the world (Brookfield, 2005).

There are many 'critical theories' that have been developed as a result of various social movements all of which attempt to eradicate domination and oppression. All critical theories share the emphasis on decreasing hegemony and increasing human freedom with 'utopian hopes for new social responses in an alienated world' (Sorrell, 2006, p. 135). As such, approaches like feminism, critical race theory, postcolonial theory, and queer theory can all be considered critical theories. Social change education, an educational application of critical theory, concerns itself with challenging injustices across social, economic, and political realms (Choules, 2007). Much of the theoretical basis of critical theory and social change education comes from Jürgen Habermas and Paulo Freire.

German philosopher and sociologist, Jürgen Habermas was a later student of the Frankfurt School and is said to be one of the more activist members from that school. Drawing heavily on the ideas of Marx and yet rejecting some of Marx's work, Habermas's approach is described as a creative blend of systems theory, pragmatism, and analytic philosophy all with the intent of application to society (Sorrell, 2006). Habermas was interested in a more equitable society and he believed that this could be achieved by empowering the members of society to action through self-reflection and dialogue. Habermas believed that we lack freedom in society and that powerful 'systems' (government, corporations, media, etc.) are manipulating individuals and therefore not meeting our needs. Habermas believed that communication has become a controlling tool primarily used to satisfy the selfish interests of the communicator regardless of the recipient's needs or interests (Heslep, 2001). He said that we have to engage in 'communicative action' (a coming together to engage in dialogue for the purpose of common action) in order to become empowered against the hegemonic system. This theory of communicative action examines everyday communication practices and Habermas believes that reason comes out of mutual understanding within ordinary human communication.

Welton and others have brought Habermas's version of critical theory to adult education and have pointed to the applicability of Habermas's ideas like reflective discourse and learning communities (Merriam et al., 2007). Habermas identifies ideal conditions for authentic reflective discourse (dialogue, discussions) to occur: comprehensibility, sincerity, truth, and legitimacy. According to Habermas, this notion of discourse should involve an honest attempt to put aside bias and be open to all sides of an argument in order to come to consensus (Merriam et al., 2007). In terms of learning communities, Habermas says we should determine whether institutions are enabling us to reach our full potential – the idea of learning organizations follows in this tradition. Additionally, in the Habermasian tradition, adult educators have been accused of being too concerned with planning classes or arranging classrooms and not considering more 'political' issues like accessibility of education for some people (Merriam et al., 2007).

Paulo Freire was a Brazilian educator and activist who proposed a social emancipatory view of learning, sometimes called popular education or liberating education, also called social change education or critical pedagogy. He follows in the footsteps of Habermas because the basis of his approach is 'critical' in nature and follows the premise of critical theory in terms of critiquing the oppressive systems of society. Freire rose in distinction during the 1960s and 1970s when anti-colonialism was strong in developing countries. Freire examined education in terms of its emancipatory potential, which appealed to the oppressed masses in developing countries. He emphasized that 'knowledge' came from those in power so people need to deconstruct that knowledge and create new knowledge that is liberatory in nature. Freire found traditional educational practices constraining and non-liberating because he believed the oppressed had been conditioned to identify with the oppressor and view them idealistically (Prabhu, 2001). Freire reasoned that if the oppressed wanted freedom they had to use critical consciousness to examine things as they truly exist in society.

Freire is well known for his participatory model of literacy described in his famous book, *Pedagogy of the Oppressed*, first published in 1970. Overall, Freire critiques the dominant 'banking model' of education and says that education in general is suffering from 'narration sickness' (1973, 2006, p. 71). He says that traditional education is one-way with the teacher narrating the content to the students – the passive recipients who should memorize the content and repeat it back to the teachers. This 'banking' idea is that teachers 'deposit' ideas into the students who become 'depositories' and 'automatons' waiting to be filled with the knowledge and wisdom of the all-powerful teachers, which inherently is an oppressive model. Freire insists that such a banking model goes directly against the idea of dialogue and gets in the way of a critical orientation to the world (Freire, 1973, 2006). Students are controlled, knowledge is static, the teacher is the authority, and the realities of life are trivialized resulting in a dehumanized and paternalistic model that reinforces the inequalities and injustices of society.

Instead Freire calls for a 'problem-posing' (authentic or liberating) education where 'men and women develop their power to perceive critically the way they exist in the world with which and in which they find themselves; they come to see the world not as a static reality but as a reality in the process of transformation' (1973, 2006, p. 83). Problem-posing education starts with a transformation of the teacher–student relationship whereby teachers become both teachers and learners and vice versa. Dialogue is an essential process within this model and the relationship between teachers and students is 'horizontal' rather than hierarchical. In this model, the educational situation is marked by posing problems that relate to the real world and critical reflection about these problems that results in a continual creating and recreating of knowledge by both teachers and students. According to Freire, problematizing is a three-phased process that involves asking questions with no predetermined answers. Phase one is a naming phase where the problem is identified. Phase two is the reflection phase to discover why or how the situation can be explained. The third phase is an action phase marked by questions about changing the situation or considering options.

Prabhu (2001) summarizes the primary differences of the banking model and the problem-posing model in terms of world, teacher, student, teacher/student relation, style of communication, social function of education, and application to extra classroom situations. He indicates that problem-posing education is dynamic and malleable; the teacher is a co-learner, the student is actively engaged in the process of learning; the teacher/student relationship is equalized; communication is dialogical and democratic; the social function of education is questioning for the purpose of transforming social reality; and learning is seen as lifelong and complex.

Ultimately such a model, according to Freire, is a 'revolutionary futurity' because teachers and students learn that dominant ideas can be challenged and oppressive systems transformed, which helps them move forward and transcend the past (Freire, 1973, 2006, p. 84). Some scholars have mistakenly labelled Freire's educational ideas as too laissez-faire, however, Freire says that problem-posing education is purposeful and rigorous. The teacher still gives structure and helps to facilitate the direction of learning through constructive feedback and goal setting.

Although critical theory and social change education certainly have their critics, the approaches bring more to the table as compared with other theories about addressing the changing diversity and socio-cultural–political issues within education and learning – their intent is 'to extend democratic socialist values and processes, to create a world in which a commitment to the common good is the foundation of individual well-being and adult development' (Brookfield, 2001, p. 21). The strength of such approaches is that they critique the existing hegemony in the hope of transforming society for the better for all people even the disenfranchised or marginalized. The main weaknesses seem to be that such approaches are not always pragmatic and although they call for change do not always offer specific strategies for affecting change (Merriam et al., 2007).

Cultural competence and education

Sue and Sue (2003) define cultural competence across three dimensions: (1) awareness of one's own assumptions, values, and biases; (2) understanding the world view of culturally diverse others; and (3) developing appropriate intervention strategies and techniques. Derald Wing Sue (2001) proposes a multidimensional model of cultural competence that includes the need to consider specific cultural group world views associated with race, gender, sexual orientation, etc.; components of cultural competence including awareness/attitudes/ beliefs, knowledge, and skills; and foci of cultural competence (individual, professional, organizational, societal).

Campinha-Bacote (1999) offers a process of cultural competence helpful for intercultural communication and within educational settings (Figure 8.2). Noteworthy is that she believes that cultural competence is a process and not an end-point. Her model of cultural competence contains five constructs: (1) cultural awareness; (2) cultural knowledge; (3) cultural encounters; (4) cultural skill; and (5) cultural desire. In her model, cultural desire fuels the process of cultural competence and motivates one to seek cultural awareness, gain cultural knowledge, seek out cultural encounters, and demonstrate cultural skill in interactions.

Another meaningful paradigm for considering intercultural communication and education is the developmental model of intercultural sensitivity, a continuum ranging from ethnocentrism, or rejection or avoidance of different cultures, to ethnorelativism, the embracing and integration of self into different cultures. Using this continuum,

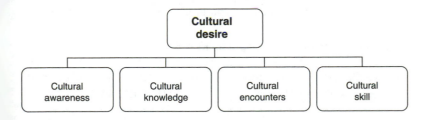

Figure 8.2 Campinha-Bacote's (1999) process of cultural competence

one can assess intercultural development relative to intercultural interactions (Bennett, 1993a; Bennett & Bennett, 2004a; Bennett & Bennett, 2004b; Bennett, 1993b; Bennett, 1998). See Table 8.3 where the following elements are considered:

(1) Denial: own culture is the only real and 'true' culture. Avoids noticing cultural difference.
(2) Defence: believe own culture is the most 'evolved'. Experience cultural difference as an attack on values ('they are taking our jobs').
(3) Minimization: elements of one's culture experienced as universal/similar to all cultures. May correct culturally different behaviour to match expectations.
(4) Acceptance: accept cultural differences as important. Own culture is just one possibility in a world of many cultures.
(5) Adaptation: take into account cultural differences by including relevant constructs from other cultural world views. Not the same as assimilation.
(6) Integration: integrate cultural differences into identity. Move in and out of different cultural world views.

And so forth (indigenous knowing)

A consideration of non-Western and indigenous knowledge allows for a broader perspective on how people learn and know within a local or community context. As George (1999) suggests, indigenous knowledge is not found in school curricula or even taught in schools in the typical manner but rather is passed down orally from one generation to the next through storytelling, poetry, ceremony, dreams

Table 8.3 Intercultural development model

Denial	Defence	Minimization	Acceptance	Adaptation	Integration
ETHNOCENTRISM			ETHNORELATIVISM		
Avoiding Cultural Difference			*Seeking Cultural Difference*		

and art, etc. Indigenous elders are often thought of as 'cultural professors' (Graveline, 2005). Other philosophical and religious systems of thought such as Buddhism, Islam, Hinduism, and Confucianism are additional non-Western approaches that suggest possibilities about other ways of learning. The Western notion of learning emphasizes the split between mind and body whereas many other cultural traditions of learning involve more somatic and spiritual aspects. In contrast, the non-Western perspectives put greater emphasis on interdependent, communal, holistic, and informal learning.

The Confucian way of thinking and learning is not to acquire a specific vocation or skill. Rather, learning for adults emphasizes spiritual development and becoming fully human. The primary notion of learning is to imitate the virtues of another person. Imitation of the sages is considered to be true learning. Another important concept according to Confucianism is to learn from everyday experiences as we journey through life. The Confucian way of learning is a continuous integrative process between the self and nature while engaging in commitment, continuous effort, and a holistic approach. To reach the highest excellence, which is considered to be the ultimate purpose of adult learning, eight steps should be followed: '(1) investigation of things; (2) extension of knowledge; (3) sincerity of will; (4) rectification of the mind; (5) cultivation of one's personal life; (6) regulation of the family; (7) national order; and (8) world peace' (Merriam et al., 2007, p. 227). In this Confucian concept, both peer learning and individual, independent learning are important. In the Confucian way of thinking, teachers are highly respected and the expectation is that learners obey their teachers (Merriam et al., 2007).

The Hindu perspective on learning emphasizes spiritual growth and a connection of the mind and body. Oral tradition is a common method of teaching and starts early with storytelling to children. The Vedas, ancient Sanskrit scriptures, are at the heart of Hinduism and are believed to be the absolute authority for Hindu culture. Messages from the Vedas are passed down orally and through dance and music, which helps to keep Hindu traditions alive. In contrast to the Western goal of knowledge acquisition in learning, the objective of Hindu learning is to understand oneself first through self-discovery and then to progress to a more holistic understanding of the universe that includes the idea of connection to the universe. Such an approach to learning allows the Hindu learner to access knowledge through various modalities (e.g., stories, meditation, music, etc.) which in turn may increase a higher level of spirituality (Merriam et al., 2007). Like Confucian learning, there is a sacred and revered relationship between teacher and learner in the Hindu tradition of learning.

People and the value of self-determination are central in the Maori concepts of learning. *Ako*, the Maori word for learning is the same word for teaching, recognizing the overlapping nature of the dispensing and receiving of knowledge. Much of the Maori approach to learning must be understood within the sociopolitical context of the Maori people alongside contemporary New Zealand dominant culture. Knowledge construction occurs through traditional tribal structure and customs. Within the tribal structure, there are smaller units of extended family that serve as a 'fundamental unit for living and learning' (Merriam et al., 2007, p. 232). Currently, the Maori are claiming their autonomy from New Zealand. One way this has occurred is that the Maori have established their own lifelong educational system with coinciding sites of learning where knowledge is defined by and constructed specifically for the Maori people. Maori educators follow in adult learning six subprinciples (Bishop & Glynn, 2003) consistent with the principles of the Treaty of Waitangi, which guides the lives of Maori people: (1) relative autonomy; (2) cultural aspirations; (3) reciprocal learning; (4) mediation of difficulties; (5) extended families; and (6) collective vision or philosophy.

The Islamic perspective gives special credence to education and seeking knowledge. The primary learning sources are the Qur'an and the *hadith* (collection of sayings from Prophet Muhammad). The Islamic religion is more than just a theological concept or religion – it is considered a way of life that affects all aspects of life from hygiene to socialization patterns (Bigby, 2003). Learning and education, according to Islam, are considered sacred – a way to become closer to Allah (God) and His creation. Cook (1999) describes that in Islam, education serves to unite a person's rational, spiritual and social dimensions. Communal learning is emphasized as a way to not only enhance the individual but to elevate the community and society at large. Like many other non-Western approaches to learning, the relationship between teacher and learner is considered sacred and one is supposed to display *adab* (discipline of body, mind, spirit) in interactions with one's teacher. Muslims believe that seeking, reflecting, and sharing knowledge are noble acts that bring one closer to Allah. The Islam perspective emphasizes that lifelong learning is expected – 'like a drop of water in the sea, one can never complete acquiring knowledge' (Merriam et al., 2007, p. 235).

In African indigenous education, the emphasis is on living harmoniously with family, community, society, and spirits of one's ancestors. This concept is reflected in the Zulu *ubuntu* philosophy that translates to 'humanism of human beings collectively' (Merriam et al., 2007, p. 235) and in the Setswana concept of *botho* that means humanism. To reach these societal values, collective learning, oral instruction, dreams and visions, and informal education are all considered valid methods of knowing and learning. Participatory education through ceremonies and rituals and other interactive customs is common in African indigenous education because of the recognition that knowledge is contingent upon the cultural and religious context that includes storytelling, myth, folklore, practical experience, and taboos. In African tradition, each person is expected to be a productive worker and participate in the dual role of teacher and learner.

Further reading

Bennett, J. M., & Bennett, M. J. (2004). Developing intercultural sensitivity: An integrative approach to global and domestic diversity. In D. Landis, J. M. Bennett & M. J. Bennett (Eds.), *Handbook of intercultural training* (3rd ed.). (pp. 147–165). Thousand Oaks: Sage.

Bishop, R., & Glynn, T. (2003). *Culture counts: Changing power relations in education*. London: Zed Books.

Freire, P. (2006). *Pedagogy of the oppressed* (30th anniversary ed.). New York: Continuum.

Merriam, S. B., Caffarella, R. S., & Baumgartner, L. M. (2007). *Learning in adulthood: A comprehensive guide* (3rd ed.). San Francisco: John Wiley & Sons, Inc.

Samovar, L. A., & Porter, R. E. (2004). *Communication between cultures* (5th ed.). Belmont, CA: Wadsworth Thompson Learning.

Chapter 9

Work/
organizations
and culture

■ Introduction   184

■ Organizational culture   185

■ Work-related values   186

■ Organizational structure   188

■ Leadership/management   189

■ Decision-making in
  organizations   191

■ Meaning of work   193

■ Multiculturalism in
  organizations   194

■ And so forth (large group
  interventions)   198

Introduction

A CROSS CULTURES, THE majority of people spend more time working, usually within an organization, than they do at any other activity. Internationalization and advances in technology and communication have forever changed work as we once knew it. Telephones, fax machines, teleconferencing, Internet, email, webinars, telecasts, telecommuting, online whiteboards, etc. allow for work to occur seemingly without boundaries; however, the boundaries that do occur are typically due to misunderstandings and mishaps related to cultural differences among the people and organizations involved. Advances in communication and transportation permit work to occur across many boundaries with large geographical and cultural distances. Intercultural issues in the workplace continue to surface as companies become increasingly dependent on companies in other countries and cultures. In particular, the workforce is becoming more diverse requiring that we adapt to ethnic, gender, and other cultural differences including interprofessional diversity.

Globally, the workforce has become increasingly diversified with many multinational and international corporations as well as the internationalization of most companies. This along with other international trends such as the changing social, linguistic, religious and other cultural differences within countries and the increase in foreign born and immigrant populations in many countries across the world (Bochner, 2003) has created the necessity for a diverse workforce. Cultural differences are important variables in understanding social and organizational behaviour and the individual members who work in organizations. Culture not only defines communication styles, decision-making, conflict resolution, leadership styles, and social structures within organizations but also directly influences organizational members' behaviour and manners within a context of an organization's particular customs and both explicit and implicit rules.

Organizational culture

Organizational culture, structure, and climate characterize culture and organizational dynamics within organizations. Organizational culture refers to 'the specific collection of values and norms that are shared by people and groups in an organization and that control the way they interact with each other and with stakeholders outside the organization' (Hill & Jones, 2001, p. 68). Organizational structure refers to how groups within an organization are constructed and how tasks are distributed across divisions and subdivisions (Hill & Jones, 2001). Organizational climate is a manifestation of organizational culture and refers to an organization's shared perception of 'the way things are around here' including the organizational policies, practices and procedures whether explicit or implicit (Reichers & Schneider, 1990).

Applebaum and colleagues (2008) offer three components of organizational culture: (1) *artifacts* signify the visible symbols of culture such as stories, rituals and symbols; (2) *values* represent beliefs about how things should be; and (3) *assumptions* reflect perceptions and thinking about the organization and guide behaviour. Factors such as size, history, employee culture, resources, and environmental and political context all play an important role in determining the organizational structure, culture, and climate. Numerous classification schemes exist for classifying organizational culture.

Similarly, well-known organizational psychologist, Edgar Schein (2004) suggests that there are three cognitive spheres that define the 'feel' of an organization and form the core of culture within an organization: (1) observable behaviours and artifacts (facilities, dress of employees, offices, etc.); (2) beliefs and values (via mission, slogans, etc.); and (3) underlying assumptions or values – unconscious basic assumptions and unspoken rules which are considered taboo within the organization.

Some have referred to the 'national character' of organizations as a way to define organizational culture and structure. Three types of general variations in organizational culture were described by Lammers and Hickson (1979) and can be applied to organizations regardless of where they are geographically located: (1) Latin – classic bureaucracy, centralized power and significant hierarchy (found in southern and Eastern Europe and many Latin American countries); (2) Anglo-Saxon – flexible, decentralized structure/power, less emphasis on hierarchy (found in North America and north-west European countries); and (3) Third World – centralized decision-making, less formalized rules, paternalistic leadership and family orientation (found in non-industrialized countries).

There are three levels of organizational culture: individual, intraorganizational, and interorganizational. The individual level is the cultural background of the individuals who make up the organization. The intraorganizational level includes the explicit and implicit rules that govern daily practice within the particular organization and the interorganizational level of organizational culture includes the explicit and implicit rules that determine how companies deal with one another nationally and internationally.

Yet another approach to organizational culture and structure includes the organizational dimensions of complexity, formalization, and centralization (Robbins, 1987). Complexity is the way that organizations differentiate tasks and activities within the employees. Formalization has to do with the degree to which there are structures, rules, and standardization in tasks to guide the operations of the organization. Centralization refers to the extent to which organizations have a limited number of business units or people concentrated together for the purpose of operations and decision-making.

Work-related values

Dutch researcher Geert Hofstede conducted a significant study of national work-related values in order to examine the role of cultures within a single organization operating across many parts of the world. He examined work-related attitudes and values of comparable groups of managers working in a multinational company (the branch offices and subsidiaries of International Business Machines, IBM) that operated in 40 countries. As a result, Hofstede (1980) established five dimensions of culture:

(1) *Power distance* – the degree of acceptance that power is distributed unequally (perception of not actual distance).

(2)   *Individualism versus collectivism* – the extent to which people define themselves independently (individualism) or as part of a group (collectivism).

(3)   *Masculinity versus femininity* – the value placed on traditionally male or female values (as defined by the Western world).

(4)   *Uncertainty avoidance* – the degree to which people minimize uncertainty through rules and structure.

(5)   *Long- versus short-term orientation* – a society's 'time horizon' in terms of importance placed on past, present or future that Hostede added as an additional dimension (1997).

With over 116,000 questionnaires in 20 languages and seven occupational levels across 50 different countries, Hofstede (1980, 2001) found that there are national and regional cultural groupings that affect the behaviour of societies and organizations, and that these groupings persist across time. For each of the dimensions, country profiles were computed that Hofstede viewed as reflecting broad dimensions of culture.

Hofstede's work has been criticized for not being representative of national populations and lack of replication with other studies not always reflecting his same dimensions. In a replication study of Hofstede's work, power distance and individualism were replicated but not uncertainty avoidance or masculinity (Merritt, 2000). Overall, Hofstede's dimension of collectivism/individualism seems to be the strongest with regard to distinguishing organizations (see for example, Triandis, Dunnette, & Hough, 1994).

Hofstede also examined regions/clusters of the world using cluster analysis. Hofstede (1980) found eight clusters that distinguished different types of organizational cultures and structures: more developed Latin, less developed Latin, more developed Asian, less developed Asian, near Eastern, Germanic, Anglo, and Nordic with Japan forming a cultural area on its own. These clusters can highlight information about particular aspects related to a country's values in the workplace. For example, harmony is more important in countries with low individualism. Ten years later, Hofstede and colleagues (1990) conducted a study with 20 organizations in Denmark and the Netherlands and found that as compared with shared values, shared daily practices were more important in capturing the core of an organization's culture.

The Organizational Culture Inventory (OCI; Human Synergistics International, 2005) is a diagnostic evaluation tool that can be used to assess the culture of an organization. The OCI is one way to get at 'cultural style' in terms of shared beliefs, values and expectations among an organization's members. The OCI identifies three cultural styles in organizations: (1) constructive (proactive, trusting, and adaptable to change); (2) aggressive/defensive; and (3) passive/defensive.

Hofstede and Bond (1988) explored values in Asian companies that were not identified in Hofstede's original dimensions. One dimension thought to be important to principles and values in Asian companies is Confucian dynamism. The principles of Confucian dynamism are related to Confucian thought, which emphasizes that unequal status in relationships signifies a stable society, the family is the unit of social organization, one should work hard using perseverance to acquire as much education and useful skills as possible, and respect for tradition and custom and thriftiness are important values (Yeh & Lawrence, 1995).

Organizational structure

The construction of groups in an organization refers to organizational structure. Formal groups that include management teams, work teams, problem-solving teams, customer teams, virtual teams all exist toward achieving a common goal in the workplace. Informal groups occur for friendship or based on similar interests. Groups tend to develop in stages. Although there are many models, one of the most popular is Tuckman's five stages: (1) forming – group comes together; (2) storming – group tests limits and experiences conflict within group and each other; (3) norming – group becomes more cohesive and difficult issues/questions are solved; (4) performing – group is working effectively using effective communication and cooperation; and (5) adjourning – the group ends their work, which leads to independence of individual group members (Tuckman, 1965) (see Figure 9.1).

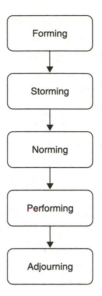

Figure 9.1 Tuckman's (1965) stages of group development

Leadership/management

Leadership and management are often not distinguished, but in the business world, they are different roles. Certainly there can be overlap in the two roles, but in general, managers have more to do with planning, organizing, controlling, directing, coordinating, and problem-solving areas of work such as management of money, time, paperwork, materials, and equipment. In contrast, leaders focus more on people within an organization using vision, inspiration, persuasion, motivation, relationships, teamwork, and listening as essential areas within their scope (McKenna, 2006). Good leaders are able to motivate and influence employees to do well and pursue the goals of the organization.

Two general categories of leadership styles have emerged in the cross-cultural literature. Originally based on work conducted in the USA, the two styles include the more authoritative/exploitative leader concerned more with production, and the more participative leader concerned with people (Likert, 1967). Cross-culturally, similar leadership styles have been noted in India and Japan. According to Sinha (1980, 1984), the 'nurturant-task leader' is concerned about the task maintaining a high level of productivity but at the same time is concerned and caring toward subordinates and their well-being. The general characterization of the nurturant-task leader is an authoritative (not authoritarian) father figure who works towards a personal relationship with employees and offers guidance and direction.

Misumi (1984) offers another conceptualization of leadership from Japan – the PM leadership theory which has two primary functions – the performance (P) function and the maintenance (M) function. P leadership emphasizes achievement whereas M leadership is concerned with interpersonal encouragement, support, and the reduction of conflict. This theory has a typology of four basic types (PM, Pm, pM, and pm leadership) and has been tested and validated in survey research and in various types of Japanese organizations. Figure 9.2 contains a summary of these four types.

What makes a good leader/manager varies across cultures. In a study examining ideas about outstanding leaders, 6000 mid-level managers from 22 European countries identified characteristics like

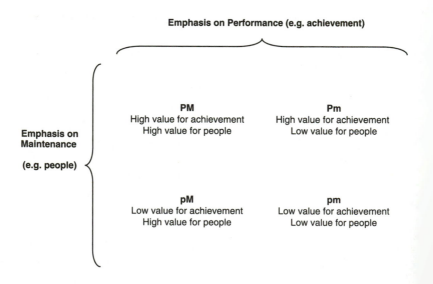

Figure 9.2 **Performance–maintenance leadership theory**

'visionary', 'inspirational', 'diplomatic', 'autocratic', and 'human orientation' that were commiserate with other global data on leadership prototypes (Brodbeck et al., 2000). However, there were differences depending on regional area. For example, participation was viewed as more valuable in north-west Europe as compared with south-eastern Europe. Administrative skills were rated higher in German-speaking countries than in Great Britain and Ireland. Overall, Brodbeck and colleagues (2000) identified three dimensions that differed across these European countries: interpersonal directness and proximity, modesty, and autonomy. With internationalization, requirements are changing for what makes a good global leader. Muczyk and Holt (2008) suggest that global leaders align their principles and practice of leadership contingent upon the cultural imperatives, their employees and the demands of the situation.

Cultural factors also influence managerial practices. For example, Japanese managers seem to focus more heavily and for a longer amount of time on a single task as compared with American managers; which may reflect the Japanese tendency toward long-term planning (Doktor, 1983). Sinha (1984) found that Indian managers emphasize job satisfaction over productivity perhaps representing the collectivistic values in India. In a study comparing managerial styles across countries, participation and a consultative system were more often used by British and US managers. The managers in Mexico, Italy, and Spain were more likely to use a 'benevolent authoritative' system of management (Silverthorne, 2005). In some countries, managers are more involved with their employees' personal lives and there is less of a distinction between work and personal life whereas in places like the United States, employees have a very clear separation between work and the rest of their life. It appears that managerial values and the effective meshing with organizational culture often contribute to the satisfaction of the employees (Silverthorne, 2005).

Decision-making in organizations

Making decisions is an essential task of organizations. Like other organizational behaviours, culture influences decision-making. In the

United States, democratic procedures are often used for decision-making typically involving a vote with the decision of the majority prevailing. Oligarchies represent an organizational structure where a few, usually at the top of the organization, make the decisions and impose them on subordinates (Ferrante, 1992). This top-down approach to decision-making is used in many American companies. The Japanese have popularized their decision-making process that is referred to as the *ringi* system. Proposals are circulated to all who will be affected regardless of rank or status in the organization with the goal of consensus before any decision is implemented (Tagaki, 2008). All decision-making processes have advantages and disadvantages. For example, the democratic approach gives everyone an equal opportunity in the decision-making process but often involves significant bureaucracy and the possibility that the majority is narrow, which leaves a large minority unhappy with the decision. The Japanese ringi system is advantageous because once consensus is reached, decisions can be implemented quickly but the disadvantage is that getting to consensus takes a significant amount of time (Tagaki, 2008).

A variety of techniques have been used in organizations in order to make decisions. Four of the most popular are brainstorming, nominal group technique, the Delphi technique, and concept mapping. Brainstorming is the group generation of ideas to solve problems with the goal of developing alternative strategies in order to infuse the decision-making process with new, creative possibilities. The nominal group technique (NGT) is a group decision-making process with the aim of generating large numbers of potential solutions to a problem, evaluating the solutions, and ranking them from most to least promising. The Delphi technique is a group problem-solving and decision-making process that gathers and evaluates information from a group without the group members having to meet face to face. It is often used for a group with different perspectives to reach consensus. The process begins with the Delphi question and the first inquiry. The first response is then analysed and feedback is given. The second inquiry is developed and an iterative process continues until a clear solution is reached (Delbecq, VandeVen, & Gustafson, 1975). Concept mapping is a participatory qualitative research method that uses a structured conceptualization process with a group. The process yields a conceptual framework for how a group views a particular topic or aspect of a topic (Trochim, 1989).

Wheeler and Janis (1980) found that it is common for people to avoid problems or make decisions – complacency and defensive avoidance. Complacency involves ignoring danger and continuing to do things the same way. Defensive avoidance is when people have little hope of finding a solution so rationalization, procrastination, or 'passing the buck' to someone else are used in place of making a decision. Another danger that can occur in relation to decision-making in organizations is groupthink (Janis, 1983). Groupthink is a collective pattern of thinking and lack of consideration for alternative approaches that gets in the way of effective group decisions. Groupthink includes the group behaviours of rationalization, avoidance of conflict, feeling of invincibility, unanimity, shared stereotypes, individual censorship, and direct pressure (Janis, 1982, 1983). Groupthink is thought to be responsible for many destructive and irrational political decisions in the United States including the Bay of Pigs invasion, the escalation of the Vietnam War, and the Bush administration's invasion of Iraq without broad-based support. Groupthink also occurs in other cultures.

Meaning of work

The meaning of work across cultures provides a helpful lens to examine the importance of work in relation to other aspects of life such as leisure, community, religion, and family. In a study conducted by the Meaning of Work International Research (MOW) team with eight countries (1987), 86% of participants across cultures said they would continue to work even if they had enough money to live in comfort for the remainder of their lives. Among leisure, community, religion, and family with family ranking as the most important, work was ranked second in importance. Across the eight countries, work was considered most important to Japan, followed by now former Yugoslavia, Israel, USA, Belgium, Netherlands, (West) Germany, and Britain. In this same study, professionals scored highest on importance of working, temporary workers scored lowest, and skilled workers and the unemployed had medium scores on the importance of working. Regarding gender, scores for women were lower than for men in all countries except for Belgium and the United States.

The significance of work in people's lives can be understood to some extent by investigating their needs and motivation. In one study with approximately 200 managers across 14 countries, researchers found that self-actualization or the realization of one's unique capacities was rated as most important by all countries when considering Maslow's hierarchy of needs (security, social, esteem, autonomy and self-actualization) (Haire, Ghiselli, & Porter, 1966). In most countries, autonomy (thinking and acting independently) was rated as next important. The most satisfied managers, as defined by a combination of all needs, were those in Japan and Nordic European countries and the least satisfied managers were those in developing countries and Latin American countries.

Collectivistic cultures appear to view work and work life as extensions of themselves thus connections and importance placed on work are stronger in collective cultures. Work in collectivistic cultures is more likely to be considered part of an obligation to the larger community or society. In contrast, people from individualistic cultures are more likely to consider work as separate from themselves and make a greater distinction between work time and personal time. It may be easier for people in individualistic cultures to perceive work as simply a way to make money in order to live (Triandis, Dunnette, & Hough, 1994).

Multiculturalism in organizations

Organizations can be examined from a perspective of power and privilege and in terms of the degree of multicultural practice in the organization. Work by Scott Page (2007) has mathematically demonstrated that diverse views from informed agents result in more accurate predictions and better decisions. Many business journals cite the benefits of cultural competency and the value of diversity as seen in the more productive, efficient, and harmonious workplace. In addition, the ability to attract and retain the most talented pool of candidates means going outside one's own culture and interacting comfortably with others (Business Week, n. d.). Being culturally competent ensures that businesses and institutions understand the populations with whom they work, value the diversity of employees, attract greater applicant pools, and are more likely to be desirable candidates for funding (Nash, 2003).

There are various types of organizations with regard to the extent of multiculturalism present. Monocultural organizations are at one end of the continuum and are generally Eurocentric and ethnocentric. Monocultural organizations generally do not value diversity and their structures and policies reinforce privilege and power of dominant groups. Generally monocultural organizations endorse the melting pot concept – that everyone should mesh together and be treated the same regardless of culture. Nondiscriminatory organizations represent more enlightened organizations who are interested in people of different cultural backgrounds however, they do not necessarily have structures and practices that support this belief. Nondiscriminatory practices are generally superficial and lack substance towards real eradication of prejudice and bias. Multicultural organizations or organizations that value diversity, actively work to end discrimination and oppression in all forms. Multicultural organizations view diversity as an asset, reflecting the contributions of its diverse members and promoting structures, practices and policies which support multiculturalism (Sue & Sue, 2003).

Organizations operate at various levels of cultural competency. One model depicts six stages of cultural competence for organizations (Cross, Bazron, Dennis, & Isaacs, 1989):

(1) *Cultural destructiveness* characterizes organizations that have been involved with forced assimilation, race/ethnic/culture-based oppression, and even genocide. Some historical examples include the Nazi sponsored medical experiments conducted with vulnerable populations (Jews, Gypsies, gays/lesbians, disabled, etc.) using torture and death and many of the federal government programmes aimed at Native American Indians.

(2) *Cultural incapacity* denotes organizations that remain biased toward the dominant group and engage in discriminatory hiring

and other practices against minorities. Stereotypical beliefs are common in this stage.

(3) *Cultural blindness* occurs in organizations that believe that all humans are the same and that dominant cultural beliefs are applicable to all cultures. These organizations may have good intentions but their services and approaches are ethnocentric and require assimilation to be effective.

(4) *Cultural pre-competence* characterizes organizations that are in an experimental stage with regard to cultural competency. The organization recognizes its weaknesses culturally. Cultural awareness and sensitivity are at least given some lip-service in these organizations although tokenism and minority staff without power and clout running multicultural programming are two common risks.

(5) *Cultural competence* marks organizations that exhibit 'continuing self assessment regarding culture, careful attention to the dynamics of difference, continuous expansion of cultural knowledge and resources, and a variety of adaptations to service models in order to better meet the needs of culturally diverse populations' (Cross et al., 1989, p. 17).

(6) *Cultural proficiency* characterizes organizations and individuals within organizations operating at a high level of multicultural competence. These organizations are not common because of the requisite shedding of many layers of racism, prejudice, and discrimination. See Figure 9.3.

All levels of the organization are invested in multicultural competence not just ethnic minorities and people of colour. Multicultural organizational competence requires constant vigilance of oppression and discrimination in organizations, recognition of power and status and the detrimental effects on the organization and its members. Culturally proficient organizations will be in a much better position to handle misunderstandings and conflict than will organizations not willing to examine their cultural practices or their lack of cultural awareness.

One important component of culturally competent organizations is that they are able to engage in successful international

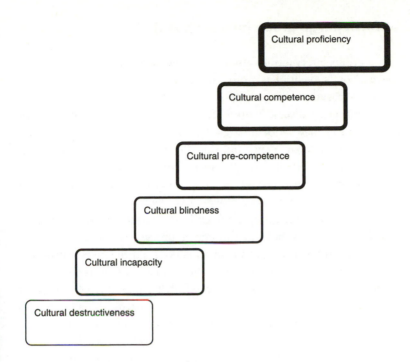

Figure 9.3 **Organizational cultural competency**

negotiation. People and organizations from different cultures approach negotiation with differing assumptions and from diverse world views. Kimmel (1994) suggests that for successful international negotiation to occur, negotiators need to consider conceptions of negotiation process, type of issue, protocol, verbal versus nonverbal behaviour, persuasive arguments, trust, risk-taking, value of time, decision-making system, and forms of agreement. Research about culture and work will continue to be dynamic. Aycan (2000) suggests that in the future, more attention will be paid to recruitment and selection, performance management, and employee health and well-being.

And so forth (large group interventions)

Large group interventions used in organizations can bring an entire 'system' or 'stakeholders' into the room at the same time to make decisions together. These approaches are particularly useful given the increasingly diverse workforce worldwide. Traditionally, assessments and change work in organizations occurred at an individual level or within departments and was directed from the top-down in a hierarchical manner (Bunker & Alban, 1997). In contrast, large group interventions give people voice, manage differences, and find common ground among diverse stakeholders. Two primary principles underlie the majority of large group interventions: (1) they create interaction among diverse stakeholders through a process where everyone can participate and be heard; 2) the focus is not on differences but instead areas of agreement from which to move forward (common ground). Large group interventions have successfully been used in communities, business organizations, at the national level to discuss dilemmas facing a nation, and in international settings with multicultural groups.

Future Search Conference (FSC) is a well-known large group intervention that brings a 'whole system' into the room to work on a task-focused agenda (Weisbord & Janoff, 2000). FSCs have been successfully used for action planning in areas as diverse as reducing infant mortality in Milwaukee, USA to decreasing child deaths due to diarrhoea in Bangladesh (Weisbord & Janoff, 2000). FSCs have been used in a variety of settings with successful results including enhanced participant involvement and awareness, confirmation of mutual values, and increased commitment to future action (Polyani, 2001). Typically 60–70 people attend a FSC and work in small groups toward five specific tasks over three days. The five major tasks involved in a typical FSC include the following. First, participants *review the past* by making time lines of important events in their own lives, the world, and the history of the topic in question – these are shared with the group and implications for the topic in question are considered. Second, participants *explore the present* by identifying the current trends that are important to the group and that impact the topic. Third, small groups work together to *create ideal future scenarios*, a brainstorming activity that generates positive opportunities. Fourth, the group *identifies common ground*, a crucial step in which the group creates a common vision that will fuel the action plan. Finally, on the last day of the FSC, the group *makes action plans* that will serve as the basis for desired future changes.

Large group interventions have been adapted over the years and include variations on the original methods. The appreciative inquiry summit (Ludema, Whitney, Mohr, & Griffin, 2003) is an adaptation of an older more individual-based method of appreciate inquiry that now is applied to organizations in order to capture the organization's positive values and practice while making changes for the future. The appreciative inquiry summit progresses through four phases and is typically held over three to five days: (1) discovery phase; (2) summit meeting; (3) dream phase; and (4) design phase. The World Café is another innovation in large group interventions particularly suited for international and multicultural audiences (Brown, 2002). The purpose of the World Café is to promote authentic conversation around a theme of interest to the invited stakeholders. It takes about two hours and involves small groups talking and drawing their conversations on tablecloths of drawing paper. One person is left at the table to communicate a summary of the conversation that just occurred. Everyone else separates and goes to a different table and the process repeats itself with at least three iterations. The final groups post a summary of the ideas developed as a result of the process. The large group then engages in a town meeting discussion and appropriate next steps are taken (e.g., action, further discussion, etc.). The World Café can be used with groups of various sizes ranging from 12 to 1200.

Many of these large group interventions have been used across different cultures. For example, non-governmental organizations in developing countries are using these methods to involve community residents in future programming. Future search has been used in Africa to demobilize child soldiers, in the Sudan to deal with problems of displaced children, and in Australia with Aboriginal peoples. Appreciative inquiry has been used in strategic planning in South Africa and Ethiopia (Bunker & Alban, 1997). Given that these large group methods allow for diverse stakeholders to have a voice amidst potentially diverging viewpoints, it is not surprising that they have been successfully used in organizations worldwide for important decisions, strategic planning, and future visions.

Further reading

Aycan, Z. (2000). Cross-cultural industrial and organizational psychology: Contributions, past developments, future directions. *Journal of Cross-Cultural Psychology*, *31*(1), 110–128.

Muczyk, J. P., & Holt, D. T. (2008). Toward a cultural contingency model of leadership. *Journal of Leadership and Organizational Studies*, *14*(4), 277–286.

Schein, E. H. (2004). *Organizational culture and leadership* (3rd ed.). San Francisco: Jossey-Bass.

Silverthorne, C. P. (2005). *Organizational psychology in cross-cultural perspective*. New York: New York University Press.

Weisbord, M., & Janoff, S. (2000). *Future search: An action guide to finding common ground in organizations and communities*. San Francisco, CA: Berrett-Koehler Publishers.

References

Abdullah, A. (1996). *Going glocal: Cultural dimensions in Malaysian management.* Kuala Lumpur: Malaysian Institute of Management.

Aboud, F. (1998). *Health psychology in global perspective.* Thousand Oaks, CA: Sage.

Abreu, J. M., Consoli, A. J., & Cypers, S. J. (2004). Treatment issues with Hispanic clients. In D. R. Atkinson (Ed.), *Counseling American minorities* (pp. 317–340). Boston: McGraw-Hill.

Adams, F., & Osgood, C. (1973). A cross-cultural study of the affective meaning of color. *Journal of Cross-Cultural Psychology, 4*(2), 135–156.

Adams, P. J., Katz, R. C., Beauchamp, K., Cohen, E., & Zavis, D. (1993). Body dissatisfaction, eating disorders, and depression: A developmental perspective. *Journal of Child and Family Studies, 2*(1), 37–46.

Åhman, E., Dolea, C., & Shah, I. (2000). *The global burden of unsafe abortion in the year 2000. Global Burden of Disease.* Retrieved September 27, 2009 from http://www.who.int/healthinfo/statistics/bod_abortions.pdf

Ainsworth, M. D. S. (1982). Attachment: Retrospect and prospect. In C. M. Parks & J. Stevenson-Hinde (Eds.), *The place of attachment in human behavior* (pp. 3–30). New York: Basic Books.

Aizenmann, N. (2002). A rebirth of traditions: Maternity wards adapt to immigrants' needs. *Washington Post, May 12*.

Allgeier, E. R., & Allgeier, A. R. (2000). *Sexual interactions* (5th ed.). Boston: Houghton Mifflin.

Allport, G. (1954). *The nature of prejudice*. Reading, MA: Addison-Wesley.

American Psychiatric Association (1994). *Diagnostic and Statistical Manual of Mental Disorders* (4th ed.). Arlington, VA: American Psychiatric Association.

American Psychiatric Association (2000). *Diagnostic and Statistical Manual of Mental Disorders* (4th ed. revised). Arlington, VA: American Psychiatric Association.

Annandale, E. (1998). *The sociology of health and medicine: A critical introduction*. Cambridge: Polity Press.

Anthias, F. (2001). New hybridities, old concepts: the limits of 'culture.' *Ethnic & Racial Studies, 24*, 619–641.

Antonucci, T. C., & Akiyama, H. (1997). Social support and the maintenance of competence. In S. Willis & K. W. Schaie (Eds.), *Societal mechanisms for maintaining competence in old age*. New York: Springer Publishing Co.

Arends-Tóth, J., & van de Vijver, F. J. R. (2006). Assessment of psychological acculturation. In D. L. Sam & J. W. Berry (Eds.), *The Cambridge handbook of acculturation psychology* (pp. 142–160). Cambridge, UK: Cambridge University Press.

Aroian, K. J., Norris, A. E., Patsdaughter, C. A., & Tran, T. V. (1998). Predicting psychological distress among former Soviet immigrants. *International Journal of Social Psychiatry, 44*(4), 284–294.

Atkinson, D. R. (2004). *Counseling American Minorities* (6th ed.). Boston: McGraw Hill.

Aune, R., & Aune, K. (1994). The influence of culture, gender, and relational status on appearance management. *Journal of Cross-Cultural Psychology, 25*(2), 258–272.

Aviera, A. (1996). 'Dichos' therapy group: A therapeutic use of Spanish language proverbs with hospitalized Spanish-speaking psychiatric patients. *Cultural Diversity and Mental Health, 2*, 73–87.

Aycan, Z. (2000). Cross-cultural industrial and organizational psychology: Contributions, past developments, future directions. *Journal of Cross-Cultural Psychology, 31*(1), 110–128.

REFERENCES

Ball, H. L. (2003). Breastfeeding, bed-sharing and infant sleep. *Birth: Issues in Prenatal Care, 30*(3), 181–188.

Bandura, A. (1977). *Social learning theory.* Englewood Cliffs, NJ: Prentice-Hall.

Barber, N. (2001). On the relationship between marital opportunity and teen pregnancy: The sex ration question. *Journal of Cross-Cultural Psychology, 32*(3), 259–267.

Barry, H., Bacon, M., & Child, I. (1957). A cross-cultural survey of some sex differences in socialization. *Journal of Abnormal and Social Psychology, 55,* 327–332.

Beal, A. C., Kuhlthau, K., & Perrin, J. M. (2003). Breastfeeding advice given to African American and white women by physicians and WIC counselors. *Public Health Report, 118*(4), 368–376.

Belenky, M. F., Clinchy, B. M., Goldberger, N. R., & Tarule, J. M. (1997). *Women's ways of knowing: The development of self, voice and mind. Tenth anniversary edition.* New York: Basic Books.

Bem, S. L. (1995). Dismantling gender polarization and compulsory heterosexuality: Should we turn the volume down or up? *Journal of Sex Research, 32,* 329–334.

Benet-Martinez, V., J., Leu, F. L., & Morris, M. D. (2002). Negotiating biculturalism: cultural frame switching in biculturals with oppositional versus compatible cultural identities. *Journal of Cross-Cultural Psychology, 33,* 492–516.

Bennett, J. M. (1993a). Cultural marginality: Identity issues in intercultural training. In R. M. Paige (Ed.), *Education for the intercultural experience.* Yarmouth, ME: Intercultural Press.

Bennett, M. J. (1993b). Towards a developmental model of intercultural sensitivity. In R. M. Paige (Ed.), *Education for the intercultural experience.* Yarmouth, ME: Intercultural Press.

Bennett, M. J. (1998). *Basic concepts of intercultural communication: Selected readings.* Boston: Intercultural Press.

Bennett, J. M., & Bennett, M. J. (2004a). *Developing intercultural competence: A reader.* Portland, OR: Intercultural Communication Institute.

Bennett, J. M., & Bennett, M. J. (2004b). Developing intercultural sensitivity: An integrative approach to global and domestic diversity. In D. Landis, J. M. Bennett & M. J. Bennett (Eds.), *Handbook of intercultural training* (3rd ed.) (pp. 147–165). Thousand Oaks CA: Sage.

Berlin, E. A., & Fowkes, W. C., Jr., (1983). A teaching framework for cross-cultural health care – Application in family practice. *Western Journal of Medicine, 12*(139), 93–98.

Bernal, H. (1996). Delivering culturally competent care. In P. D. Barry (Ed.), *Psychosocial nursing care of physically ill patients* and *their families* (3rd ed.). pp. 78–99. Philadelphia: Lippincott-Raven.

Berry, J. W. (1966). Temne and Eskimo perceptual skills. *International Journal of Psychology, 4*, 119–128.

Berry, J. W. (1997). Immigration, acculturation and adaptation. *Applied Psychology: An International Review, 46*, 5–68.

Berry, J. W. (1998). Social psychological costs and benefits of multiculturalism: A view from Canada. *Trames, 2*, 209–233.

Berry, J. W. (2001). A psychology of immigration. *Journal of Social Issues, 57*(3), 615–631.

Berry, J. W., Dalal, A., & Pande, N. (1994). *Disability attitudes, beliefs and behaviors: A cross-cultural study.* Kingston: International Centre for Community-Based Rehabilitation.

Berry, J. W., Poortinga, Y. H., Segall, M. H., & Dasen, P. R. (2002). *Cross-cultural psychology: Research and applications* (2nd ed.). Cambridge, UK: Cambridge University Press.

Betancourt, J. R. (2003). Cross-cultural medical education: Conceptual approaches and frameworks for evaluation. *Academic Medicine, 78*(6), 560–569.

Betancourt, J. R., Green, A. R., & Carrillo, J. E. (2007). *Quality interactions.* Retrieved September 27, 2009, from http://www.qualityinteractions.org/prod_overview/index.html

Betancourt, J. R., Green, A. R., Carrillo, J. E., & Park, E. R. (2005). Cultural competence and health care disparities: key perspectives and trends. *Health Aff (Millwood), 24*(2), 499–505.

Bigby, J. (2003). *Cross-cultural medicine.* Philadelphia: American College of Physicians.

Bishop, R., & Glynn, T. (2003). *Culture counts: Changing power relations in education.* London: Zed Books.

Black, R., Morris, S., & Bryce, J. (2003). Where and why are 10 million children dying every year. *Lancet, 361*, 2226–2234.

Blaine, B. (2007). *Understanding the psychology of diversity.* Los Angeles: Sage.

Bochner, S. (1994). Cross-cultural differences in the self concept. *Journal of Cross-Cultural Psychology, 25*, 273–283.

Bochner, S. (2003). Culture shock due to contact with unfamiliar cultures. In W. J. Lonner, D. L. Dinnel, S. A. Hayes & D. N. Sattler (Eds.), *Online readings in psychology and culture* (Vol. unit 8, chapter 7). Retrieved September 27, 2009 from http://www.ac.wwu.edu/~culture/Bochner.htm

Bolton, R. (1994). Sex, science, and social responsibility: Cross-cultural research on same-sex eroticism and sexual intolerance. *Cross-Cultural Research, 28,* 134–190.

Bond, R., & Smith, P. B. (1996). Culture and conformity: A meta-analysis of studies using Asch's line judgment task. *Psychological Bulletin, 119,* 111–137.

Boog, B. W. M. (2003). The emancipatory character of action research, its history and the present state of the art. *Journal of Community & Applied Social Psychology, 13,* 426–438.

Borgatti, S. P., & Cross, R. (2003). A relational view of information seeking and learning in social networks. *Management Science, 49*(4), 432–445.

Born, M., Bleichrodt, N., & Van der Flier, H. (1987). Cross-cultural comparison of sex-related differences on intelligence tests: A meta-analysis. *Journal of Cross-Cultural Psychology, 18,* 283–314.

Bornstein, M. H., Tal, J., Rahn, C., Galperín, C. Z., Pecheux, M.-G., Lamour, M., et al. (1992). Functional analysis of the contents of maternal speech to infants of 5 and 13 months in four cultures: Argentina, France, Japan and the United States. *Developmental Psychology, 28,* 593–603.

Bostok, J., & Freeman, J. (2003). 'No limits': Doing participatory action research with young people in Northumberland. *Journal of Community & Applied Social Psychology, 13,* 464–474.

Brace, C. (2005). *Race is a four letter word.* New York: Oxford University Press.

Breger, R., & Hill, R. (Eds.). (1998). *Cross-cultural marriage: Identity and choice.* New York: Berg.

Brehm, S. S. (1985). *Intimate relationships.* New York: Random House.

Brenner, R. A., Simons-Morton, B. G., Bhaskar, B., Revenis, M., Das, A., & Clemens, J. D. (2003). Infant-parent bedsharing in an inner-city population. *Archives of Pediatrics and Adolescent Medicine, 157,* 33–39.

Brislin, R. W. (1981). *Cross-cultural encounters, face-to-face interaction.* New York: Pergamon Press.

Brislin, R. W. (2000). *Understanding culture's influence on behavior* (2nd ed.). Fort Worth: Harcourt College Publishers.

Brodbeck, F. C., Frese, M., Akerblom, S., Andia, G., Bakacsi, G., Bendova, H., et al. (2000). Cultural variation of leadership prototypes across 22 European countries. *Journal of Occupational and Organizational Psychology, 73,* 1–29.

Bronfenbrenner, U. (1979). *The ecology of human development: Experiments by nature and design.* Cambridge, MA: Harvard University Press.

Brookfield, S. (2001). Repositioning ideology critique in a critical theory of adult learning. *Adult Education Quarterly, 52*(1), 7–22.

REFERENCES

Brookfield, S. (2005). *The power of critical theory: Liberating adult learning and teaching.* San Francisco: Jossey-Bass.

Brooks, J. B. (2004). *The process of parenting* (6th ed.). Boston: McGraw-Hill.

Brown, J. (2002). *The world café: A resource guide for hosting conversations that matter.* Mill Valley, CA: Whole-Systems Associates.

Brydon-Miller, M. (2003). Health research and social change. In M. Murray (Ed.), *Critical health psychology* (pp. 187–202). London: Palgrave Publishers.

Budryte, D., Vaughn, L. M., & Riegg, N. (Eds.). (2009). *Feminist conversations: Women, trauma and empowerment in post-transitional societies.* New York: University Press of America.

Bullock, M. (2006). Toward a global psychology. *Monitor on Psychology, 37*(5), 9.

Bunker, B. B., & Alban, B. T. (1997). *Large group interventions: Engaging the whole system for rapid change.* San Francisco, CA: Jossey-Bass.

Burgos-Ocasio, H. (1996). Understanding the Hispanic community. In M. C. Julía (Ed.), *Multicultural awareness in the health care professions* (pp. 111–130). Boston: Allyn & Bacon.

Business Week (n.d.). *Cultural competence: establishing a knowledge structure.* Retrieved October 7, 2008 from http://www.businessweek.com/adsections/diversity/diversecompet.htm

Buss, D. (1985). Human mate selection. *American Scientist, 73,* 47–51.

Buss, D. (1988). The evolution of human intrasexual competition: Tactics of mate attraction. *Journal of Personality and Social Psychology, 54,* 616–628.

Buss, D. (1989). Sex differences in human mate preferences: Evolutionary hypotheses tested in 37 cultures. *Behavioral and Brain Sciences, 12,* 1–49.

Buss, D. (1994). *The evolution of desire: Strategies of human mating.* New York: Basic Books.

Byrne, D., & Murnen, S. K. (1988). Maintaining love relationships. In R. J. Sternberg & M. L. Barnes (Eds.), *The psychology of love* (pp. 293–310). New Haven, CT: Yale University Press.

Caldwell, J. C., Orubuloye, I. O., & Caldwell, P. (1997). Male and female circumcision in Africa from a regional to a specific Nigerian examination. *Social Science & Medicine, 44*(8), 1181–1193.

Cameron, R., Manske, S., Brown, S., Jolin, M. A., Murnaghan, D., & Lovato, C. (2007). Integrating public health policy, practice, evaluation, surveillance, and research: The school health action planning and evaluation system. *Health Policy and Ethics, 97,* 648–654.

Camilleri, C., & Malewska-Peyre, H. (1997). Socialization and identity strategies. In J. W. Berry, P. R. Dasen & T. S. Saraswathi (Eds.), *Handbook of cross-cultural psychology: Basic processes and human development* (Vol. 2, pp. 41–67). Boston: Allyn & Bacon.

Campbell, C., & Jovchelovitch, S. (1999). Health community and development towards a social psychology of participation. *Journal of Community & Applied Social Psychology, 9*, 144–169.

Campinha-Bacote, J. (1999). A model and instrument for addressing cultural competence in health care. *Journal of Nursing Education, 38*(5), 203–207.

Cannon, W. B. (1927). The James-Lange theory of emotions: A critical examination and an alternative theory. *American Journal of Psychiatry, 39*, 106–124.

Carpo, R. H. (1995). Factors in the cross-cultural patterning of male homosexuality: A reappraisal of the literature. *Cross-Cultural Research, 29*, 178–202.

Carroll, J. L., & Wolpe, P. R. (1996). *Sexuality and gender in society*. New York: HarperCollins.

Centers for Disease Control and Prevention (1991). Screening for hepatitis B virus infection among refugees arriving in the United States, 1979–1991. *MMWR Morb Mortal Wkly Rep, 40*(45), 784–786.

Chalmers, B. (1996). Western and African conceptualizations of health. *Psychology & Health, 12*(1), 1–10.

Cheetham, R. W. S., & Griffiths, J. A. (1982). Sickness and medicine – an African paradigm. *South African Medical Journal, 62*(11), 954–956.

Chen, J., & Rankin, S. H. (2002). Using the resiliency model to deliver culturally sensitive care to Chinese families. *Journal of Pediatric Nursing, 17*, 157–166.

Chen, S., & Ravallion, M. (2008). *The developing world is poorer than we thought, but no less successful in the fight against poverty*. Washington, DC: The World Bank.

Chen, X., French, D. C., & Schneider, B. H. (2006). *Peer relationships in cultural context*. Cambridge, UK: Cambridge University Press.

Chipfakacha, V. (1994). The role of culture in primary health care. *South African Medical Journal, 84*(12), 860–861.

Chiu, C., & Hong, Y. (2006). *Social psychology of culture*. New York: Psychology Press.

Choi, S.-C., Kim, U., & Choi, S.-H. (1993). Indigenous analysis of collective representations: A Korean perspective. In U. Kim & J. W. Berry (Eds.),

Indigenous psychologies: Research and experience in cultural context (pp. 193–210). Thousands Oaks, CA: Sage.

Chopra, A. S. (2003). Ayurveda. In H. Selin & H. Shapiro (Eds.), *Medicine across cultures: History and practice of medicine in non-western cultures*. The Netherlands: Kluwer Academic Publishers.

Choules, K. (2007). Social change education: Context matters. *Adult Education Quarterly, 57*(2), 159–176.

Christakis, N. A., & Fowler, J. H. (2007). The spread of obesity in a large social network over 32 years. *The New England Journal of Medicine, 357*(4), 370–379.

Clarke, V., & Peel, E. (Eds.). (2007). *Out in psychology: Lesbian, gay, bisexual, trans and queer perspectives*. Chichester, England: John Wiley & Sons.

Cochran, P. A. L., Marshall, C. A., Garcia-Downing, C., Kendall, E., Cook, D., McCubbin, L., et al. (2008). Indigenous ways of knowing: Implications for participatory research and community. *Health Policy and Ethics, 98*(1), 22–27.

Cohen, D. (2007). Methods in cultural psychology. In S. Kitayama & D. Cohen (Eds.), *Handbook of cultural psychology* (pp. 196–236). New York: The Guilford Press.

Committee on Community Health Services (2005). Providing care for immigrant, homeless, and migrant children. *Pediatrics, 115*(4), 1095–1100.

Conn, P. (2008). The politics of international adoption. *Origins, 1*(4). Retrieved March 9, 2009 from http://ehistory.osu.edu/osu/origins/article.cfm?articleid=6

Cook, B. J. (1999). Islam versus Western conceptions of education: Reflections on Egypt. *International Review of Education, 45*(3/4), 339–357.

Coontz, S. (2005). *Marriage, a history: How love conquered marriage*. New York: Penguin Books.

Coontz, S. (2007). The origins of modern divorce. *Family Process, 46*(1), 7–16.

Cousins, S. D. (1989). Culture and self-perception in Japan and the United States. *Journal of Personality and Social Psychology, 56*, 124–131.

Crawford, M., & Unger, R. (2004). *Women and gender: A feminist psychology* (4th ed.). Boston: McGraw-Hill.

Cross, W. E. (1971). The Negro-to-Black conversion experience: Towards a psychology of Black liberation. *Black World, 20*, 13–27.

Cross, W. (1978). The Thomas and Cross models of psychological nigrescence: A literature review. *Journal of Black Psychology, 4*, 13–31.

Cross, T., Bazron, B., Dennis, K., & Isaacs, M. (1989). *Towards a culturally competent system of care: A Monograph on effective services for minority children who are severely emotionally disturbed* (Vol I). Washington, DC: Georgetown University Child Development Center.

Cross, R., Borgatti, S. P., & Parker, A. (2002). Making invisible work visible: Using social network analysis to support strategic collaboration. *California Management Review, 44*(2), 25–46.

Crystal, S. (2004). Back Translation: Same questions – different continent. *Communicate, 5*. Retrieved September 27, 2009 from http://www.atc.org.uk/winter2004.pdf

Cushner, K., & Brislin, R. W. (1996). *Intercultural interactions: a practical guide* (2nd ed.). Thousand Oaks, CA: Sage.

Daibo, I., Murasawa, H., & Chou, Y. (1994). Attractive faces and affection of beauty: A comparison in preference of feminine facial beauty in Japan and Korea. *Japanese Journal of Research on Emotions, 1*(2), 101–123.

Davenport, W. (1965). Sexual patterns and their regulation in a society of the Southwest Pacific. In F. A. Beach (Ed.), *Sex and behavior* (pp. 164–207). New York: Wiley.

Dawson, J. (1975). Socioeconomic differences in size judgments of discs and coins by Chinese primary VI children in Hong Kong. *Perceptual and Motor Skills, 41*, 107–110.

Dawson, R., Prewitt, K., & Dawson, K. (1977). *Political socialization.* Boston: Little, Brown.

Daya, R. (2000). Buddhist psychology, a theory of change process: Implications for counsellors. *International Journal for the Advancement of Counselling, 22*, 257–271.

de Munck, V. C., & Korotayev, A. V. (2007). Wife-husband intimacy and female status in cross-cultural perspective. *Cross-Cultural Research: The Journal of Comparative Social Science, 41*(4), 307–335.

Delbecq, A. L., VandeVen, A. H., & Gustafson, D. H. (1975). *Group techniques for program planners.* Glenview, IL: Scott Foresman and Company.

Denmark, F. L., & Paludi, M. A. (Eds.). (2008). *Psychology of women: A handbook of issues and theories* (2nd ed.). Westport, CT: Praeger.

Desjarlais, R. R. (1991). Dreams, divination, and Yolmo ways of knowing. *Dreaming: Journal of the Association for the Study of Dreams, 1*(3), 211–224.

Devi, S. (2008). US health care still failing ethnic minorities. *Lancet, 371*, 1903–1904.

Dhikav, V., Aggarwal, N., Gupta, S., Jadhavi, R., & Singh, K. (2008). Depression in dhat syndrome. *The Journal of Sexual Medicine, 5*(4), 841–844.

Diener, E., Diener, M., & Diener, C. (1995). Factors predicting the subjective well-being of nations. *Journal of Personality and Social Psychology, 69,* 851–864.

Diener, E., Oishi, S., & Lucas, R. E. (2002). Subjective well-being: The science of happiness and life satisfaction. In C. R. Snyder & S. J. Lopez (Eds.), *Oxford handbook of positive psychology* (pp. 187–194). Oxford: Oxford University Press.

Diener, E., & Suh, E. M. (Eds.). (2000). *Culture and subjective well-being.* Cambridge, MA: MIT Press.

Directgov (2009). *Marriage, cohabitation and civil partnerships.* Retrieved September 29, 2009 from http://www.direct.gov.uk/en/GovernmentCiti zensandrights/yourrightsandresponsibilities/DG_10026937

Doescher, M. P., Saver, B. G., Franks, P., & Fiscella, K. (2000). Racial and ethnic disparities in perceptions of physician style and trust. *Archives of Family Medicine, 9,* 1156–1163.

Doi, T. (1973). *The anatomy of dependence.* Tokyo: Kodansha.

Doktor, R. (1983). Culture and the management of time: A comparison of Japanese and American top management top practice. *Asia Pacific Journal of Management, 1,* 65–70.

Donini-Lenhoff, F. G., & Hedrick, H. L. (2000). Increasing awareness and implementation of cultural competence principles in health professions education. *J Allied Health, 29*(4), 241–245.

Draguns, J. G. (1990). Applications of cross-cultural psychology in the field of mental health. In R. Brislin (Ed.), *Applied cross-cultural psychology* (pp. 302–324). Thousand Oaks, CA: Sage.

Eagley, A. (1987). *Sex differences in social behavior: A social role interpretation.* Hillsdale, NJ: Lawrence Erlbaum Associates, Inc.

Earley, P. C. (2002). Redefining interactions across cultures and organizations: Moving forward with cultural intelligence. In B. M. Staw & R. M. Kramer (Eds.), *In Research in Organizational Behaviour.* Amsterdam, NL: Jai-Elsevier.

Eisenberg, D. M., Davis, R. B., Ettner, S. L., Appel, S., Wilkey, S., Van Rompay, M., et al. (1998). Trends in alternative medicine use in the United States, 1990–1997: Results of a follow-up national survey. *Journal of the American Medical Association, 280,* 1569–1575.

Ekman, P. (1994). Strong evidence of universals in facial expression: A reply to Russall's mistaken critique. *Psychological Bulletin, 115,* 268–278.

Ekman, P., & Friesen, W. V. (1975). *Unmasking the face.* Englewood Cliffs, NJ: Prentice Hall.

Ember, C. R., Ember, M., & Peregrine, P. N. (2006). *Anthropology* (12th ed.). Upper Saddle River, NJ: Prentice Hall.

Emirbayer, M., & Goodwin, J. (1994). Network analysis, culture, and the problem of agency. *American Journal of Sociology, 99*, 1411–1454.

Ergenekon-Ozelci, P., Elmaci, N., Ertem, M., & Saka, G. (2006). Breast-feeding beliefs and practices among migrant mothers in slums of Diyarbakir, Turkey, 2001. *European Journal of Public Health, 16*(2), 143–148.

Ezzati, M., Friedman, A. B., Kulkarni, S. C., & Murray, C. J. L. (2008). The reversal of fortunes: Trends in county mortality and cross-county mortality disparities in the United States. *PLoS Medicine, 5*(4), e66.

Fennelly, K. (2006). *State and local policy responses to immigration in Minnesota.* Report to the Century Foundation. Retrieved October 3, 2007 from http://www.hhh.umn.edu/img/assets/3755/slp_immigration_in_mn.pdf

Fernald, A. (1992). Meaningful melodies in mothers' speech to infants. In H. Papoušek, U. Jurgens & M. Papoušek (Eds.), *Nonverbal vocal communication: Comparative and developmental approaches* (pp. 263–281). Cambridge, UK: Cambridge University Press.

Ferrante, J. (1992). *Sociology: A global perspective.* Belmont, CA: Wadsworth.

Fiscella, K., Franks, P., Gold, M. R., & Clancy, C. M. (2000). Inequality in quality: Addressing socioeconomic, racial, and ethnic disparities in health care. *Journal of the American Medical Association, 283*(19), 2579–2584.

Fisher, H. (1992). *Anatomy of love: A natural history of monogamy, adultery, and divorce.* New York: W. W. Norton.

Fiske, S. T. (1995). Social cognition. In A. Tesser (Ed.), *Advanced social psychology.* New York: McGraw-Hill.

Fitness, J., Fletcher, G., & Overall, N. (2007). Interpersonal attraction and intimate relationships. In M. A. Hogg & J. Cooper (Eds.), *The SAGE handbook of social psychology.* Thousand Oaks, CA: Sage.

Flanagan, O. (2000). *Dreaming souls: Sleep, dreams, and the evolution of the conscious mind.* Oxford: Oxford University Press.

Food and Agriculture Organization of the United Nations (2004). *The state of food insecurity in the world 2004.* Retrieved May 25, 2009 from ftp://ftp.fao.org/docrep/fao/007/y5650e/y5650e00.pdf

Forsterling, F. (2001). *Attribution: an introduction to theories, research, and applications.* Hove, UK: Psychology Press.

Freire, P. (1973). *Pedagogy of the oppressed.* New York: Seabury Press.

Freire, P. (1973, 2006). *Pedagogy of the oppressed (30th anniversary ed.).* New York: Continuum.

French, D. C., Bae, A., Pidada, S., & Lee, O. (2006). Friendships of Indonesian,

South Korean, and U.S. college students. *Personal Relationships, 13,* 69–81.

Furnham, A. (1994). Explaining health and illness: Lay perceptions on current and future health, the causes of illness, and the nature of recovery. *Social Science and Medicine, 39*(5), 715–725.

Furnham, A., Akande, D., & Baguma, P. (1999). Beliefs about health and illness in three countries: Britain, South Africa and Uganda. *Psychology, Health & Medicine, 4*(2), 189–201.

Gardiner, H. W., & Kosmitzki, C. (2008). *Lives across cultures: Cross-cultural human development (4th ed.)*. Boston, MA: Allyn & Bacon.

Gardner, H. (2000). *Intelligence reframed: Multiple intelligences for the 21st century.* New York: Basic Books.

Gartner, L. M., Morton, J., Lawrence, R. A., Naylor, A. J., O'Hare, D., Schanler, R. J., et al. (2005). American Academy of Pediatrics Policy statement: Breastfeeding and the use of human milk. *Pediatrics, 115*(2), 496–506.

Gavagan, T., & Brodyaga, L. (1998). Medical care for immigrants and refugees. *Am Fam Physician, 57*(5), 1061–1068.

Geertz, C. (1973). *The interpretation of cultures: Selected essays.* New York: Basic Books.

Gelfand, M. (1981). African customs in relation to preventive medicine. *Cent Afr J Med, 27*(1), 1–8.

Generations United (2006). *Fact sheet: Multigenerational households.* Retrieved March 4, 2009 from http://www.gu.org/documents/A0/Multigenerational_Families.pdf

Georgas, J., Berry, J. W., van de Vijver, F. J. R., Kagitçibasi, C., & Poortinga, Y. H. (Eds.). (2006). *Families across cultures: A 30-nation psychological study.* Cambridge, UK: Cambridge University Press.

Georgas, J., Poortinga, Y. H., Angleitner, A., Goodwin, R., & Charalambous, N. (1997). The relationship of family bonds to family structure and function across cultures. *Journal of Cross-Cultural Psychology, 28*(3), 303–320.

George, D., & Yancey, G. (2004). Taking stock of America's attitudes on cultural diversity: An analysis of public deliberation on multiculturalism, assimilation, and intermarriage. *Journal of Comparative Family Studies, 35*(1), 1–19.

George, J. M. (1999). Indigenous knowledge as a component of the school curriculum. In L. M. Semali & J. L. Kincheloe (Eds.), *What is indigenous knowledge? Voices from the academy* (pp. 79–94). New York: Falmer Press.

Giannotti, F., Cortesi, F., Sebastiani, T., & Vagnoni, C. (2005). Sleeping habits in Italian children and adolescents. *Sleep and Biological Rhythms*, 3, 15–21.

Gibbon, J. L. (2000). Adolescence in international and cross-cultural perspective: An introduction. *International Journal of Group Tensions*, 29(1/2), 3–16.

Giger, J. N., & Davidhizar, R. E. (1995). *Transcultural nursing: Assessment and intervention* (2nd ed.). St. Louis: Mosby.

Gilbert, J., & Galanti, G. (2005). *Cultural competence and pediatric care*. Pediatric Grand Rounds. Los Angeles: Los Angeles County Department of Health Services and University of Southern California Women's Hospital.

Gilligan, C. (1982). *In a different voice: Psychological theory and women's development*. Cambridge, MA: Harvard University Press.

Glass Jr, J. C., & Huneycutt, T. L. (2002). Grandparents parenting grandchildren: Extent of situation, issues involved, and educational implications. *Educational Gerontology*, 28(2), 139–161.

Gloria, A. M., & Segura-Herrera, T. A. (2004). !Somos! Latinas and Latinos in the United States. In D. R. Atkinson, G. Morten, & D. W. Sue (Ed.), *Counseling American minorities*. Boston: McGraw-Hill.

Goleman, D. (2006). *Social intelligence: The new science of human relationships*. New York: Bantam Books.

Goodwin, R. (1990). Sex differences among partner preferences: Are the sexes really very similar? *Sex Roles*, 23, 501–503.

Grand Challenges in Global Health (2008). *The grand challenges*. Retrieved July 2, 2009 from http://www.grandchallenges.org/Pages/default.aspx

Graveline, F. J. (2005). Indigenous learning. In L. M. English (Ed.), *International encyclopedia of adult education* (pp. 304–309). New York: Palgrave Macmillan.

Green, A. R., Betancourt, J. R., & Carrillo, J. E. (2002). Integrating social factors into cross-cultural medical education. *Academic Med*, 77(3), 193–197.

Greenfield, P. M. (1997). You can't take it with you: Why ability assessments don't cross cultures. *American Psychologist*, 52, 1115–1124.

Gregg, J., & Curry, R. H. (1994). Explanatory models for cancer among African-American women at two Atlanta neighborhood health centers: The implications for a cancer screening program. *Social Science and Medicine*, 39(4), 519–526.

Grossoehme, D. H., Ragsdale, J., Dixon, C., Berz, K., & Zimmer, M. (2009). The changing face of medical education: The role of religion, integrative medicine and osteopathy. *Open Medical Education*, 2, 80–87.

Guarnaccia, P. J., De La Cancela, V., & Carrillo, E. (1989). The multiple meanings of ataques de nervios in the Latino community. *Medical Anthropology*, *11*, 47–62.

Gummerum, M., & Keller, M. (2008). Affection, virtue, pleasure, and profit: Developing an understanding of friendship closeness and intimacy in western and Asian societies. *International Journal of Behavioral Development*, *32*(3), 218–231.

Guthrie, R. V. (2004). *Even the rat was white: A historical view of psychology* (2nd ed.). Boston: Pearson.

Haire, M., Ghiselli, E. E., & Porter, L. W. (1966). *Managerial thinking: An international study*. New York: John Wiley & Sons.

Hales, A. (1996). West African beliefs about mental illness. *Perspectives in Psychiatric Care*, *32*(2), 23–30.

Hall, B. (1981). Participatory research, popular knowledge and power: A personal reaction. *Convergence*, *14*, 6–17.

Halligan, P. W., & Aylward, M. (Eds.). (2006). *The power of belief: Psychosocial influence on illness, disability and medicine*. Oxford: Oxford University Press.

Hambleton, R. K. (1994). Guidelines for adapting educational and psychological tests: A progress report. *European Journal of Psychological Assessment*, *10*, 229–244.

Hancock, T., & Perkins, F. (1985). The mandala of health: A conceptual model and teaching tool. *Health Education*, *24*(1), 8–10.

Hanscom, K. L. (2001). Treating survivors of war, trauma and torture. *American Psychologist*, *56*(11), 1032–1039.

Hansen, L. S. (1997). *Integrative life planning*. San Francisco: Jossey-Bass.

Harkness, S., & Super, C. M. (2002). Culture and parenting. In M. H. Bornstein (Ed.), *Handbook of parenting* (2nd ed.) (pp. 253–280). Mahwah, NJ: Lawrence Erlbaum Associates, Inc.

Harlow, H. F., & Harlow, M. K. (1962). Social deprivation in monkeys. *Scientific American*, *207*, 136–146.

Hatfield, E., & Sprecher, S. (1995). Men's and women's preferences in marital partners in the United States, Russia, and Japan. *Journal of Cross-Cultural Psychology*, *26*(6), 728–750.

Haugh, R. (2005). Diversity and the bottom line. *H&HN: Hospitals & Health Networks*. Retrieved September 27, 2009 from http://www.hhnmag.com/hhnmag_app/hospitalconnect/search/article.jsp?dcrpath=HHNMAG/PubsNewsArticle/data/0506HHN_FEA_Summit_Preview&domain=HHNMAG

Heine, S. J., Lehman, D. R., Markus, H. R., & Kitayama, S. (1999). Is there a universal need for positive self-regard? *Psychological Review, 106,* 766–794.

Helman, C. G. (2001). *Culture, health and illness.* London: Arnold.

Hendrick, C., & Hendrick, S. (1983). *Liking, loving, and relating.* Pacific Grove, CA: Brooks/Cole.

Hermans, J. M., & Kempen, J. G. (1998). Moving cultures: The perilous problems of cultural dichotomies in a globalizing society. *American Psychologist, 53*(10), 1111–1120.

Heslep, R. D. (2001). Habermas on communication in teaching. *Educational Theory, 51*(2), 191–207.

Heymann, J., Earle, A., & Hayes, J. (2007). *The work, family and equity index: How does the United States measure up?* Retrieved July 13, 2009 from http://www.mcgill.ca/files/ihsp/WFEIFinal2007.pdf

Hill, C. W. L., & Jones, G. R. (2001). *Strategic management* (5th ed.). Boston: Houghton Mifflin.

Ho, D. (1998). Indigenous psychologies: Asian perspectives. *Journal of Cross-Cultural Psychology, 29*(1), 88–103.

Hobson, J. A. (1999). The new neuropsychology of sleep: Implications for psychoanalysis. *Neuropsychoanalysis, 1,* 157–183.

Hofstede, G. (1980). *Culture's consequences: International differences in work related values.* Beverly Hills, CA: Sage.

Hofstede, G. (1997). *Culture and organizations.* New York: McGraw Hill.

Hofstede, G. H. (2001). *Culture's consequences: Comparing values, behaviors, institutions, and organizations across nations.* Thousand Oaks, CA: Sage.

Hofstede, G., & Bond, M. (1988). Confucious and economic growth: New trends in culture's consequences. *Organizational Dynamics, 16*(4), 4–21.

Hofstede, G., Neuijen, B., Ohayv, D. D., & Sanders, G. (1990). Measuring organizational cultures: A qualitative/quantitative study across twenty cases. *Academy of Management Journal: Administrative Science Quarterly, 35,* 286–316.

Holland, A. (2000). *Voices of Qi: An Introductory Guide to Traditional Chinese Medicine.* Berkeley, CA: North Atlantic Books.

Hong, Y., Morris, M. W., Chiu, C., & Benet-Martínez, V. (2000). Multicultural minds: A dynamic constructivist approach to culture and cognition. *American Psychologist, 55*(7), 709–720.

Hopkins, B. (1977). Considerations of comparability of measures in cross-cultural studies of early infancy from a study on the development of black and white infants in Britain. In Y. H. Poortinga (Ed.), *Basic problems in cross-cultural psychology* (pp. 36–46). Lisse, Netherlands: Swets and Zeitlinger.

Horowitz, C. R., Davis, M. H., Palermo, A. G., & Vladeck, B. C. (2000). Approaches to eliminating sociocultural disparities in health. *Health Care Financ Rev*, *21*(4), 57–74.

Hortacsu, N., Bastug, S., & Muhammetberdiev, O. (2001). Desire for children in Turkmenistan and Azerbaijan: Son preference and perceived instrumentality for value satisfaction. *Journal of Cross-Cultural Psychology*, *32*(3), 309–321.

Hsu, L. K. G., & Zimmer, B. (2009). Eating disorders in old age. *International Journal of Eating Disorders*, *7*(1), 133–138.

Hubbard, E. E. (2008). The business case for diversity. *The Multicultural Advantage*. Retrieved September 27, 2009 from http://www.multiculturaladvantage.com/recruit/metrics/The-Business-Case-for-Diversity.asp

Human Synergistics International (2005). Organizational Culture Inventory. Retrieved July 12, 2009 from http://www.humansynergistics.com/products/oci.aspx

Institute for Women's Policy Research (2007). *Maternity leave in the United States*. Retrieved July 13, 2009 from http://www.iwpr.org/pdf/parentalleaveA131.pdf

Institute of Medicine (1998). *From generation to generation: The health and well-being of children in immigrant families*. Washington, DC: National Academy Press.

Intercountry Adoption (2008). *Total adoptions to the United States*. Retrieved October 1, 2009 from http://www.adoption.state.gov/news/total_chart.html

Isaacs, M. R., & Benjamin, M. P. (1991). *Towards a culturally competent system of care (Vol. II)*. Washington, DC: CASSP Technical Assistance Center, Georgetown University Child Development Center.

Israel, B., Schulz, A., Parker, E., & Becker, A. (2001). Community-based participatory research: Policy recommendations for promoting a partnership approach in health research. *Education for Health*, *14*(2), 182–197.

Ito, T. A., Larsen, J. T., Smith, N. K., & Cacioppo, J. T. (1998). Negative information weighs more heavily on the brain: the negativity bias in evaluative categorizations. *J Pers Soc Psychol*, *75*(4), 887–900.

Jablensky, A., Sartorious, N., Ernberg, G., Anker, M., Korten, A., Cooper, J. E., et al. (1992). Schizophrenia: Manifestations, incidence and course in different cultures. *Psychological Medicine, Monograph, Supplement* *20*, 1–97.

Janis, I. L. (1982). *Groupthink: Psychological studies of policy decisions and fiascoes* (2nd ed.). New York: Houghton Mifflin.

Janis, I. L. (1983). *Group think*. Boston: Hougton Mifflin.

Jansen, F. E. (1983). The medical system as an aspect of culture and some acculturative effects of western cross-culture medical services. *South African Journal of Ethnology*, 6, 11–17.

Jegede, O. J. (1999). Science education in nonwestern cultures: Toward a theory of collateral learning. In L. M. Semali & J. L. Kincheloe (Eds.), *What is indigenous knowledge? Voices from the academy* (pp. 119–142). New York: Falmer Press.

Jenni, O. G., & O'Connor, B. B. (2005). Children's sleep: An interplay between culture and biology. *Pediatrics*, 115(1), 204–216.

Jobanputra, R., & Furnham, A. (2005). British Gujarati Indian immigrants' and British Caucasians' beliefs about health and illness. *International Journal of Social Psychiatry*, 51(4), 350–364.

Karp, I. (1986). Laughter at marriage: Subversion in performance. In D. Parkin (Ed.), *The transformation of African marriage*. London: International African Institute.

Kim, H. S., Sherman, D. K., & Taylor, S. E. (2008). Culture and social support. *American Psychologist*, 63(6), 518–526.

Kimmel, P. R. (1994). Cultural perspectives on international negotiation. *Journal of Social Issues*, 50(1), 179–196.

Kitayama, S., & Uchida, Y. (2003). Explicit self-criticism and implicit self-regard: Evaluating self and friend in two cultures. *Journal of Experimental Social Psychology*, 39, 476–482.

Kleinman, A. (1981). *Patients and healers in the context of culture*. Berkeley, CA: University of California Press.

Kline, S. L., Horton, B., & Zhang, S. (2008). Communicating love: Comparisons between American and East Asian university students. *International Journal of Intercultural Relations*, 32, 200–214.

Klonoff, E. A., & Landrine H. (1996). Belief in healing powers of prayer: prevalence and health correlates for African-Americans. *The Western Journal of Black Studies*, 20(4), 207–210.

Kohlberg, L. (1976). Moral stages and moralization: The cognitive-developmental approach. In T. Lickona (Ed.), *Moral development and behavior*. New York: Holt, Rinehart and Winston.

Kosmitzki, C. (1996). The reaffirmation of cultural identity in cross-cultural encounters. *Personality and Social Psychology Bulletin*, 22, 238–248.

Kottak, C. P. (2008). *Cultural anthropology* (12th ed.). Boston: McGraw Hill.

Kumari, R. (1988). *Female sexuality in Hinduism.* Delhi: Joint Women's Programme by ISPCK.

Kunda, Z. (1999). *Social cognition: Making sense of people.* Cambridge, MA: MIT Press.

La Roche, M. J. (2002). Psychotherapeutic considerations in treating Latinos. *Harvard Review of Psychiatry, 10,* 115–122.

LaFromboise, T., Coleman, H. L., & Gerton, J. (1993). Psychological impact of biculturalism: evidence and theory. *Psychological Bulletin, 114,* 395–412.

Lam, T. K., McPhee, S. J., Mock, J., Wong, C., Doan, H. T., Nguyen, T., et al. (2003). Encouraging Vietnamese-American women to obtain pap tests through lay health worker outreach and media education. *Journal of General Internal Medicine, 18*(7), 516–524.

Lammers, C. J., & Hickson, D. J. (Eds.). (1979). *Organizations alike and unlike: International and interinstitutional studies in the sociology of organizations.* London: Routledge & Kegan Paul.

Landrine, H., & Klonoff, E. A. (1992). Cultural and health-related schemas: a review and proposal for interdisciplinary integration. *Health Psychology, 11*(4), 267–276.

Landrine, H., & Klonoff, E. A. (1994). Cultural diversity in causal attributions for illness: The role of the supernatural. *Journal of Behavior Medicine, 17*(2), 181–193.

Lang, S. (2005). *Interracial relationships are on the increase in U.S., but decline with age, Cornell study finds.* Retrieved September 27, 2009 from www.news.cornell.edu/stories/Nov05/interracial.couples.SSL.html.

Lange, C. G. (1922) (Original work published 1885). The emotions: A psychophysiological study. In C. G. Lange & W. James (Eds.), *Psychology classics* (Vol. 1). Baltimore: Williams & Wilkins.

Laroia, N., & Sharma, D. (2006). The religious and cultural bases for breastfeeding practices among the Hindus. *Breastfeeding Medicine, 1*(2), 94–98.

Latz, S., Wolf, A. W., & Lozoff, B. (1999). Cosleeping in context: Sleep practices and problems in young children in Japan and the United States. *Archives of Pediatrics and Adolescent Medicine, 153*(4), 339–346.

Laumann, E. O., Nicolosi, A., Glasser, D. B., Paik, A., Gingell, C., Moreira, E., et al. (2005). Sexual problems among women and men aged 40 to 80 years: Prevelence and correlates identified in the Global Study of Sexual Attitudes and Behaviors. *International Journal of Impotence Research 17,* 39–57.

Lawson, H. M., & Leck, K. (2006). Dynamics of internet dating. *Social Science Computer Review, 24*(2), 189–208.

Leach, M. L. (1975). The effect of training in the pictorial depth perception of Shona children. *Journal of Cross-Cultural Psychology, 6,* 457–470.

Leclere, F. B., Jensen, L., & Biddlecom, A. E. (1994). Health care utilization, family context, and adaptation among immigrants to the United States. *J Health Soc Behav, 35*(4), 370–384.

Lee, S. (1995). Reconsidering the status of anorexia nervosa as a culture-bound syndrome. *Social Science & Medicine, 42,* 21–34.

Lee S., Sobal, J., & Frongillo, E. A. (2003). Comparison of models of acculturation: the case of Korean-Americans. *Journal of Cross-Cultural Psychology 34,* 282–296.

Leff, S. S., Power, T. J., Costigan, T. E., & Manz, P. H. (2003). Assessing the climate of the playground and lunchroom: Implications for bullying prevention programming. *School Psychology Review, 32,* 418–430.

Lehman, D. R., Chiu, C., & Schaller, M. (2004). Psychology and culture. *Annual Review of Psychology, 55,* 689–714.

Lessard, G., & Ku, L. (2003). Gaps in coverage for children in immigrant families. *Future Child, 13*(1), 101–115.

Levin, S. J., Like, R. C., & Gottlieb, J. E. (2000). ETHNIC: A framework for culturally competent clinical practice. In Appendix: Useful clinical interviewing mnemonics. *Patient Care, 34*(9), 188–189.

Levine, R., Sato, S., Hashimoto, T., & Verma, J. (1995). Love and marriage in eleven cultures. *Journal of Cross-Cultural Psychology, 26,* 554–571.

Lewin, S. A., Dick, J., Pond, P., Zwarenstein, M., Aja, G., van Wyk, B., et al. (2005). Lay health workers in primary and community health care. *Cochrane Database of Systematic Reviews (1, Art. No.: CD004015).*

Lewis, M. (1989). Culture and biology: The role of temperamental factors. In P. R. Zelazo & R. G. Barr (Eds.), *Challenges to developmental paradigms: Implications for theory, assessment, and treatment* (pp. 203–223). Hillsdale, NJ: Lawrence Erlbaum Associates, Inc.

Li, F. P., & Pawlish, K. (1998). Cancers in Asian Americans and Pacific Islanders: Migrant Studies. *Asian Am Pac Isl J Health, 6*(2), 123–129.

Lia-Hoagberg, B., Rode, P., Skovholt, C. J., Oberg, C. N., Berg, C., Mullett, S., et al. (1990). Barriers and motivators to prenatal care among low-income women. *Social Science & Medicine, 30*(4), 487–495.

Likert, R. (1967). *The human organization: Its management and values.* New York: McGraw-Hill.

Lincoln, Y., & Guba, E. G. (2000). Paradigmatic controversies, contradictions, and emerging conflicts. In N. K. Denzin & Y. Lincoln (Eds.), *Handbook of qualitative research* (pp. 163–188). Thousand Oaks, CA: Sage.

Linley, P. A., & Joseph, S. (Eds.). (2004). *Positive psychology in practice.* Hoboken, NJ: John Wiley & Sons.

Liu, Z., Shilkret, K. L., Tranotti, J., Freund, C. G., & Finelli, L. (1998). Distinct trends in tuberculosis morbidity among foreign-born and US-born persons in New Jersey, 1986 through 1995. *Am J Public Health, 88*(7), 1064–1067.

Loue, S. (Ed.). (1998). *Handbook of immigrant health.* New York: Plenum Press.

Ludema, J. D., Whitney, D., Mohr, B. J., & Griffin, T. J. (2003). *The appreciative inquiry summit: A practitioner's guide for leading large-group change.* San Francisco: Berrett-Koehler.

Lustig, S. L., Weine, S. M., Saxe, G. N., & Beardslee, W. R. (2004). Testimonial psychotherapy for adolescent refugees: A case series. *Transcultural Psychiatry, 41*(1), 31–45.

Lyubomirksy, S., Sheldon, K. M., & Schkade, D. (2005). Pursuing happiness: The architecture of sustainable change. *Review of General Psychology, 9*, 111–131.

McCann, D., & Delmonte, H. (2005). Lesbian and gay parenting: babes in arms or babes in the woods? *Sexual & Relationship Therapy, 20*(3), 333–347.

McCargar, D. F. (1993). Teacher and student role expectations: Cross-cultural differences and implications. *Modern Language Journal, 77*(2), 197–207.

McCrae, R. R. (2001). Trait psychology and culture: Exploring intercultural comparisons. *Journal of Personality, 69*(6), 819–848.

McIntosh, P. (1988). Working paper 189. *White privilege and male privilege: A personal account of coming to see correspondences through work in women's studies.* Retrieved September 27, 2009 from: http://www.iub.edu/~tchsotl/part2/McIntosh%20White%20Privilege.pdf

McKenna, E. (2006). *Business psychology and organisational behaviour: A student's handbook.* Hove, UK: Psychology Press.

McLeod, K. A. (1984). Multiculturalism and multicultural education: Policy and practice. In R. Samuda, J. W. Berry & M. Laferriere (Eds.), *Multiculturalism in Canada: Social and educational perspectives* (pp. 30–49). Toronto: Allyn and Bacon.

Maccoby, E. E. (1998). *The two sexes: Growing up apart, coming together.* Cambridge, MA: Harvard University Press.

Madge, C. (1998). Therapeutic landscapes of the Jola, The Gambia, West Africa. *Health Place, 4*(4), 293–311.

Magen, Z. (1998). *Exploring adolescent happiness: Commitment, purpose, and fulfillment*. Thousand Oaks, CA: Sage.

Management of Social Transformations Programme (MOST) (1995). *Multiculturalism: A policy response to diversity*. Paris: UNESCO.

Mardiros, M. (2001). Reconnecting communities through community-based action research. *International Journal of Mental Health*, 30(2), 58–78.

Marín, G., & Marín, B. V. (1991). *Research with Hispanic populations* (Vol. 23). Thousand Oaks, CA: Sage.

Markus, H., & Kitayama, S. (1991). Culture and the self: Implications for cognition, emotion, and motivation. *Psychological Review*, 98, 224–253.

Martín-Baró, I. (1994). *Writings for a liberation psychology*. Cambridge, MA: Harvard University Press.

Martin, P. L., & Midgley, E. (2003). *Immigration: Shaping and reshaping America*. Washington, DC: Population Reference Bureau.

Matsumoto, D. (1994). *People: Psychology from a cultural perspective*. Pacific Grove, CA: Brooks/Cole.

Matsumoto, D., & Juang, L. (2008). *Culture and psychology (4th ed.)*. Florence, KY: Wadsworth, Cengage Learning.

Matsumoto, D., LeRoux, J., Ratzlaff, C., Tatani, H., Uchida, H., Kim, C., et al. (2001). Development and validation of a measure of intercultural adjustment potential in Japanese sojourners: The Intercultural Adjustment Potential Scale (ICAPS). *International Journal of Intercultural Relations*, 25, 483–510.

Mead, H., Cartwright-Smith, L., Jones, K., Ramos, C., Woods, K., & Siegel, B. (2008). Racial and ethnic disparities in U.S. health care: A chartbook. New York: Commonwealth Fund.

Mead, M. (1978). *Culture and commitment*. Garden City, NY: Anchor.

Meaning of Work International Research Team (MOW) (1987). *The meaning of working*. London: Academic Press.

Merriam, S. B., Caffarella, R. S., & Baumgartner, L. M. (2007). *Learning in adulthood: A comprehensive guide (3rd ed.)*. San Francisco: John Wiley & Sons, Inc.

Merritt, A. (2000). Culture in the cockpit: Do Hofstede's dimensions replicate? *Journal of Cross-Cultural Psychology*, 31, 283–301.

Messenger, J. C. (1993). Sex and repression in an Irish folk community. In D. N. Suggs & A. W. Miracle (Eds.), *Culture and human sexuality* (pp. 240–261). Pacific Grove, CA: Brooks/Cole.

Miller, L. (2006). The terrorist mind: I. A psychological and Political Analysis. *International Journal of Offender Therapy and Comparative Criminology*, 50(2), 121–138.

REFERENCES

Miller, N. B. (1982). Social work services to urban Indians. In J. Green (Ed.), *Cultural awareness in the human services*. Upper Saddle River, NJ: Prentice-Hall.

Miller, B. (2008). *Cultural anthropology in a globalizing world*. Boston: Pearson.

Minkler, M., & Wallerstein, N. (Eds.). (2003). *Community-based participatory research for health*. San Francisco: Jossey-Bass.

Mir, G., & Tovey, P. (2002). Cultural competency: Professional action and South Asian carers. *Journal of Management in Medicine, 16*(1), 7–19.

Misumi, J. (1984). Decision-making in Japanese groups and organizations. In B. Wilpert & A. Sorge (Eds.), *International perspectives on organizational democracy* (vol. II) (pp. 525–539). Chichester: Wiley.

Monroe, K., & Kreidie, L. (1997). The perspective of Islamic fundamentalists and the limits of Rational Choice Theory. *Political Psychology, 18*(1), 19–44.

Moseley, K. L., Clark, S. J., Gebremariam, A., Sternthal, M. J., & Kemper, A. R. (2006). Parents' trust in their child's physician: Using an adapted trust in physician scale. *Ambulatory Pediatrics, 6*(1), 58–61.

Moss, R. (1996). Dreaming with the Iroquois. *Dream Time, 13*(2), 6–7.

Muczyk, J. P., & Holt, D. T. (2008). Toward a cultural contingency model of leadership. *Journal of Leadership and Organizational Studies, 14*(4), 277–286.

Mulatu, M. S. (2000). Perceptions of mental and physical illness in Northwestern Ethiopia: Causes, treatments and attitudes. *Journal of Health Psychology, 4*, 531–549.

Murguía, A., Zea, M. C., Reisen, C. A., & Peterson, R. A. (2000). The development of the cultural health attributions questionnaire (CHAQ). *Cultural Diversity and Ethnic Minority Psychology, 6*(3), 268–283.

Nash, K. A. (2003). *Cultural competence: a guide for human service agencies* (Rev. ed.). Washington, DC: CWLA Press.

National Center for Cultural Competence (NCCP) (2004). *Bridging the cultural divide in health care settings: The essential role of cultural broker programs*. Retrieved May 10, 2007 from http://www11.georgetown.edu/research/gucchd/nccc/documents/Cultural_Broker_Guide_English.pdf

Neto, F., Mullet, E., Deschamps, J. C., Barros, J., Benvindo, R., Camino, L., et al. (2000). Cross-cultural variations in attitudes toward love. *Journal of Cross-Cultural Psychology, 31*(5), 626–635.

News-Medical.Net (2008). *Denmark the happiest nation in the world, Zimbabwe the unhappiest*. June 30, 2008. Retrieved September 29, 2009 from http://www.news-medical.net/net/news/2008/ob/30/39599.aspx

Noh, S., & Kaspar, V. (2003). Diversity and immigrant health. In P. Anisef & M. Lamphier (Eds.), *The world in a city*. Toronto: Buffalo: University of Toronto Press.

Noller, P., & Feeney, J. A. (Eds.). (2006). *Close relationships: Functions, forms, and processes*. New York: Psychology Press.

Nuestra Communidad Sana (NCS) (n. d.). Lay health promoters. Retrieved September 29, 2009 from http://community.gorge.net/ncs/background/promoters.htm

O'Malley, J. M., & Chamot, A. U. (1990). *Learning strategies in second language acquisition*. Cambridge: Cambridge University Press.

Offer, D., Ostrov, E., Howard, K. I., & Atkinson, R. (1988). *The teenage world: Adolescents' self-image in ten countries*. New York: Plenum.

Okitikpi, T., & Aymer, C. (2003). Social work with African refugee children and their families. *Child and Family Social Work*, 8, 213–222.

Okun, B. F., Fried, J., & Okun, M. L. (1999). *Understanding diversity: A Learning-as-Practice Primer*. Pacific Grove, CA: Brooks/Cole Publishing Company.

Olowu, A. A. (1990). The self-concept in cross-cultural perspective. In A. A. Olowu (Ed.), *Contemporary issues in self-concept studies*. Ibadan, Kenya: Shaneson C.I. Ltd.

Oyserman, D. (1993). The lens of personhood: Viewing the self and others in a multicultural society. *Journal of Personality and Social Psychology*, 65(5), 993–1009.

Oyserman, D., Gant, L., & Ager, J. (1995). A socially contextualized model of African American identity: Possible selves and school persistence. *Journal of Personality and Psychology*, 69(6), 1216–1232.

Padilla, M. B., Hirsch, J. S., Muñoz-Laboy, M., Sember, R. E., & Parker, R. G. (2007). Introduction: Cross-cultural reflections on an intimate intersection. In M. B. Padilla, J. S. Hirsch, M. Muñoz-Laboy, R. E. Sember & R. G. Parker (Eds.), *Love and globalization: Transformations of intimacy in the contemporary world* (pp. ix–xxi). Nashville, TN: Vanderbilt University Press.

Page, S. E. (2007). *The difference: How the power of diversity creates better groups, firms, schools, and societies*. Princeton, NJ: Princeton University Press.

Parham, T. A., & Helms, J. E. (1985). Relation of racial identity attitudes to self-actualization and affective status of Black students. *Journal of Counseling Psychology*, 32, 431–440.

Paxton, S. J., Schutz, H. K., Wertheim, E. H., & Muir, S. L. (1999). Friendship clique and peer influences on body image concerns, dietary restraint, extreme weight-loss behaviors, and binge eating in adolescent girls. *Journal of Abnormal Psychology, 108*(2), 255–268.

Payne, R. K., DeVol, P. E., & Smith, T. D. (2006). *Bridges out of poverty: Strategies for professionals and communities (Rev. ed.).* Highlands, TX: Aha Process, Inc.

Peat, M. (1997). *Community-based rehabilitation.* London: Saunders.

Pérez, M. A., & Luquis, R. R. (2008). *Cultural competence in health education and health promotion.* San Francisco, CA: Jossey-Bass.

Peterson, C., & Seligman, M. E. P. (2004). *Character strengths and virtues: A handbook and classification.* Oxford: Oxford University Press.

Phinney, J. S. (1992). The multigroup ethnic identity measure: A new scale for use with diverse groups. *Journal of Adolescent Research, 7*(2), 156–176.

Phinney, J. (2000). Identity formation across cultures: The interaction of personal, societal, and historical change. *Human Development, 43,* 27–31.

Piaget, J. (1972). Intellectual evolution from adolescence to adulthood. *Human Development, 15,* 1–12.

Pines, A. M. (2001). The role of gender and culture in romantic attraction. *European Psychologist, 6*(2), 96–102.

Pinker, S. (1995). *The language instinct: How the mind creates language.* New York: HarperCollins.

Plant, E. A., Hyde, J. S., Keltner, D., & Devine, P. G. (2000). The gender stereotyping of emotions. *Psychology of Women Quarterly, 24,* 81–92.

Polyani, M. (2001). Toward common ground and action on repetitive strain injuries: An assessment of a future search conference. *Journal of Applied Behavioral Sciences, 37*(4), 465–487.

Pontius, A. A. (1997). Lack of sex differences among east Ecuadorian school children on geometric figure rotation and face drawings. *Perceptual and Motor Skills, 85*(1), 72–74.

Portes, A. (1998). Social capital: Its origins and applications in modern society. *Annual Review of Sociology, 24,* 1–24.

Prabhu, J. (2001). Some challenges facing multiculturalism in a globalized world. *ReVision, 24*(1), 30–38.

Prochaska, J. O., & Norcross, J. C. (2003). *Systems of psychotherapy: a transtheoretical analysis* (5th ed.). Pacific Grove, CA: Brooks/Cole Pub.

Putnam, R. (2000). *Bowling alone: The collapse and revival of American community.* New York: Simon and Schuster.

Rao, V., & Rao, V. (1985). Sex-role attitudes across two cultures: United States and India. *Sex Roles, 13*(11–12), 607–624.

Rathus, S., Nevid, J., & Fischer-Rathus, L. (1993). *Human sexuality in a world of diversity.* Boston: Allyn & Bacon.

Reason, P., & Bradbury, H. (Eds.). (2008). *The SAGE handbook of action research: Participative inquiry and practice* (2nd ed.). Los Angeles, CA: Sage.

Reichers, A. E., & Schneider, B. H. (1990). Climate and culture: An evolution of constructs. In B. H. Schneider (Ed.), *Organizational climate and culture* (pp. 5–39). San Francisco: Jossey-Bass.

Reiter, M., Krause, J., & Stirlen, A. (2005). Intercouple dating on a college campus. *College Student Journal, 39*(3), 449–454.

Renshon, S. (1989). Psychological perspectives on theories of adult development and the political socialization of leaders. In R. Sigel (Ed.), *Political learning in adulthood: A sourcebook of theory and research*. Chicago: University of Chicago Press.

Reynolds, A. L. (2001). Multidimensional cultural competence: Providing tools for transforming psychology. *The Counseling Psychologist, 29*(6), 833–841.

Richmond, A. (1993). Reactive migration: Sociological perspectives on refugee movements. *Journal of Refugee Studies, 6*, 7–24.

Robbins, S. R. (1987). *Organization theory: Structure, design and applications*. Englewood Cliffs, NJ: Prentice-Hall.

Robins, L. S., Fantone, J. C., Hermann, J., Alexander, G. L., & Zweifler, A. J. (1998). Improving cultural awareness and sensitivity training in medical school. *Acad Med, 73*(10 Suppl), S31–34.

Romano, D. (2008). *Intercultural marriage: Promises and pitfalls* (rev. ed.). Boston: Intercultural Press.

Rose, A. J., & Rudolph, K. D. (2006). A review of sex differences in peer relationship processes: Potential trade-offs for the emotional and behavioral development of girls and boys. *Psychological Bulletin, 132*, 98–131.

Royal Anthropological Institute (1951). *Notes and queries on anthropology* (6th ed.). London: Routledge and Kegan Paul.

Rudy, D., & Grusec, J. (2001). Correlates of authoritarian parenting in individualist and collectivist cultures and implications for understanding the transmission of values. *Journal of Cross-Cultural Psychology, 32*(2), 202–212.

Saha, S., Komaromy, M., Koepsell, T. D., & Bindman, A. B. (1999). Patient-physician racial concordance and the perceived quality and use of health care. *Archives of Internal Medicine, 159*, 997–1004.

Samovar, L. A., & Porter, R. E. (2004). *Communication between cultures* (5th ed.). Belmont, CA: Wadsworth Thompson Learning.

Saraswathi, T. S. (1999). Adult-child continuity in India: Is adolescence a myth or an emerging reality? In T. S. Saraswathi (Ed.), *Culture, socialization and human development: Theory, research and applications in India* (pp. 213–232). New Delhi: Sage.

Scarr, S. (1993). Biological and cultural diversity: The legacy of Darwin for development. *Child Development, 64*, 1333–1353.

Schachter, F. F., Fuchs, M. L., Bijur, P. E., & Stone, R. K. (1989). Cosleeping and sleep problems in Hispanic-American urban young children. *Pediatrics, 84*(3), 522–530.

Schein, E. H. (2004). *Organizational culture and leadership* (3rd ed.). San Francisco: Jossey-Bass.

Schlegel, A., & Barry, H. (1991). *Adolescence: An anthropological enquiry.* New York: Free Press.

Schulze, P., Harwood, R., & Schoelmerich, A. (2001). Feeding practices and expectations among middle-class Anglo and Puerto Rican mothers of 12-month old infants. *Journal of Cross-Cultural Psychology, 32*(4), 397–406.

Scott, J. (1991). *Social network analysis: A handbook.* London: Sage.

Seeman, T. E. (1996). Social ties and health: The benefits of social integration. *Annals of Epidemiology, 6*, 442–451.

Segall, M. H., Campbell, D. T., & Herskovits, M. J. (1966). *The influence of culture on visual perception.* Indianapolis, IN: Bobbs-Merrill.

Segall, M. H., Dasen, P. R., Berry, J. W., & Poortinga, Y. H. (1999). *Human behavior in global perspective.* Boston: Allyn & Bacon.

Seligman, M. E. P. (2002). *Authentic happiness: Using the new positive psychology to realize your potential for lasting fulfillment.* New York: Simon and Schuster.

Shane, S., Venkataraman, S., & MacMillan, I. (1995). Cultural differences in innovation championing strategies. *Journal of Management, 21*(5), 931–952.

Shiraev, E., & Levy, D. (2010). *Cross-cultural psychology: Critical thinking and contemporary applications* (4th ed.). Boston, MA: Allyn & Bacon.

Short, K. H., & Johnston, C. (1997). Stress, maternal distress, and children's adjustment following immigration: the buffering role of social support. *J Consult Clin Psychol, 65*(3), 494–503.

Shweder, R. (1991). *Thinking through cultures.* Cambridge, MA: Harvard University Press.

Siegel, J. E., Horan, S. A., & Teferra, T. (2001). Health and health care status of African-born residents of Metropolitan Washington, DC. *Journal of Immigrant Health, 3*(4), 213–224.

Silverthorne, C. P. (2005). *Organizational psychology in cross-cultural perspective*. New York: New York University Press.

Sinha, D. (1980). *The nurturant task leader*. New Delhi: Concept Publishing House.

Sinha, D. (1984). A model of effective leadership styles in India. *International Studies of Management and Organization, 14*, 86–98.

Sinha, D. (1993). Indigenization of psychology in India and its relevance. In U. Kim & J. W. Berry (Eds.), *Indigenous psychologies: Research and experience in cultural context* (pp. 30–43). Newbury Park, CA: Sage.

Skinner, B. F. (1953). *Science and human behavior*. New York: The Free Press.

Smart, J. F., & Smart, D. W. (1995). Acculturative stress: The experience of the Hispanic immigrant. *Counseling Psychologist, 23*, 25–42.

Smedley, B. D., Stith, A. Y., & Nelson, A. R. (Eds.). (2003). *Unequal treatment: Confronting racial and ethnic disparities in healthcare*. Washington, DC: National Academies Press.

Smith, A. G. (2008). The implicit motives of terrorist groups: How the needs for affiliation and power translate into death and destruction. *Political Psychology, 29*(1), 55–75.

Smith, D. E., & Reynolds, T. E. (1992). Adolescents' self image: A cross-cultural perspective. *Child Study Journal, 22*, 303–315.

Snowden, L. (2001). Social embeddedness and psychological well-being among African Americans and Whites. *American Journal of Community Psychology, 29*(4), 519–536.

Sonko, S. (1994). Family and culture in sub-Saharan Africa. *International Social Sciences Journal, 46*, 397–411.

Sorrell, J. H. (2006). The pleasure of dissent: A critical theory of psychotherapy as an emancipatory practice. *American Journal of Psychotherapy, 60*(2), 131–145.

Sparrow, L. M. (2000). Beyond multicultural man: Complexities of identity. *Journal of Intercultural Relations, 24*, 173–201.

Spearman, C. E. (1927). *The abilities of man*. New York: Macmillan.

Spector, R. E. (2004). *Cultural diversity in health and illness* (6th ed.). Upper Saddle River, NJ: Prentice Hall.

Spiro, M. E. (1993). Is the Western conception of the self 'peculiar' within the contexts of world cultures? *Ethos, 21*, 107–153.

Srivastava, R. (2007). *The healthcare professional's guide to clinical cultural competence*. Toronto: Mosby Elsevier.

Stainton Rogers, W. (1991). *Explaining health and illness: An exploration of diversity*. London: Wheatsheaf.

Stanton, B. F., Aronson, R., Borgatti, S., Galbraith, J., & Feigelman, S. (1993).

Urban adolescent high-risk sexual behavior: Corroboration of focus group discussions through pile-sorting. The AIDS Youth Research Team. *AIDS Education & Prevention*, 5(2), 162–174.

Steinberg, L., & Morris, A. S. (2001). Adolescent development. *Annual Review of Psychology*, 52, 83–110.

Stephens, W. N. (1963). *The family in cross-cultural perspective*. New York: Holt, Rinehart & Winston.

Sternberg, R. J. (1986). *Intelligence applied: Understanding and increasing our intellectual skills*. New York: Harcourt Brace Jovanovich.

Sternberg, R. J. (1988). Triangulating love. In R. J. Sternberg & M. L. Barnes (Eds.), *The psychology of love* (pp. 119–138). New Haven, CT: Yale University Press.

Suárez-Orozco, C., & Suárez-Orozco, M. M. (2001). *Children of immigration*. Cambridge, MA: Harvard University Press.

Sue, D. W. (2001). Multidimensional facets of cultural competence. *The Counseling Psychologist*, 29(6), 790–821.

Sue, D. W., & Sue, D. (2003). *Counseling the culturally diverse: theory and practice* (4th ed.). New York: John Wiley & Sons.

Super, C. M. H. S., Van Tijen, N., Van der Vlugt, E., Fintelman, M., & Dijkstra, J. (1996). The three R's of Dutch childrearing and the socialization of infant arousal. In S. Harkness & C. M. Super (Eds.), *Parents' cultural belief systems: Their origins, expressions, and consequences* (pp. 447–465). New York: Guilford.

Sussman, N. M. (2002). Sojourners to another country: the psychological roller-coaster of cultural transitions. In W. J. Lonner, D. L. Dinnel, S. A. Hayes & D. N. Sattler (Eds.), *Online readings in psychology and culture* (Unit 8, chapter 1). Retrieved September 27, 2009 from http://www.ac.wwu.edu/~culture/sussman.htm

Sy, S., & Schulenburg, J. (2005). Parent beliefs and children's achievement trajectories during the transition to school in Asian American and European American families. *International Journal of Behavioral Development*, 29(6), 505–515.

Tagaki, K. (2008). A social psychological approach to the ringi-system. *Applied Psychology*, 18(1), 53–57.

Tajfel, H. (1978). *Differentiation between social groups*. London: Academic Press.

Takaki, R. (1998). *Strangers from a different shore: A history of Asian Americans* (rev. ed.). Boston: Back Bay Books.

Tannen, D. (1990). *You just don't understand: Women and men in conversation*. New York: Morrow.

Tedlock, B. (1992). The role of dreams and visionary narratives in Mayan cultural survival. *Ethos*, *20*(4), 453–476.

Thamer, M., Richard, C., Casebeer, A. W., & Ray, N. F. (1997). Health insurance coverage among foreign-born US residents: the impact of race, ethnicity, and length of residence. *Am J Public Health*, *87*(1), 96–102.

Thomas, A., & Chess, S. (1977). *Temperament and development*. New York: Brunner/Mazel.

Thomas, D. C., & Inkson, K. (2004). *Cultural intelligence: People skills for global business*. San Francisco, CA: Berrett-Koehler.

Thomas, T. N. (1995). Acculturative stress in the adjustment of immigrant families. *Journal of Social Distress and the Homeless*, *4*(2), 131–142.

Torsch, V. L., & Xueqin Ma, G. (2000). Cross-Cultural Comparison of Health Perceptions, Concerns, and Coping Strategies among Asian and Pacific Islander American Elders. *Qualitative Health Research*, *10*(4), 471–489.

Triandis, H. C. (1989). The self and social behavior in differing cultural contexts. *Psychological Review*, *96*, 506–520.

Triandis, H. C. (2007). Culture and psychology: A history of the study of their relationship. In S. Kitayama & D. Cohen (Eds.), *Handbook of cultural psychology*. New York: The Guilford Press.

Triandis, H. C., Bontempo, R., Villareal, M. J., Asai, M., & Lucca, N. (1988). Individualism and collectivism: Cross-cultural perspectives on self-ingroup relationships. *Journal of Personality and Social Psychology*, *4*, 323–338.

Triandis, H. C., Dunnette, M. D., & Hough, L. M. (Eds.). (1994). *Handbook of industrial and organizational psychology* (Vol IV, 2nd ed.). Palo Alto, CA: Consulting Psychologists Press.

Trochim, W. (1989). An introduction to concept mapping for program planning and evaluation. *Evaluation and Program Planning*, *12*, 1–16.

Tuckman, B. (1965). Developmental sequence in small groups. *Psychological Bulletin*, *63*(6), 384–399.

U.S. Census Bureau (2008). *International data base*. Retrieved May 15, 2009 from http://www.census.gov/ipc/www/idb/

U.S. Department of Health & Human Services (2008). *The 2008 HHS poverty guidelines*. Retrieved September 27, 2009 from http://aspe.hhs.gov/poverty/08Poverty.shtml

UNAIDS (2008). *2008 Report on the global AIDS epidemic*. Retrieved July 1, 2009 from http://www.unaids.org/en/KnowledgeCentre/HIVData/GlobalReport/2008/

United Nations (2009). *The United Nations world water development report,*

WWDR (3rd ed.). Retrieved July 2, 2009, from http://www.unesco.org/water/wwap/wwdr/index.shtml

Valentin, S. R. (2005). Sleep in German infants – The 'cult' of independence. *Pediatrics*, *115*(1), 269–271.

Valsiner, J., & Rosa, A. (Eds.). (2007). *The Cambridge handbook of sociocultural psychology*. Cambridge, UK: Cambridge University Press.

Vamus, H., Klausner, R., Zerhouni, E., Acharya, T., Daar, A. S., & Singer, P. A. (2003). Grand challenges in global health. *Science*, *302*, 398–399.

Van de Poel, E., Hosseinpoor, A. R., Speybroeck, N., Van Ourti, T., & Vega, J. (2008). Socioeconomic inequality in malnutrition in developing countries. *Bulletin of the World Health Organization*, *86*(4), 241–320.

Van den Heuvel, H., Tellegen, G., & Koomen, W. (1992). Cultural differences in the use of psychological and social characteristics in children's self-understanding. *European Journal of Social Psychology*, *22*, 353–362.

Van der Zee, K. I., & Van Oudenhoven, J. P. (2001). The multicultural personality questionnaire: Reliability and validity of self- and other ratings of multicultural effectiveness. *Journal of Research in Personality*, *35*, 278–288.

Van Dyk, G. A. J., & Nefale, M. C. (2005). The split-ego experience of Africans: Ubuntu therapy as a healing alternative. *Journal of Psychotherapy Integration*, *15*(1), 48–66.

Van Hook, J., & Fix, M. (2000). A profile of the immigrant student population. In M. Fix & T. Clewell (Eds.), *Overlooked and Undeserved: Immigrant Children in U.S. Secondary Schools*. Washington, DC: The Urban Institute Press.

Vasquez, M. J. T. (1994). Latinas. In L. Comas-Diaz & B. Greene (Eds.), *Women of color: Integrating ethnic and gender identities in psychotherapy*. New York: The Guilford Press.

Vaughn, L. M. (2009). Familes and cultural competency: Where are we? *Family & Community Health*, *32*(3), 247–256.

Vaughn, L. M., & Phillips, R. (2009). Intercultural adjustment for cultural competence in shared context: 'The company we keep'. *The International Journal of Interdisciplinary Social Sciences*, *3*(11), 1–12.

Veenhoven, R. (2009). *World Database of Happiness. Distributional findings in nations*. Erasmus: University Rotterdam. Retrieved September 29, 2009 from http://worlddatabaseofhappiness.eur.nl

Verkuyten, M. (2005). *The social psychology of ethnic identity*. New York: Psychology Press.

Victoroff, J. (2005). The mind of the terrorist: A review and critique of psychological approaches. *Journal of Conflict Resolution*, *49*(1), 3–42.

Viste, T. T., & Ahtonen, M. (2007). Child-rearing values of Estonian and Finnish mothers and fathers. *Journal of Cross-Cultural Psychology*, 38(2), 137–155.

Vygotsky, L. S. (1978). *Mind in society: The development of higher psychological processes.* Cambridge, MA: Harvard University Press.

Ward, C. (1994). Culture and altered states of consciousness. In W. J. Lonner & R. Malpass (Eds.), *Psychology and culture.* Boston: Allyn & Bacon.

Ward, C. A., Bochner, S., & Furnham, A. (2001). *The psychology of culture shock* (2nd ed.). Hove, UK: Routledge.

Ward, R. (Ed.). (2003). *Foundations of osteopathic medicine* (2nd ed.). Philadelphia: Lippincot Williams and Wilkins.

Warheit, G. J., Vega, W. A., Auth, J., & Meinhardt, K. (1985). Mexican-American immigration and mental health: A comparative analysis of psychosocial stress and dysfunction. In W. A. Vega & M. R. Miranda (Eds.), *Stress and Hispanic mental health: Relating research to service delivery.* Bethesda, MD: National Institute of Mental Health.

Weeks, M. R., Clair, S., Borgatti, S. P., Radda, K., & Schensul, J. J. (2002). Social networks of drug users in high-risk sites: Finding the connections. *AIDS and Behavior*, 6(2), 193–206.

Weisbord, M., & Janoff, S. (2000). *Future search: An action guide to finding common ground in organizations and communities.* San Francisco: Berrett-Koehler Publishers.

Welles-Nystrom, B. (2005). Co-sleeping as a window into Swedish culture: Considerations of gender and health care. *Scandinavian Journal of Caring Sciences*, 19(4), 354–360.

Whaley, A. L., & Davis, K. E. (2007). Cultural competence and evidence-based practice in mental health services. *American Psychologist*, 62(6), 563–574.

Wheeler, D., & Janis, I. L. (1980). *A practical guide for making decisions.* New York: Free Press.

White, A. (2007). A global projection of subjective well-being: A challenge to positive psychology? *Psychtalk*, 56, 17–20.

Whitty, M. T., & Carr, A. N. (2006). *Cyberspace romance: The psychology of online relationships.* Basingstoke: Palgrave Macmillan.

Williams, J., & Best, D. L. (1982). *Measuring sex stereotypes: A thirty-nation study.* Beverly Hills, CA: Sage.

Williams, J., & Best, D. L. (1990). *Measuring sex stereotypes: A multination study.* Beverly Hills, CA: Sage.

Willms, L., & St Pierre-Hansen, N. (2008). Integrating integrative medicine. *Canadian Family Physician*, 54(8), 1085–1087.

Wills, T. A. (1991). Social support and interpersonal relationships. In M. S. Clark (Ed.), *Prosocial behavior* (pp. 265–289). Thousand Oaks, CA: Sage.

Wilson, T. D., & Gilbert, D. T. (2005). Affective forecasting: Knowing what to want. *Current Directions in Psychological Science, 14*, 131–134.

Witkin, H. A., Dyk, R. B., Paterson, H. F., Goodenough, D. R., & Karp, S. (1962). *Psychological differentiation.* New York: Wiley.

World Health Organization (1978). *Primary health care: Report of the international conference in Alma Ata.* Geneva: WHO.

World Health Organization (1986). *Ottawa Charter for Health Promotion.* Ottawa, Ontario, Canada.

World Health Organization (2004). *The global burden of disease: 2004 update.* Retrieved July 2, 2009 from http://www.who.int/healthinfo/global_burden_disease/2004_report_update/en

Yan, M. C., & Lam, C. M. (2009). Intersecting social capital and Chinese culture: Implications for services assisting unemployed youths. *International Social Work, 52*(2), 195–207.

Yan, W., & Gaier, L. E. (1994). Causal attributions for college success and failure: An Asian-American comparison. *Journal of Cross-Cultural Psychology, 25*, 146–158.

Yao, L. E. (1985). A comparison of family characteristics of Asian American and Anglo American high achievers. *International Journal of Comparative Sociology, 26*(3–4), 198–206.

Yeh, R.-S., & Lawrence, J. J. (1995). Individualism and Confucian dynamism: A note on Hofstede's cultural root to economic growth. *Journal of International Business Studies, 26*(3), 655–669.

Zebrowitz-McArthur, L. (1988). Person perception in cross-cultural perspective. In M. H. Bond (Ed.), *Cross-cultural research and methodology series: Volume 11 The cross-cultural challenge to social psychology* (pp. 245–265). Beverly Hills, CA: Sage.

Zuñiga, M. E. (1991). 'Dichos' as metaphorical tools for resistant Latino clients. *Psychotherapy: Theory, Research, Practice, and Training, 28*, 480–483.

Glossary

abantu   Zulu word describing a humanized being.

absolutism   Paradigm that culture plays a limited role in human differences.

acculturative stress   Psychological effects of adapting to a new culture.

adab   Discipline of body, mind and spirit.

altered states of consciousness (ASC)   Include mystical perceptual and sensory experiences such as meditation, hypnosis, trance, and possession.

alternation   The act of switching between two or more cultural identities, depending upon the situation.

amae   Feature of the Japanese personality referring to the passive, childlike dependence of one person on another.

amulet   An object that protects its owner.

androgyny   Possession and expression of both masculine and feminine characteristics.

appreciative inquiry summit   Process by which an organization acknowledges its positive traits and works to make changes for the future.

arranged marriages   Matrimony set up by someone other than the people getting married.

assimilation   Acculturation strategy that involves relinquishing one's culture and seeking out interactions with dominant culture.

asylum seeker   Someone forced to leave home to find sanctuary from perceived danger or persecution.

ataques de nervios   Latino culture-bound illness – nervous breakdowns.

attachment styles   Characterizes the relationship between infant and mother.

authoritarian parenting   Style of parenting in which parents are highly demanding, and yet not responsive to their children.

ayurvedic medicine   Indian system of medicine based on the idea that every human must have equal amounts of wind/spirit/air, bile, and phlegm.

back translation   Approach to address linguistic equivalence in tests involving the translation of the test into a different language(s) and then having a different person translate it back to the original language and repeated with the goal of semantic equivalence.

Berdache   Two-spirit people displaying mixed genders; from Native American and Canadian First Nations groups.

bicultural identity   Individuals belonging to two cultural groups.

biopsychosocial model   Model used in medicine emphasizing biological, psychological, and social factors in human functioning.

brainstorming   Techniques used to come up with ideas and make decisions.

bridewealth   The money a man pays to the family of his future wife.

cao gio   Asian medical practice of coin rubbing.

carpentered world hypothesis   Attributes Western susceptibility to misjudging the length of lines in the Ponzo illusion to being used to seeing geometric shapes (buildings, etc.) and subsequently applying perspective to even nonrectangular shapes.

cheong   Korean concept that means human affection.

clitordiction   Removal of the clitoris.

cognitive misers   Describes people who use stereotypes and generalizations about others and their behaviour in order to simplify their view of the world.

cognitive style   The way a person thinks.

collateral households   Families including siblings with their spouses and children.

collectivism   Perspective that self and society are inextricably linked.

community-based participatory research A participatory approach to research that engages community members in health research initiatives.

compartmentalization When two or more cultural identities are kept separate.

Computer mediated relationships Internet dating.

concept mapping Organizational method in which ideas and their relationship to other ideas are represented graphically.

confucian dynamism Organizational mindset in Asia that values unequal distribution of power, perseverance, respect for tradition, and thriftiness.

conscientization Freire's terms meaning the awakening of critical consciousness.

constructivism Philosophy that knowledge is relative and reality is socially constructed.

co-sleeping Bed-sharing between parents and children.

critical theory Philosophy that knowledge is subjective and bound by values and sociocultural and historical context.

cross-cultural psychology The study of human behaviour as it is affected by cultures in general, with data collected across many different cultures.

cultural awareness Consciousness of cultural similarities and differences.

cultural brokers Liaisons working to bridge connections between patients and health care providers.

cultural competence The ability of an individual to reflect upon his or her own biases, understand people from different cultures, and develop effective strategies for sensitive and effective cross-cultural interaction.

cultural diversity Cultural differences.

cultural empathy Ability to empathize with members from different cultural groups.

cultural frame switching The process of switching between two or more culturally prescribed thoughts and behaviours.

cultural identity An individual's feeling of belonging within a specific cultural group.

cultural intelligence The ability to be effective within different cultural contexts.

cultural mixtures approach Psychological approach presented by Hermans and Kempen (1998) that emphasizes the need to study intersections in culture to truly understand its effect on people.

cultural psychology The study of human behaviour as it is affected by a specific culture.

cultural reaffirmation Crystallization of the native culture.

cultural sensitivity Knowledge that cultural similarities and differences exist.

cultural world views Belief systems about a person's culture.

culture desire The force that motivates an individual to seek cultural competence.

culture shock The negative psychological and/or emotional effects of settling into an unfamiliar culture.

culture-bound syndromes Physical and mental illnesses that are unique to particular cultures and are influenced directly by cultural belief systems and other cultural factors.

delphi technique Problem-solving strategy developed to avoid face-to-face negotiation; ideas are submitted anonymously.

dhat Indian culture-bound syndrome characterized by fear of losing semen.

dichos/refranes Spanish proverbs/folklore sayings.

didactic teaching Style of instruction in which teachers lecture and children listen.

disability Physical impairment.

discrimination Enacted unjust behaviour resulting from prejudice.

diversity See cultural diversity.

ecological systems approach Model introduced by Urie Bronfenbrenner (1979) that describes how four 'layers' of a child's environment – each differing in their proximity to the child – affects the child's development.

emics Culture-specific principles or aspects of life that differ across cultures.

emotional stability Ability to stay calm while stressed.

equity attributions The attribution of health to moral behaviour.

ethnic identity Knowledge of belonging to a certain cultural group, coupled with the value attached to this inclusion.

ethnicity Cultural heritage of a group of people with common ancestral origin, language, traditions, and often religion and geographic territory.

ethnocentrism The belief that your own ethnic or cultural group is better in comparison to others.

ethno-medical approach Belief that assumes that good deeds are rewarded and bad deeds are punished by some force or deity.

etics   Universal principles across cultures or aspects of behaviour that are consistent across cultures.

expanded family households   Families including non-nuclear relatives.

family bed   See co-sleeping.

family of orientation   Family in which a person is raised.

family of procreation   Family which a person creates when he or she marries and has children.

female genital mutilation   Female circumcision generally performed without anaesthesia.

five factor model of personality   Model of personality with five dimensions – extroversion, neuroticism, agreeableness, conscientiousness, and openness.

folk remedies   Treatments to cure a disease typically passed on through tradition (e.g., herbs used in teas; chicken soup to cure a cold).

folklore therapy   The use of cultural sayings/proverbs and cultural customs to convey helpful information in therapy.

future search conference   A large group planning meeting that brings a 'whole system' into the room to work on a task-focused agenda.

gender   Norms and expectations that are culturally assigned to men and women.

gender role socialization   The process of enculturating males and females into gender-based groups based on culturally prescribed behaviours and other social factors.

gender stereotypes   Generalizations made about women or men as a whole.

groupthink   A cohesive group's pattern of thinking in which alternative options are not considered in decision-making.

guanxi   Chinese cultural practice of nurturing and networking within social relations.

hadith   Islamic collection of sayings from the Prophet Muhammad.

healthy migrant phenomenon   The temporary health advantage that immigrants have been observed to have upon arriving to Westernized countries.

hegemony   When the dominant culture secures power over all other cultures by establishing the status quo.

hierbistas   Latino folk healers knowledgeable in herbal remedies.

high-context cultures   Cultures in which nothing needs to be stated directly; information is gleaned from situations.

hishkarma karma   Indian concept of detachment.

homogeneity   Similarity of characteristics within a group.

immigrant   Anyone who leaves his or her native country to establish residence in another country.

indigenous personalities   Personality characteristics understood within the context of a particular culture.

indigenous psychologies   Maintains the belief that a culture can only be fully understood by studying its social, historical, political, ideological, and religious factors.

individualism   Perspective that emphasizes the self as independent from society.

infibulations   The stitching together of the vulva.

integration   The blending of two cultures into one multicultural identity.

integrative medicine   Growing field of medicine that seeks to combine conventional and alternative medical practices.

intercultural adjustment   Becoming accustomed to a new culture.

international adoption   Adoption of a child across national borders.

lay health workers   People who provide public health care service to those who have typically been denied equitable and adequate health care – usually come from community with which they work. 'Lay Health Promoters have gone by many names including: Village Health Workers, Primary Health Care Workers, Indigenous Health Care Workers, Community Health Workers, Community Health Assistants, Community Health Representatives, Medical Auxiliaries, Rural Health Assistants, Community Health Aides, Brigadistas, Promotores y Promotoras de Salud, Indigenous Health Aides, Lay Health Advisors, Auxiliary Health Workers, Front Line Health Workers, Barefoot Doctors, Feldsher, Community Health Promoters, Kaders, Prokesa. These terms are not necessarily interchangeable, since each has its own practical, historical and political significance' (Nuestra Communidad Sana (NCS), n.d.).

learning styles   The way a person takes in new information.

levirate   When a man inherits a widow from his brother.

linguistic relativity   See Sapir–Whorf hypothesis.

low-context cultures   Cultures that use more explicit communication; less information is inferred compared with high-context cultures.

machismo   Regard for masculine ability.

macho   Male.

mal de ojo   Known as 'evil eye' in Latin American cultures; designates a syndrome triggered by the admiring glance of an adult over a child (evil eye is also found in other cultures).

marginalization   Acculturation strategy that involves relinquishing one's culture and avoiding contact with dominant culture.

marianismo   Sanctification of women/reverence of the Virgin Mary.

matching hypothesis   Attraction theory that posits that people who are equal in physical attractiveness select each other as partners.

meditation   Deepened state of relaxation or awareness.

melting pot   Perspective that sees that minorities are absorbed completely into the dominant culture.

migration motivation   Reason for migration.

monocultural organizations   Organizations that generally do not value diversity and their structures and policies reinforce privilege and power of dominant groups.

monogamy   Having a single romantic partner.

morita therapy   Japanese psychological therapy of social isolation.

mosaic   Perspective that argues that minority cultures retain their individual characteristics even as people assimilate into the dominant culture.

multicultural identity   Individuals belonging to multiple cultural groups.

multicultural organizations   Organizations that value diversity and aim to end discrimination and oppression.

multiculturalism   Idea that all cultural groups should be recognized as equal and that each cultural group is unique with its own set of shared values, norms, and customs that should be respected in their own right.

multigenerational family   Three or more generations of a family living together.

nationality   A person's country of origin.

nominal group technique   Group problem-solving process in which potential solutions are ranked from most to least promising.

nuclear household   Nuclear family composed of one adult couple with or without children.

nurturant-task leader   An authoritative father-figure who works toward a personal relationship with employees and offers guidance.

oligarchies   Organizations in which a few individuals have the majority of the power. Optical illusions like the Mueller–Lyer illusion (two lines with arrowheads pointing outward or inward).

organizational climate   The procedures and policies that characterize an organization.

organizational culture   The values that determine how members of an organization interact with others.

organizational structure   The distribution of roles and responsibilities within an organization.

osteopathic medicine   Branch of medicine that maintains that the body is a unit that possesses self-regulatory mechanisms, and that structure and function are interrelated.

participatory action research   A collaborative, partnership approach to research that equitably involves all stakeholders in all aspects of the research process.

pathic relationships   When two men of similar age share a relationship similar to marriage.

pluralism   Coexistence of different cultural groups.

polyandry   Marriage between one woman and more than one man.

polygamy   Matrimony in which an individual has multiple spouses.

polygyny   The marriage of one man with more than one woman.

Ponzo illusion   Two lines of the same length are set against two converging lines that look like a railroad track. The line on top appears longer because we interpret it as receding into the distance.

positivism   Philosophy that true knowledge is obtainable, verifiable and results from an objective reality.

possession   Invasion of the body by spirits.

post-positivism   Philosophy that knowledge of reality is imperfect and based on conjecture but can be examined through systematic inquiry and critical experimentation.

power distance   The degree of acceptance that power is distributed unequally.

prejudice   A usually negative and generally unjustified judgement of another person on the basis of his or her social or cultural group identity.

problem posing education   Freire's notion of authentic or liberating education.

proxemics   A form of nonverbal communication signifying distance between people.

psychological acculturation   The process of adjusting psychologically to a new culture.

qualitative research   Research that emphasizes inquiry and exploration through analysis of words, views of respondents, and the social construction of experience and meaning.

quantitative research   The measure of human behaviour comparatively through empirical means.

race A way to classify people based on physical characteristics; some have argued it is a social construct.

reciprocity hypothesis The opposite of the similarity hypothesis – proposes that 'opposites attract'.

refugee Someone forced to leave his or her native country to evade persecution.

relativism Paradigm that human variation is due to sociocultural factors.

ringi system Japanese decision-making process.

rites of passage Certain culture-specific experiences that mark the transition from child- to adulthood.

santeros Practitioners of Santería (Caribbean religion emphasizing saints).

Sapir–Whorf hypothesis Posits that language structure and function determine how speakers think.

schizophrenia Mental disorder exhibiting bizarre delusions.

self-actualization The 'peak' of Maslow's Hierarchy of Needs – the desire to reach one's full potential.

self-concept An individual's beliefs about him/herself.

self-esteem How people feel about themselves.

separation Acculturation strategy that involves maintaining one's culture and avoiding contact with dominant culture.

sex The defining of a person as either 'male' or 'female' based on physical characteristics.

Similarity hypothesis Attraction theory that posits that people seek out partners like themselves.

simpatia Mexican concept meaning avoidance of conflict.

Social capital Refers to the value of connections within and between various social networks.

social initiative The inclination to instigate social interactions.

social network A complex web of relationships among people.

social support Feeling of inclusion and of being loved that one experiences through relationships with others; can help combat negative effects of stress.

socialization The process by which a person develops to interiorize the norms and values of his or her culture.

sociocultural psychology The study of human behaviour as it is affected by culture and its resulting social practices.

sojourners People who visit a country with the intention of returning back to their native country.

somatization Physical ailments due to stress or emotional distress.

sororate   When two sisters are married to the same man.

stakeholder   Any individual or group affected by the actions of an organization.

stereotypes   Overgeneralized beliefs about people from social groups.

susto   Latin American culture-bound syndrome – when the soul flees the body after a frightening episode.

synergy   The creation of a new multicultural identity that is different than simply the combination of two cultures.

tarawads   Indian family compounds headed by an older woman and her brother.

temperament   A biologically based way of interacting with the world; specific to each individual.

testimonial therapy   Strategy used to gather information and help treat patients in a way that seeks to maintain patients' autonomy.

the world café   Brainstorming session during which invited stakeholders illustrate their ideas on paper tablecloths to initiate discussion and/or change.

third gender   Intermediate gender/sex between men and women.

traditional Chinese medicine   Branch of medicine that links health with equilibrium within the body.

trances   Mental states usually induced by singing or music in order to access the unconscious mind.

transgendered   A person who is neither a man or a woman or has elements of both males and females.

transnational adoption   See international adoption.

Turnim man   Alternative sexual category for a person with ambiguous sexuality or an intersexed person; from New Guinea.

ubuntu philosophy   South African Zulu philosophy that emphasizes the collective nature of human beings.

uncertainty avoidance   The degree to which people minimize uncertainty through rules and structure.

universalism   Paradigm that basic psychological processes are the same across cultures but that culture influences the different expressions and variations of behaviour.

validity   The extent to which an item or test measures what it purports to measure.

Western biomedical model   Perspective that posits that illness originates inside the body due to a specific, identifiable 'medical' cause or pathogen.

yang   The opposing, yet interrelated complement to the Chinese *yin* – symbolizes masculinity, light, and dominance.

yin   The opposing, yet interrelated complement to the Chinese *yang* – symbolizes femininity, darkness, and passivity.

zadruga   In Yugoslavia, several nuclear families living together.

Author Index

Abdullah, A. 164
Aboud, F. 134
Abreu, J. M. 101
Acharya, T. 157
Adams, F. 84
Adams, P. J. 148
Ager, J. 29
Aggarwal, N. 148
Åhman, E. 48
Ahtonen, M. 63
Ainsworth, M. D. S. 51
Aizenmann, N. 49
Aja, G. 154
Akande, D. 137, 138, 141
Akerblom, S. 191
Akiyama, H. 114
Alban, B. T. 198, 199
Alexander, G. L. 2
Allgeier, A. R. 125, 126
Allgeier, E. R. 125, 126
Allport, G. 10

American Psychiatric
    Association 146
Andia, G. 191
Angleitner, A. 57, 58
Anker, M. 146
Annandale, E. 141
Anthias, F. 30
Antonucci, T. C. 114
Appel, S. 143
Arends-Tóth, J. 108, 153
Aroian, K. J. 97
Aronson, R. 72
Asai, M. 77
Atkinson, D. R. 25, 26, 140
Atkinson, R. 55
Aune, K. 117
Aune, R. 117
Auth, J. 96, 98
Aviera, A. 156
Aycan, Z. 197, 200
Aylward, M. 77

Aymer, C. 95, 97

Bacon, M. 61
Bae, A. 112, 113, 114
Baguma, P. 137, 138, 141
Bakacsi, G. 191
Ball, H. L. 58
Bandura, A. 48
Barber, N. 48
Barros, J. 127
Barry, H. 55, 61
Bastug, S. 48
Baumgartner, L. M. 172, 174,
    176, 179, 180, 181
Bazron, B. 195, 196
Beal, A. C. 51
Beardslee, W. R. 156
Beauchamp, K. 148
Becker, A. 17
Belenky, M. F. 170
Bem, S. L. 39
Bendova, H. 191
Benet-Martínez, V. 30, 31, 100,
    101
Benjamin, M. P. 152
Bennett, J. M. 108, 178, 181
Bennett, M. J. 108, 178, 181
Benvindo, R. 127
Berg, C. 48
Berlin, E. A. 152
Bernal, H. 143
Berry, J. W. 3, 4, 6, 7, 19, 32, 35,
    37, 38, 46, 54, 67, 73, 94, 95,
    98, 99, 100, 108, 138, 139
Berz, K. 142
Best, D. L. 35
Betancourt, J. R. 102, 105, 106,
    150, 151, 152, 159
Bhaskar, B. 59

Biddlecom, A. E. 144
Bigby, J. 143, 160, 180
Bijur, P. E. 59
Bindman, A. B. 141
Bishop, R. 180, 181
Black, R. 158
Blaine, B. 9, 10, 19, 41, 70
Bleichrodt, N. 37
Bochner, S. 12, 23, 28, 94, 95,
    105, 107, 109, 184
Bolton, R. 123
Bond, M. 188
Bond, R. 7
Bontempo, R. 77
Boog, B. W. M. 27
Borgatti, S. P. 72, 73
Born, M. 37
Bornstein, M. H. 53
Bostok, J. 19
Brace, C. 8
Bradbury, H. 16, 19, 106
Breger, R. 124
Brehm, S. S. 105, 115
Brenner, R. A. 59
Brislin, R. W. 12, 29, 30, 37, 83,
    101, 104, 153
Brodbeck, F. C. 191
Brodyaga, L. 144
Bronfenbrenner, U. 46, 47, 68,
    73
Brookfield, S. 173, 176
Brooks, J. B. 60, 61
Brown, J. 199
Brown, S. 19
Bryce, J. 158
Brydon-Miller, M. 19
Budryte, D. 6
Bullock, M. 8
Bunker, B. B. 198, 199

Burgos-Ocasio, H. 38
Business Week 195
Buss, D. 115, 116
Byrne, D. 115

Cacioppo, J. T. 10, 104
Caffarella, R. S. 172, 174, 176,
    179, 180, 181
Caldwell, J. C. 40
Caldwell, P. 40
Cameron, R. 19
Camilleri, C. 38, 56
Camino, L. 127
Campbell, C. 17
Campbell, D. T. 84
Campinha-Bacote, J. 177
Cannon, W. B. 80
Carpo, R. H. 123
Carr, A. N. 130, 131
Carrillo, E. 140
Carrillo, J. E. 102, 105, 106, 152
Carroll, J. L. 117
Cartwright-Smith, L. 159
Casebeer, A. W. 144
Centers for Disease Control and
    Prevention 144
Chalmers, B. 139
Chamot, A. U. 86
Charalambous, N. 58
Cheetham, R. W. S. 140
Chen, J. 96, 160
Chen, S. 40
Chen, X. 68, 113, 131
Chess, S. 50
Child, I. 61
Chipfakacha, V. 140, 154
Chiu, C. 4, 5, 7, 19, 31, 100, 101
Choi, S.C. 32
Choi, S.H. 32

Chopra, A. S. 143
Chou, Y. 117
Choules, K. 173
Christakis, N. A. 72
Clair, S. 72
Clancy, C. M. 159
Clark, S. J. 141
Clarke, V. 41, 131
Clemens, J. D. 59
Clinchy, B. M. 170
Cochran, P. A. L. 16
Cohen, D. 15, 16, 19
Cohen, E. 148
Coleman, H. L. 29, 31
Committee on Community
    Health Services 144
Conn, P. 65
Consoli, A. J. 101
Cook, B. J. 180
Cook, D. 16
Coontz, S. 119
Cooper, J. E. 146
Cortesi, F. 59
Costigan, T. E. 19
Cousins, S. D. 23
Crawford, M. 37, 39, 60, 114,
    126, 148
Cross, R. 72, 73
Cross, T. 195, 196
Cross, W. E. 25, 27
Crystal, S. 16
Curry, R. H. 140
Cushner, K. 101
Cypers, S. J. 101

Daar, A. S. 157
Daibo, I. 117
Dalal, A. 138, 139
Das, A. 59

Dasen, P. R. 3, 4, 6, 7, 32, 35, 37, 38, 46, 54, 95, 99
Davenport, W. 127
Davidhizar, R. E. 134, 137
Davis, K. E. 154, 160
Davis, M. H. 12
Davis, R. B. 143
Dawson, J. 82
Dawson, K. 54
Dawson, R. 54
Daya, R. 154
De La Cancela, V. 140
de Munck, V. C. 49
Delbecq, A. L. 192
Delmonte, H. 65
Denmark, F. L. 35, 36, 39, 40, 42
Dennis, K. 195, 196
Deschamps, J. C. 127
Desjarlais, R. R. 87
Devi, S. 159
Devine, P. G. 36
DeVol, P. E. 41
Dhikav, V. 148
Dick, J. 154
Diener, C. 7
Diener, E. 77, 88, 89, 90
Diener, M. 7
Dijkstra, J. 53, 54
Directgov 122
Dixon, C. 142
Doan, H. T. 154
Doescher, M. P. 141
Doi, T. 32, 210
Doktor, R. 191
Dolea, C. 48
Donini-Lenhoff, F. G. 2
Draguns, J. G. 149
Dunnette, M. D. 187, 194
Dyk, R. B. 79

Eagley, A. 37
Earle, A. 49, 50
Earley, P. C. 33, 104
Eisenberg, D. M. 143
Ekman, P. 80, 91
Elmaci, N. 52
Ember, C. R. 64, 66, 67, 68, 117, 118, 123, 124, 126, 127, 128
Ember, M. 64, 66, 67, 68, 117, 118, 123, 124, 126, 127, 128
Emirbayer, M. 73
Ergenekon-Ozelci, P. 52
Ernberg, G. 146
Ertem, M. 52
Ettner, S. L. 143
Ezzati, M. 157

Fantone, J. C. 2
Feeney, J. A. 112, 131
Feigelman, S. 72
Fennelly, K. 144, 145
Fernald, A. 53
Ferrante, J. 192
Finelli, L. 144
Fintelman, M. 53, 54
Fiscella, K. 141, 159
Fischer-Rathus, L. 117
Fisher, H. 117
Fiske, S. T. 10, 91, 101, 104
Fitness, J. 12
Fix, M. 96
Flanagan, O. 87
Fletcher, G. 12
Food and Agriculture Organization of the United Nations 158
Forsterling, F. 10, 104
Fowkes, W. C., Jr. 152
Fowler, J. H. 72

Franks, P. 141, 159
Freeman, J. 19
Freire, P. 17, 18, 173, 174, 175, 176, 181
French, D. C. 68, 112, 113, 114, 131
Frese, M. 191
Freund, C. G. 144
Fried, J. 34, 35, 49, 71, 80, 81, 163, 164, 165, 166, 167, 168, 169
Friedman, A. B. 157
Friesen, W. V. 80, 91
Frongillo, E. A. 31
Fuchs, M. L. 59
Furnham, A. 94, 107, 109, 137, 138, 141

Gaier, L. E. 70, 169
Galanti, G. 151
Galbraith, J. 72
Galperín, C. Z. 53
Gant, L. 29
Garcia-Downing, C. 16
Gardiner, H. W. 37, 60, 62, 63, 69, 73
Gardner, H. 78, 91, 169, 170
Gartner, L. M. 51, 52
Gavagan, T. 144
Gebremariam, A. 141
Geertz, C. 2
Gelfand, M. 139
Generations United 64, 65
Georgas, J. 57, 58, 67, 73
George, D. 125
George, J. M. 178
Gerton, J. 29, 31
Ghiselli, E. E. 194
Giannotti, F. 59

Gibbon, J. L. 54, 55, 73
Giger, J. N. 134, 137
Gilbert, D. T. 88
Gilbert, J. 151
Gilligan, C. 48
Gingell, C. 127
Glass Jr, J. C. 56, 65
Glasser, D. B. 127
Gloria, A. M. 38, 96, 140
Glynn, T. 180, 181
Gold, M. R. 159
Goldberger, N. R. 170
Goleman, D. 33, 104
Goodenough, D. R. 79
Goodwin, J. 73
Goodwin, R. 58, 73, 116
Gottlieb, J. E. 152
Grand Challenges in Global Health 157
Graveline, F. J. 179
Green, A. R. 102, 105, 106, 152
Greenfield, P. M. 78
Gregg, J. 140
Griffin, T. J. 199
Griffiths, J. A. 140
Grossoehme, D. H. 142
Grusec, J. 63
Guarnaccia, P. J. 140
Guba, E. G. 13
Gummerum, M. 113
Gupta, S. 148
Gustafson, D. H. 192
Guthrie, R. V. 76

Haire, M. 194
Hales, A. 146, 147
Hall, B. 17
Halligan, P. W. 77
Hambleton, R. K. 79

Hancock, T. 134, 135
Hanscom, K. L. 154
Hansen, L. S. 35
Harkness, S. 53, 54, 57, 73
Harlow, H. F. 51
Harlow, M. K. 51
Harwood, R. 53
Hashimoto, T. 119, 121
Hatfield, E. 116
Haugh, R. 102
Hayes, J. 49, 50
Hedrick, H. L. 2
Heine, S. J. 23
Helman, C. G. 136, 137
Helms, J. E. 25
Hendrick, C. 115
Hendrick, S. 115
Hermann, J. 2
Hermans, J. M. 8
Herskovits, M. J. 84
Heslep, R. D. 174
Heymann, J. 49, 50
Hickson, D. J. 185
Hill, C. W. L. 185
Hill, R. 124
Hirsch, J. S. 120, 131
Ho, D. 8
Hobson, J. A. 80, 87
Hofstede, G. H. 186, 187, 188
Holland, A. 142
Holt, D. T. 191, 200
Hong, Y. 7, 31, 100, 101
Hopkins, B. 49
Horan, S. A. 145
Horowitz, C. R. 12
Hortacsu, N. 48
Horton, B. 122
Hosseinpoor, A. R. 59
Hough, L. M. 187, 194

Howard, K. I. 55
Hsu, L. K. G. 148
Hubbard, E. E. 102
Human Synergistics
    International 188
Huneycutt, T. L. 56, 65
Hyde, J. S. 36

Inkson, K. 33, 104
Institute for Women's Policy
    Research 50
Institute of Medicine 144
Intercountry Adoption 66
Isaacs, M. 152, 195, 196
Israel, B. 17
Ito, T. A. 10, 104

Jablensky, A. 146
Jadhavi, R. 148
Janis, I. L. 193
Janoff, S. 198, 200
Jansen, F. E. 139
Jegede, O. J. 171
Jenni, O. G. 58
Jensen, L. 144
Jobanputra, R. 137
Johnston, C. 97
Jolin, M. A. 19
Jones, G. R. 185
Jones, K. 159
Joseph, S. 72, 88, 89
Jovchelovitch, S. 17
Juang, L. 12, 24, 36, 38, 51, 77,
    78, 167

Kagitçibasi, C. 67, 73
Karp, I. 118
Karp, S. 79
Kaspar, V. 145

Katz, R. C. 148
Keller, M. 113
Keltner, D. 36
Kempen, J. G. 8
Kemper, A. R. 141
Kendall, E. 16
Kim, C. 33, 34, 95, 104, 106, 108
Kim, H. S. 71, 73
Kim, U. 32
Kimmel, P. R. 197
Kitayama, S. 22, 23, 24, 42, 71
Klausner, R. 157
Kleinman, A. 106, 149, 152
Kline, S. L. 122
Klonoff, E. A. 137, 140, 141
Koepsell, T. D. 141
Kohlberg, L. 48
Komaromy, M. 141
Koomen, W. 23
Korotayev, A. V. 49
Korten, A. 146
Kosmitzki, C. 29, 37, 60, 62, 63, 69, 73
Kottak, C. P. 67, 68, 118, 122, 124, 127, 128, 129
Krause, J. 125
Kreidie, L. 6
Ku, L. 141
Kuhlthau, K. 51
Kulkarni, S. C. 157
Kumari, R. 118
Kunda, Z. 10, 104

La Roche, M. J. 32
LaFromboise, T. 29, 31
Lam, C. M. 72
Lam, T. K. 154
Lammers, C. J. 185
Lamour, M. 53

Landrine, H. 137, 140, 141
Lang, S. 125
Lange, C. G. 80
Laroia, N. 52
Larsen, J. T. 10, 104
Latz, S. 58
Laumann, E. O. 127
Lawrence, R. A. 51, 52
Lawson, H. M. 130, 131
Leach, M. L. 83
Leck, K. 130, 131
Leclere, F. B. 144
Lee, O. 112, 113, 114
Lee, S. 29, 31
Leff, S. S. 19
Lehman, D. R. 4, 5, 19, 23
LeRoux, J. 33, 34, 95, 104, 106, 108
Lessard, G. 141
Leu, F. L. 30
Levin, S. J. 152
Levine, R. 119, 121
Levy, D. 10, 48, 52, 53, 57, 81, 85, 116, 117
Lewin, S. A. 154
Lewis, M. 50
Li, F. P. 145
Lia-Hoagberg, B. 48
Like, R. C. 152
Likert, R. 189
Lincoln, Y. 13
Linley, P. A. 72, 88, 89
Liu, Z. 144
Loue, S. 148
Lovato, C. 19
Lozoff, B. 58
Lucas, R. E. 90
Lucca, N. 77
Ludema, J. D. 199

Luquis, R. R. 11
Lustig, S. L. 156
Lyubomirksy, S. 90, 91

Maccoby, E. E. 113, 114
MacMillan, I. 80
Madge, C. 139
Magen, Z. 55
Malewska-Peyre, H. 38, 56
Management of Social
    Transformations Programme
    (MOST) 11
Manske, S. 19
Manz, P. H. 19
Mardiros, M. 19
Marín, B. V. 140
Marín, G. 140
Markus, H. 22, 23, 24, 42, 71
Marshall, C. A. 16
Martin, P. L. 18, 145
Martín-Baró, I. 18
Matsumoto, D. 12, 24, 33, 34,
    36, 38, 51, 77, 78, 81, 95, 104,
    106, 108, 167
McCann, D. 65
McCargar, D. F. 168
McCrae, R. R. 32
McCubbin, L. 16
McIntosh, P. 31
McKenna, E. 189
McLeod, K. A. 172
McPhee, S. J. 154
Mead, H. 159
Mead, M. 69
Meaning of Work International
    Research Team (MOW) 193
Meinhardt, K. 96, 98
Merriam, S. B. 172, 174, 176,
    179, 180, 181

Merritt, A. 187
Messenger, J. C. 127
Midgley, E. 18, 145
Miller, B. 66, 118, 122, 123
Miller, L. 41
Miller, N. B. 152
Minkler, M. 16, 18
Mir, G. 143
Misumi, J. 190
Mock, J. 154
Mohr, B. J. 199
Monroe, K. 6
Moreira, E. 127
Morris, A. S. 55
Morris, M. D. 30
Morris, M. W. 31, 100, 101
Morris, S. 158
Morton, J. 51, 52
Moseley, K. L. 141
Moss, R. 87
Muczyk, J. P. 191, 200
Muhammetberdiev, O. 48
Muir, S. L. 72
Mulatu, M. S. 138
Mullet, E. 127
Mullett, S. 48
Muñoz-Laboy, M. 120, 131
Murasawa, H. 117
Murguía, A. 140
Murnaghan, D. 19
Murnen, S. K. 115
Murray, C. J. L. 157

Nash, K. A. 195
National Center for Cultural
    Competence (NCCP) 96, 153
Naylor, A. J. 51, 52
Nefale, M. C. 156
Nelson, A. R. 141, 159

Neto, F. 127
Neuijen, B. 187
Nevid, J. 117
News-Medical.Net 89, 90
Nguyen, T. 154
Nicolosi, A. 127
Noh, S. 145
Noller, P. 112, 131
Norcross, J. C. 12
Norris, A. E. 97
Nuestra Communidad Sana
    (NCS) 238

O'Connor, B. B. 58
O'Hare, D. 51, 52
O'Malley, J. M. 86
Oberg, C. N. 48
Offer, D. 55
Ohayv, D. D. 187
Oishi, S. 90
Okitikpi, T. 95, 97
Okun, B. F. 34, 35, 49, 71, 80,
    81, 163, 164, 165, 166, 167,
    168, 169
Okun, M. L. 34, 35, 49, 71, 80,
    81, 163, 164, 165, 166, 167,
    168, 169
Olowu, A. A. 24
Orubuloye, I. O. 40
Osgood, C. 84
Ostrov, E. 55
Overall, N. 12
Oyserman, D. 29, 43

Padilla, M. B. 120, 131
Page, S. E. 194
Paik, A. 127
Palermo, A. G. 12
Paludi, M. A. 35, 36, 39, 40, 42

Pande, N. 138, 139
Parham, T. A. 25
Park, E. R. 102
Parker, A. 72
Parker, E. 17
Parker, R. G. 120, 131
Paterson, H. F. 79
Patsdaughter, C. A. 97
Pawlish, K. 145
Paxton, S. J. 72
Payne, R. K. 41
Peat, M. 134
Pecheux, M.-G. 53
Peel, E. 41, 131
Peregrine, P. N. 64, 66, 67, 68,
    117, 118, 123, 124, 126, 127,
    128
Pérez, M. A. 11
Perkins, F. 134, 135
Perrin, J. M. 51
Peterson, C. 88
Peterson, R. A. 140
Phillips, R. 103
Phinney, J. S. 24, 28, 43
Piaget, J. 46, 54
Pidada, S. 112, 113, 114
Pines, A. M. 116
Pinker, S. 163
Plant, E. A. 36
Polyani, M. 198
Pond, P. 154
Pontius, A. A. 37
Poortinga, Y. H. 3, 4, 6, 7, 32,
    35, 37, 38, 46, 54, 57, 58, 67,
    73, 95, 99
Porter, L. W. 194
Porter, R. E. 164, 181
Portes, A. 72
Power, T. J. 19

Prabhu, J. 175, 176
Prewitt, K. 54
Prochaska, J. O. 12
Putnam, R. 72

Radda, K. 72
Ragsdale, J. 142
Rahn, C. 53
Ramos, C. 159
Rankin, S. H. 96, 160
Rao, V. N. 36
Rao, V. V. P. 36
Rathus, S. 117
Ratzlaff, C. 33, 34, 95, 104, 106, 108
Ravallion, M. 40
Ray, N. F. 144
Reason, P. 16, 19, 106
Reichers, A. E. 185
Reisen, C. A. 140
Reiter, M. 125
Renshon, S. 56
Revenis, M. 59
Reynolds, A. L. 12
Reynolds, T. E. 24
Richard, C. 144
Richmond, A. 99
Riegg, N. 6
Robbins, S. R. 186
Robins, L. S. 2
Rode, P. 48
Romano, D. 125
Rose, A. J. 113, 114
Royal Anthropological Institute 118
Rudolph, K. D. 113, 114
Rudy, D. 63

Saha, S. 141

Saka, G. 52
Samovar, L. A. 164, 181
Sanders, G. 187
Saraswathi, T. S. 55, 120
Sartorious, N. 146
Sato, S. 119, 121
Saver, B. G. 141
Saxe, G. N. 156
Scarr, S. 77, 91
Schachter, F. F. 59
Schaller, M. 4, 5, 19
Schanler, R. J. 51, 52
Schein, E. H. 185, 200
Schensul, J. J. 72
Schkade, D. 90, 91
Schlegel, A. 55
Schneider, B. H. 68, 113, 131, 185
Schoelmerich, A. 53
Schulenburg, J. 70
Schulz, A. 17
Schulze, P. 53
Schutz, H. K. 72
Scott, J. 73
Sebastiani, T. 59
Seeman, T. E. 71
Segall, M. H. 3, 4, 6, 7, 32, 35, 37, 38, 46, 54, 84, 95, 99
Segura-Herrera, T. A. 38, 96, 140
Seligman, M. E. P. 88, 89
Sember, R. E. 120, 131
Shah, I. 48
Shane, S. 80
Sharma, D. 52
Sheldon, K. M. 90, 91
Sherman, D. K. 71, 73
Shilkret, K. L. 144

Shiraev, E. 10, 48, 52, 53, 57, 81, 85, 116, 117
Short, K. H. 97
Shweder, R. 165
Siegel, B. 159
Siegel, J. E. 145
Silverthorne, C. P. 191, 200
Simons-Morton, B. G. 59
Singer, P. A. 157
Singh, K. 148
Sinha, D. 32, 190, 191
Skinner, B. F. 46
Skovholt, C. J. 48
Smart, D. W. 97
Smart, J. F. 97
Smedley, B. D. 141, 159
Smith, A. G. 42
Smith, D. E. 24
Smith, N. K. 10, 104
Smith, P. B., 7,
Smith, T. D. 41
Snowden, L. 140
Sobal, J. 31
Sonko, S. 118
Sorrell, J. H. 173
Sparrow, L. M. 31, 43
Spearman, C. E. 78
Spector, R. E. 136, 148, 160
Speybroeck, N. 59
Spiro, M. E. 23
Sprecher, S. 116
Srivastava, R. 143
St Pierre-Hansen, N. 142
Stainton Rogers, W. 138
Stanton, B. F. 72
Steinberg, L. 55
Stephens, W. N. 118
Sternberg, R. J. 78, 120, 121
Sternthal, M. J. 141

Stirlen, A. 125
Stith, A. Y. 141, 159
Stone, R. K. 59
Suárez-Orozco, C. 97
Suárez-Orozco, M. M. 97
Sue, D. W. 11, 25, 27, 31, 103, 177, 195
Sue, D. 11, 25, 27, 31, 103, 177, 195
Suh, E. M. 88, 89
Super, C. M. 53, 54, 57, 73
Sussman, N. M. 30, 105, 107, 108
Sy, S. 70

Tagaki, K. 192
Tajfel, H. 24
Takaki, R. 29
Tal, J. 53
Tannen, D. 166
Tarule, J. M. 170
Tatani, H. 33, 34, 95, 104, 106, 108
Taylor, S. E. 71, 73
Tedlock, B. 87
Teferra, T. 145
Tellegen, G. 23
Thamer, M. 144
Thomas, A. 50
Thomas, D. C. 33, 104
Thomas, T. N. 96, 98
Torsch, V. L. 139
Tovey, P. 143
Tran, T. V. 97
Tranotti, J. 144
Triandis, H. C. 4, 6, 7, 22, 77, 187, 194
Trochim, W. 193
Tuckman, B. 188, 189

US Census Bureau 49, 64
US Department of Health &
    Human Services 96
Uchida, H. 33, 34, 95, 104, 106,
    108
Uchida, Y. 23
UNAIDS 158
Unger, R. 37, 39, 60, 114, 126,
    148
United Nations 95, 126, 157,
    158

Vagnoni, C. 59
Valentin, S. R. 58, 59
Valsiner, J., & Rosa, A. 7,
    19
Vamus, H. 157
Van de Poel, E. 59
van de Vijver, F. J. R. 67, 73, 108,
    153
Van den Heuvel, H. 23
Van der Flier, H. 37
Van der Vlugt, E. 53, 54
Van der Zee, K. I. 33, 34, 104
Van Dyk, G. A. J. 156
Van Hook, J. 96
Van Oudenhoven, J. P. 33, 34,
    104
Van Ourti, T. 59
Van Rompay, M. 143
Van Tijen, N. 53, 54
van Wyk, B. 154
VandeVen, A. H. 192
Vasquez, M. J. T. 38
Vaughn, L. M. 6, 103, 105, 109,
    151, 153, 160
Veenhoven, R. 89
Vega, J. 59
Vega, W. A. 96, 98

Venkataraman, S. 80
Verkuyten, M. 24, 43
Verma, J. 119, 121
Victoroff, J. 41, 42, 43
Villareal, M. J. 77
Viste, T. T. 63
Vladeck, B. C. 12
Vygotsky, L. S. 46

Wallerstein, N. 16, 18
Ward, C. A. 94, 107, 109
Ward, C. 87
Ward, R. 142
Warheit, G. J. 96, 98
Weeks, M. R. 72
Weine, S. M. 156
Weisbord, M. 198, 200
Welles-Nystrom, B. 58,
    59
Wertheim, E. H. 72
Whaley, A. L. 154, 160
Wheeler, D. 193
White, A. 89
Whitney, D. 199
Whitty, M. T. 130, 131
Wilkey, S. 143
Williams, J. 35
Willms, L. 142
Wills, T. A. 71
Wilson, T. D. 88
Witkin, H. A. 79
Wolf, A. W. 58
Wolpe, P. R. 117
Wong, C. 154
Woods, K. 159
World Health Organization 51,
    59, 126, 134, 158, 159

Xueqin Ma, G. 139

Yan, M. C. 72
Yan, W. 70, 169
Yancey, G. 125
Yao, L. E. 168
Yeh, R.S., & Lawrence, J. J.
   188

Zavis, D. 148
Zea, M. C. 140

Zebrowitz-McArthur, L.
   115, 116
Zerhouni, E. 157
Zhang, S. 122
Zimmer, B. 148
Zimmer, M. 142
Zuñiga, M. E. 155
Zwarenstein, M. 154
Zweifler, A. J. 2

Subject Index

Abortion 48
Acculturation 94–95
    process of 100–101
    strategies toward 98–99
Action research 16
Adolescence
    changes during 54–55
    happiness and 55
    self-image and 55
Adoption
    international 65–66
    transnational,
      see international
Adulthood
    openness model of 55
    persistence model of
      55
    social roles of 55
Aging
    declines and 56
    views on 56–57

*Alma Ata Declaration
    of Health* 134
Appreciative inquiry
    summit 199
Asylum seeker 95
Attachment patterns 51
Attraction
    Buss evolutionary study
      115–116
    cultural differences 115–116
    matching hypothesis 115
    physical 116
    proximity and 114
    reciprocity hypothesis 115
    similarity hypothesis 115
    social construction
      perspective 116
    standards of beauty and 117

Biopsychosocial model 77
Brainstorming 192

Breastfeeding 50, 158
  beliefs and 52
  benefits of 51–52
  low rates 51
  recommendations 51
Bridewealth 128
Buddhist psychology 154

Childbirth 48–49
Childhood
  eating preferences and 53
  play and 54, 60
  sleeping patterns and, 53–54,
    60, see also sleep
Childrearing 60
  dimensions of 61
Cognition 78
  creativity and 79–80
Cognitive development theory
  46
Cognitive misers 10, 104
Cognitive style
  field independence/
    dependence 79
Collectivism 22
Communication
  conversational traits 163–164
  gender and 166
  intercultural 162, 165–166
  nonverbal 162, 164
  style 164
  verbal 162
Communicative action
  discourse and 174
Community-based
  participatory research 16
  Aboriginal peoples and 18
  vulnerable communities and
    18

Competence
  cultural, see cultural
    competence
  interpersonal 103–104
  intrapersonal 103–104
  linguistic 150
Computer mediated
  relationships
  benefits of 130
  internet dating 129,
    130
  problems 130–131
Concept mapping 192–193
Consciousness
  altered states of 86–87
  dreams and 87
  sleep and 87
  states of 86–87
Core virtues 88
Critical theory 172–174, 176
Cross-cultural psychology 6–7,
  9
Cultural awareness 11
Cultural brokers 153
Cultural competence 11–12
  approaches to 105–106,
    150–153
  benefits of 102
  critical incidents and 153
  definition 105, 177
  dimensions of 177
  healthcare and 149
  multidimensional model of
    177
  organizations and 195–197
  process of 177
  techniques 105–106
Cultural diversity 11
Cultural frame switching 31

Cultural psychology 6, 9
Cultural reaffirmation 29
Cultural sensitivity 150
   dimensions 11
Culture
   aspects of 3–4
   behaviors and 3
   beliefs and 3
   cultural-mixtures approach
     8
   definition 2
   elements of 5
   functions of 4, 6
   intelligence and 33, 104
   interpersonal interaction and
     5
   national identity and 2
   philosophical paradigms and
     13
   research paradigms and 13
   social differences and 3
   social-psychological
     approach 7, 9
   symbolic immortality and
     5
   theoretical orientations 13
Culture shock 95, 101
   stages 107–108

Delphi technique 192
Developmental niche 57
Disability 9
Discrimination 10, 12
Diversity 8
Divorce
   changes in 129
   cultural practice 128–129
   rates 129
   reasons for 129

Eating disorders 148
Ecological systems approach
   46–47
Education
   banking model of 175–176
   effort vs. ability 70, 169
   extracurricular activities and
     69–70, 168–169
   formal vs. informal 167
   intercultural schooling and
     172
   language and 169
   multicultural 166, 171–172
   parent and family view
     168
   popular/liberating, 174,
     see also education, social
     change
   problem-oriented 172
   problem-posing 175–176
   school and 166, 171
   social change, 172–174, 176,
     see also education,
     popular
   socialization and 69, 166
Emics 11
Emotion
   Cannon and Bard theory
     80
   display rules and 80
   expression of 81
   James Lange theory 80
   universal 80
Erikson's life stage approach
   47
Ethnicity 8–9
Ethnocentrism 10
Etics 11
Evil eye 49, 148

Family
    expanded 68
    extended 57, 67
    family bed, 58,
        see also co-sleeping
    households and 66–68
    multigenerational 64–65
    nuclear 57, 67
    of orientation 67
    single-parent 63–64
    structure of 57
Family and Medical Leave Act
    50
Female circumcision, see female
    genital mutilation
Female genital mutilation 40,
    126
Friendships
    as a buffer 113
    cultural factors 113
    developmental sequence of
        113
    gender and 113–114
    purpose of 112–113
    women and 114
Future Search Conference
    198–199

Gender 9
    androgyny and 38–39
    Berdache and 39, 123
    bias 39
    concept of machismo and 38
    concept of marianismo and
        38
    differences 36
    global views 35
    inequality 40
    male aggression and 37

patriarchal cultures and 35
    physically 35–36
    roles 34
    socialization 37
    societal roles and 35
    stereotypes 35–37
    third sex 39
    Williams and Best study 35
Gene-environment interactions
    77
Global psychology 8–9
Grandparents 56, 64–65
Groups
    developmental stages
        188–189
Groupthink 193

Happiness 87–88
    nations and 89–90
    set point 90
    World Database of
        Happiness 89
    World Map of Happiness 89
    World Values Survey 89
Health
    access to healthcare 143, 159
    African immigrants and 139,
        145
    alternative practices/models
        143, 156–157
    causal attributions and 138,
        140–141
    causes of illness 136
    cultural beliefs about 136
    cultural variables 134–137
    definition 134
    ethno-medical approach to
        139–140
    global 157–158

immigrants and 141–144
insurance and 144, 159
life domains approach 153
mandala of 134–135
minorities and 159
models of 134–135, 138
Western beliefs on 141
Western biomedical model
  141
Health disparities 157–159
High/low context cultures 164
HIV/AIDS 158
Hofstede's dimensions of
  culture 186–187
Homosexuality 126
Human development,
  see socialization

Identity
  appearance and 41
  bicultural 25, 28
  cultural 24, 27
  disability and 41
  dominant 31
  ethnic 24
  measurement of 27–28
  multicultural, 28–29,
    see also multicultural
    individuals
  negotiation strategies 29–30
  religious differences and 40
  social class and 40
  socioeconomic status and,
    see social class
Identity development models 24
  African-American 25
  Asian-American 25
  Cross model of psychological
    Nigrescence 25

Latino/Hispanic American
  25
minority identity model
  25–26
racial/cultural 25, 27
Third World consciousness
  and 25
Immigration and immigrants
  94–95
  acculturative stress and
    97–98
  children and 96, 144, 145
  health and, *see* health,
    immigrants and
  health disparities and 145
  health problems and 145
  healthy migrant
    phenomenon and 144–145
  migration motivation and 99
  poverty and 97, 145
  psychosocial factors of 144
Indigenous knowledge 178
  African 181
  Confucian 179
  Hindu 179–180
  Islamic 180
  Maori 180
Indigenous psychologies 7–9
Individualism 22
Infancy
  language and 52–53
  mortality and 49
  touch and massage during 49
Intelligence
  as protective factor 78
  benefits of 71–72
  cultural, *see* culture and
    intelligence
  multiple 78, 169–170

social support 71, 77–78
  types of 78
Intercultural adjustment 33, 95,
  103
Intercultural development
  177–178
Intercultural frameworks
  levels 11
Intercultural interactions 94
  barriers to 101
  benefits 102
  model of 103
  successful 102–103
Internet dating, *see* computer
  mediated relationships

Kissing 117

Language 85
  linguistic relativity,
    see Sapir-Whorf
    hypothesis
  multilingual 86
  Sapir-Whorf hypothesis 86,
    162–163
Lay health workers 153–154
Leadership
  nuturant-task leader 190
  PM theory 190
  styles 189
Learning 167, 171
  cultural factors 168
  formal vs. informal 167, 179
  motivation and 167
  role of student and 168
  social organization aspects
    167
  styles 167
  Western notion of 179

Love 119
  attitudes 121
  in marriage 122
  Sternberg's triangular theory
    120–121

Managers 189, 191
Marriage 129
  anthropological view
    118
  arranged 119
  civil 118
  common-law 118
  forms of 122
  functions of 120
  intercultural 124–125
  interracial, *see* intercultural
  reasons for 118–119
  replacement 128
  romantic love and 119
  same-sex 122
  transformation of 120
  woman-woman 122
Mate selection 116
Maternity leave 49–50
Medicine
  allopathic 142
  ayurvedic 142–143
  complementary and
    alternative medicine
    (CAM) 142
  integrative 142
  Kleinman's view on 149
  osteopathic 142
  traditional chinese medicine
    (TCM) 142
Meditation 87
Menarche, *see* menstruation
Menstruation 60

Mental health 158–159
  attributions 147
  beliefs about 146
  causes of 146–147
  cultural-bound syndromes
    148–149
  mental illness, 146–147,
    see also psychological
    disorders
  treatments 147–148
Monocultural individuals 31
Monogamy 122
Moral development 48
Multicultural individuals 28,
  31
  coping skills 29–30
Multicultural mind 31
Multicultural Personality
  Questionnaire (MPQ) 33
Multiculturalism 10
Multigroup Ethnic Identity
  Measure (MEIM) 28

Nationality 9
Nominal group technique 192
Non-Western knowledge,
  see indigenous knowing

Organizations
  climate and 185
  cognitive spheres of 185
  Confucian dynamism 188
  cultural competence and
    195–197
  culture and 185, 188
  decision-making in 191–192
  dimensions of 186
  international negotiation
    and 197

large group interventions and
    198–200
  monocultural 195
  multiculturalism and
    194–197
  national character of
    185–186
  ringi system 192
  stakeholders and 198
  structure and 185, 188
Organizational Culture
  Inventory (OCI) 188
Ottawa Charter 134

Parenting
  authoritarian style 63
  gay 65
  involvement 63
  models of 61–62
  mother-child interactions 62
Participatory action research,
  16–18, *see also* community-
  based participatory research
  advantages 17
  conscientization and 17
Pedagogy of the Oppressed 175
Peers
  influence on socialization 69
  pressure 68
  schooling and 68–69
Perception
  art and 84
  beauty and 85
  carpentered world
    hypothesis 84
  children's coin study 82
  colour and 84
  expectations 81
  music and 86

optical illusions and 82–83
pain and 81
tastes 84
time and 85, 136
touch 85
vision 84
Personality
African model 32
five factor model 32
indigenous 32
multicultural 33–34
successful factors 33, 104
terrorist 41–42
Phrenology 76
Pluralism
cultural 99
melting pot view 94
mosaic view 94
Polyandry 124
Polygamy 68, 123
Polygyny 123–124
Possession 87
Poverty 40
effects of 60
health and 158
malnutrition and 59
Pregnancy 48–49
Prejudice 10, 12
Prenatal period 48
Privilege 32
Proxemics
zones 165
Psychological acculturation,
see acculturation
Psychological disorders,
see also mental illness
depression 158–159
schizophrenia 145
therapy for 154

Psychological Engine of
Adjustment 33–34, 104
Psychological processes 76
Psychotherapy
folklore 155–156
HEARTS model 154–155
survivors of trauma and 156
Ubuntu 156

Race 8
Refugee 95
Relationships 112
common-law partnerships
118, 124
homosexual, 123, 126,
see also homosexuality
online, see computer
mediated relationships
Religion 70
Research
back translation and 15–16
ethical issues 16
methods 14
mixed methods approach 14
political issues 16
qualitative 14
quantitative 14
sample selection 15
test translation and 15
tools 14
types 15
validity 15
Rites of passage 60

Schizophrenia 145
Self-concept
Asian 22
collective 22–23
independent 22–23

interdependent 22
multiple 29
Western 22
Self-esteem 23–24
Sex roles, 34, *see also* gender
    roles
Sexuality 41
    chastity and 125
    cultural beliefs 125
    extramarital sex and 127
    practices and 127
    privacy and 128
    problems and 127
    restrictions and 128
Sleep 87
    co-sleeping 58–59
    Germans and 59
    Hispanic-Americans and 59
    Italians and 59
    private bedroom and 58
    solitary 58
    Swedish and 59
Social capital
    guanxi 72
    types 7
Social learning theory 48
Social network analysis 72–73
Socialization
    agents of 66
    nature vs. nurture debate and
        46
    orientations 46

Sociocultural psychology 7, 9
Sojourners 95
Somatization 149
Stereotypes 10

Teaching
    cultural factors 168
    didactic 167
    modeling 168
    role of teacher and
        168
Temperament 50
Testing
    cognitive 79
    guidelines 79
    intelligence 78–79
    standardized 79
Trances 87

Women's Ways of Knowing
        170–171
Work
    collectivistic cultures and
        194
    diverse workforce and
        184
    importance of 193–194
    individualistic cultures and
        194
    meaning of 193
    values and 186
World Café 199

Offending Identities